JONES

PORTRAIT OF A MUGGER

BY
James Willwerth

M. Evans and Company, Inc. NEW YORK, N.Y. 10017

M. Evans and Company titles are distributed
in the United States by the J. B. Lippincott Company,
East Washington Square, Philadelphia, Pa. 19105
and in Canada by McClelland and Stewart Limited,
25 Hollinger Road, Toronto M4B 3G2, Ontario

Library of Congress Catalog Card Number: 73-87707
ISBN 0-87131-136-4

Designed by Paula Wiener

Manufactured in the United States of America

9 8 7 6 5 4 3 2 1

For my father, Vic Willwerth

For Ardis

And for a certain street lady

"The source of every crime is some defect of the understanding; or some error in reasoning; or some sudden force of the passions . . ."
—Thomas Hobbes, from *Leviathan*

"Something is happening here
But you don't know what it is
Do you, Mr. Jones?"
—Bob Dylan,
from *Ballad of a Thin Man*

Foreword

1

During the spring of 1973, I was assigned part of a *Time* Magazine national roundup on "crime in America"—a good assignment but a frustrating one. My copy, along with that of the other reporters, would be boiled down by a rewrite man to three columns of abstractions and random quotations. It is almost impossible to have an individual stamp on such a story.

I wanted a more substantial role; so I suggested that the story include an interview with a mugger.

They went along with this. The next problem was to find one. I'd never tried. I had no idea what a mugger would say —give me your money?—once I found him. But I happened to know people who counseled runaway kids on Manhattan's Lower East Side. I assumed that their clients— gang members, junkies, young male and female prostitutes—turned occasionally to mugging when other hustles failed. Or they would know someone who had.

So I put out the word that I would take someone to dinner, forget to ask his name, and make him a "famous outlaw" if he had the credentials. He would have to convince a go-between that he was the real thing.

I was introduced to an articulate black kid who'd spent five years with a teen-age gang in Harlem. He and I and a white friend of his who sometimes did his work with a hatchet went to a Chinese restaurant one night and talked about the business of mugging people. The black gang frequented parks, dark streets, and elevator buildings. They surrounded people, took what they wanted, and moved out, fast. They were chased sometimes, but never caught. Once they put an uncooperative victim in the hospital for two weeks. The white kid talked very little that night. He usually threw his victims down on the sidewalk and brandished his ax until they gave up their money. The black kid had "retired"; he was returning to school with the help of a social worker.

I never saw either of them again. I never wanted to.

When the article appeared, I was approached by an editor of a major publishing house. Could I find a "working" mugger? The publisher wanted no convert to good citizenship. He wanted the sense of ongoing war with the larger society; more drama, perhaps more truth. It seemed an enormous challenge; it also was a chance to change my own life, for I'd become terribly frustrated with news writing. A news magazine goes to press every Saturday; the stories week after week become faces in a rushing crowd. You talk to people quickly, grabbing at them, talking whatever you can back to the typewriter. Here was a chance to get into something.

I shook hands with the publisher and said my agent would call to settle the details. I took a leave of absence from my job and began looking for Mr. Jones.

That week, the publisher backed out. His lawyers said the project was "too controversial."

I went ahead anyway. The more I thought about it, the more it fascinated me. What kind of person *is* a mugger? This would be a reporter's rare chance to get beyond the stereotypes. In any event, this would be no instant analysis of a passing face.

For I'd have to force myself into this man's life: walk with him, share his problems, live in his world. It sounded frightening, difficult, dangerous, even crazy; it sounded perfect. Adventure is the blood of good journalism; it will lure most writers—certainly me—far beyond the bounds of common sense.

2

Down on the Lower East Side, the idea proved less romantic. I was looking for an "articulate mugger"—and the street talk was negative. How could I be trusted? What if I brought the police? I told people that I expected the mugger to give himself a pseudonym, that we would meet at his convenience— a pizza shop, a street corner, or whatever—and that we were in this together. I assumed I had a *lot* to worry about if I crossed him.

A connection was finally made. The man who calls himself Jones heard about the book from a street kid who knew some people in a storefront agency on lower Second Avenue. A volunteer worker talked to Jones and called me. The storefront has since closed; the street kid dropped out of sight shortly after I began the book—it was as if the earth opened briefly to reveal a secret, then slammed shut before too many escaped. On a Wednesday, after a week of messages, Jones called; we arranged to meet at a subway stop on Houston Street.

Why did he do it?

At first, ego. Most people's lives do not include a biographer, and Jones' vanity is considerable. He saw immediately that my interest in him would be relentless and pervasive; he was flattered. And beneath the vanity, he was a lonely, troubled human being bent on self-destruction; I was a sympathetic ear, perhaps a therapist in some ways.

As time passed, our relationship gathered even more complexity. A bond of fascination, even confession, formed; in effect, a friendship. We did keep a certain distance by using the pseudonyms "Jones" and "Sam" (we still use them on the rare occasions that I hear from him), but it was clear that each of us had something to learn from the other. Jones coveted my stability, my career; a perverse part of me envied his rogue status. And I had a book to write.

During the four months we spent together, our relationship exhausted nearly all of my emotions. My fear surfaced immediately (and reappeared often). Then came fascination, then affection; at the end, anger. We became enmeshed in an easy street camaraderie. I met his family, his women, his street friends. We got high together, and sometimes—though I kept him largely ignorant of my personal life—I told him my problems. He never asked about my life, as it happened, unless I volunteered the information; it was not his way. And I was frightened by the idea of getting too close to him. The difference in our life-styles, I told myself, would bring unnecessary tension to the relationship. Besides he might somehow hurt me.

But at various times, I came to like him enormously, to wish him the best, to wish that he would pull his life together. I even wished he would become "respectable" so he could meet my friends without them cringing. And then in the end I became very upset with him. I saw how deeply he was hurting people who loved and depended on him (not to mention—all along—those he encountered as a mugger, whom I had difficulty perceiving except in abstractions of pity or outrage). For the burden of his self-indulgence even on those he loved had become obvious. He took from them constantly; he rarely gave anything back.

Still, the fact remains that I came to see Jones as a human being and as a friend. In my eyes he shed his mugger sheen by the second or third meeting; after that I saw a human being who happened to be a mugger. It is not enough, of course, that he happens to be likable; he is a dangerous, unstable man, and he is a burden to our society. It isn't even possible to be sure of the measure of fact and fantasy in his stories. Criminals are often pathological liars. The stories I checked always proved true, sometimes even understated. But I didn't always believe him. There is a story of murder in this book which doesn't—I hope—ring true.

We met on the average of three times a week, ending our sessions when I filled a notebook or developed cramps in my writing hand or simply got too stoned to take more notes. Each session had a wild, unpredictable life of its own.

Take election day, for example. That was when I learned he was a registered Republican.

It was during the city's 1973 mayoral primary election. One candidate, State Senator John Marchi, a conservative Republican, was talking loudly of law and order. "A vote for my opponents," he said at one point, "is a vote for mugging."

Senator Marchi would have been pleased to know that he and Jones belonged to the same party. In 1968 Jones had voted for Richard Nixon, who promised his supporters stern anti-crime legislation, conservative court appointments, and preventive detention. Another Republican, Nelson Rockefeller, had recently pushed a bill through New York's state legislature providing long jail sentences for drug pushers and users.

I happened to meet with Jones the day of one of the mayoral primaries. I mentioned I'd voted that morning to see what he'd say.

"Wow, yeah . . . voting. I should do that thing. But I'm not gonna."

"Why not?"

"Everybody who's running is a crook. One guy is Puerto Rican, which is cool—but he's probably a crook like the rest of them. You don't have to be white to steal."

"Are you registered?"

"Yeah. I'm a Republican. I got registered at St. Mark's Place a few years ago. I wanted to make some money."

"Uh . . . what?"

"I was running a con and I needed a front, you know? I had this dude with me, and I wanted to sell him some smoke [marijuana] that was catnip. We were going by this registration table, and this white-haired lady was sitting at it. I figured I would show the dude I wasn't a dope fiend . . . which I *was*, of course. No dope fiend would have time for petty shit like registering.

"I told this dude to wait. I said I had business with the

lady at the table. I went over to get a voting card, and the lady filled it out. I don't remember saying what I was to be registered as, but she put down Republican. I would have said Democrat—but there I was, a registered Republican."

"You've voted?"

"Once or twice. I voted in 1968. My mother and father were voting for Nixon, so I did it, too. The Republicans fucked me up, though."

He lit a cigarette, cupping his hands around it.

"When they had that other election a while back [the city had two Democratic primaries in 1973] Moms told me to go vote for Biaggi [the Brooklyn Democratic congressman running for mayor]. She said I could get a job working for the campaign; she knew someone down there. So I went down to vote. It was hot, and I had to stand in line a long time. Then the lady told me I couldn't vote! I was a Republican."

"Did you score with the catnip?"

"Yeah." He grinned.

One

1

His world is small, a whirlpool of lower New York street corners, tense friendships, family problems, small-change business deals, people without last names—and sudden violence. It is a world where "uptown" means a girlfriend's apartment north of Houston Street, where "the Bronx" is your brother's apartment on 287th Street, and "the projects" is your parents' place near the Brooklyn Bridge. It is the world of New York's Lower East Side: long rows of orange-brick housing projects, Chinatown's noisy streets, runaway kids in the East Village, the Bowery's squalor, grimy tenements, and dirty streets connecting everything.

"Moms" and "Pops" still live in the apartment where he grew up, a tiny shelter in a forest of tall project buildings. One son remains at home; a daughter and another son are living in the Bronx. Jones lives at his parents' home when it suits him; when it doesn't, he stays with one of his women, Carol, on Clinton Street, about a mile away.

His closest friend is a tall ex-Marine named Jeff, who wears broad-brimmed hats, flared pants with big cuffs, translucent shirts, and platform shoes. Jeff talks fast and furiously, lots of palm slapping, lots of motion, you-can-dig-it-Jack.

Jeff was a junkie who kicked with methadone. He dealt "smoke," for a while, but now he works in a bank and goes to night school. He gets GI Bill money for school and veterans' benefits for a bullet he took in Vietnam, and he's doing all right. His father has Family connections, but the cops caught his father with some cocaine, and he's doing one to five now.

Jeff has some good smoke tonight—he calls it wacky weed —and he comes by Clinton Street, and he and Jones get down with a little wine and some weed, and they rap.

Jones and Jeff are down at the door of Clinton Street— Carol's place—smoking one of the joints and tripping on the good vibes of the warm spring night. They are slapping palms and stomping feet and laughing and bending over and working on that weed, and Jeff says some jive-ass thing and it is so funny they both explode in laughter.

But they don't see these two Puerto Rican dudes walking down the block with a girl between them, who somehow figure that Jones and Jeff are laughing at them.

The dudes keep walking by.

And Jeff and Jones work on that smoke, the joint down to the roach now.

Then the two dudes come back without the girl, and one of them has a gun!

One dude is saying they insulted his woman. And he wants an apology. Jones and Jeff tell him he can shove the apology up his motherfuckin' ass, and he doesn't go for that, and he starts screaming something in Spanish. And they look across the street, and the other dude is *aiming that gun* and yelling something about how he's going to shoot their fucking heads off. It is time to split.

Just then the B bus pulls up and Jones and Jeff move fast and run behind it. But Jones is going to see them again. And when he does, it'll be time to take care of business.

2

The street corner friend wears his hair in corn rows, and he is sitting on a stool and leaning forward. Call him J. C. He is tall and thin and keen-eyed; he has an air of strength and quickness. He knows things.

"Jones draws the shit, the violence, *to* him. I used to think he was exaggerating, but wow, when I started going around with him, I saw it. I've seen him in stages from almost comatose to where he was, like, *vibrating*. It seemed like he was trying to destroy himself. He would be afraid to do things—but somehow he was compelled to do them."

J. C. and Jones worked once as a burglary team, then as muggers. J. C. was into heroin, too.

"He's got a crafty-type mind, you know? But he also has, like, a conscience. I could do something and not think about it. But he goes back to it. It really bothers him. And if he's worried about how it'll come out, he won't do it. He's very apprehensive. If he doesn't feel right, he'll say 'later.' He can be very paranoid.

"I remember times we went sick when we couldn't find the right hit. We couldn't hit a woman—it was his code. The dudes who hit women, he feels they are sick. And he's smarter than the average street dude—he's seen more than most of them. And he knows you have to be careful when you work where you live; people will get down on you—fast."

J. C. has a job now. He spends time at one of the storefront centers on Second Avenue. He talks to the workers and the counselors, and he is articulate about many of the places he has been.

"Jones has got his conflict. Everybody in the projects hangs out in cliques, you know? He hangs out with anybody he wants to. He has his maneuverability of color, you know? This gets the other dudes uptight. But people who speak about him will think twice before they do anything. He has worked for years to build himself a reputation—he's known."

What about the law? What about values? J. C. pokes his finger into the air and draws imaginary lines—then slices through the pattern with the flat of his hand, a law student examining the system from a street perspective.

"You don't think about *laws*. It's all irrelevant, man. That's what's been done to Third World cats. A lot of cats on the street scene are very talented, very smart. But unless some cat says, look at this, check it out, the dude is too used to depending on himself. He'll go out and pull a rip rather than go through the changes. Jones has been into this world for twenty years. The way he thinks is as natural as turning on the TV. The community works this way, and perpetuates itself this way. It doesn't give a shit about the laws of the land. *They don't apply.*"

But J. C. got off the streets. "It was like getting ulcers—having to look over my back all the time."

What about Jones? Is his toughness a mask?

"Of course." J. C. is staring into the distance.

"What is underneath it?"

"I don't know . . . it's inadequacy, man. He's afraid to succeed in the straight way. He's been into this world so long that it's the safest thing he knows. Switching over is a whole different thing. You have to break routines, you have to change. Some people won't do it."

J. C. turns and looks directly at me.

"The man is capable of doing anything he wants to do. But it's him, *he's* got to decide what *he's* gonna do. Society can punish him as many times as it wants to, but in the end it comes down to him. *He* decides what he's gonna do."

3

We are walking through the tall buildings, and the day is breezy. I am left to stand near the handball courts while Jones makes a smoke connection on the other side of the asphalt. Roland stays with me. He is short and wiry with a small round face set over chunky shoulders; his hair is close-cropped and curly. Roland talks carefully at first.

"He wants to make it big. He thinks about having the green, and he has plans and schemes. That's how he sees it, you know? That is his aim in life, to get over in a way that makes him big. He doesn't want to deal with all the petty shit."

Roland was a junkie, too. He left his habit at Odyssey House, where he was trained as a carpenter. He laughs oddly —almost self-consciously—when I ask about the mugging days; he and Jones were frequent partners. They shoot coke together now and hang out and sometimes talk about jobs and the future. But Roland has left the life; he subcontracts for construction jobs with a crew of three men. Work is spotty, but he is doing reasonably well.

"One summer me and Jeff was talking about jobs, and Jones was right there, planning, suggesting things. But you know he makes plans and never follows them through. I don't think it's in his mind to work eight hours a day. He lives *off* people."

Roland looks at me.

"He has this eye; he knows where the money is. I would go to mug a dude, and he would have two dollars in his pocket. Jones goes after a dude and comes up with a hundred. He has really got the Eye. He can make good money."

I looked at Roland. "What if you had this gift?"

Roland cackles happily. "Oh yeah! I would be right out there, man."

4

"I was sick, and I needed some dope," Jones remembers of his first mugging. "I was with Ronnie, and mugging was his *thing*. This was in 1968, and we were in this building in the projects."

As he talks, he is slightly removed, technical, coldly professional. Yet his eyes betray him, showing a mist of ambivalence. His fingers, interlocked as he begins, fly apart to make urgent, convoluted motions.

"Ronnie knew what he was doing—I didn't know my way at all. We were in a lobby, and we saw this dude about as old as my father. We followed him into the elevator." He describes a man in a long coat. He has gray, thinning hair, and he is stocky, muscle turning to middle-aged flesh.

"The dude knew what we were up to, and he tried to fight his way out of the elevator. Ronnie hit him in the jaw twice. He tried to grab the elevator door. Ronnie closed the door on his hands. He took his money—it was about twelve dollars—and we got out at the next stop and ran down the stairs."

"What did you feel?" I ask. "What was happening inside your head?"

"Wow, I was scared! I was scared of the dude—and then I was scared that the police would come behind all the noise and bust us. It was a learning time for me—I just watched Ronnie do his thing, and I backed him up. I was just out of the Navy—my thoughts were on getting a job or going back to school."

Jones drags on a filter Kool. He is braced tightly, reliving the fear and confusion. If he felt compassion, he doesn't remember it.

"I wasn't doing anything else in crime then. I still had some money left over from the Navy, but it was in bonds, and bonds are hard to cash. It was late at night, nine-thirty or so, and we went and found a connection and copped. We had only gotten twelve dollars, but bags at that time were six dollars, so we got off okay."

5

Handball and basketball games fill the asphalt near the tall buildings, making small circles of energy below them.

I've followed Jones onto the handball court to meet Pinky. The dealer, a high school kid, doesn't want to talk; he looks at me strangely and I move away. I'm wearing street clothes —dungarees, wool shirt, Levi jacket—but I stand out. I am an owl trying to infiltrate a flock of crows.

I ask Jones if I cause problems for him or for his friends. I feel uncomfortable, a little frightened, even guilty that my presence somehow . . . disrupts things. He looks at me without blinking. His response is astonishingly crisp.

"Don't worry about it. They see in you what they lack—class. If you grow up around here, you see one thing; when you meet people who see more, it is hard to relate. People get nervous. If you stay with me, everything is cool. They know I wouldn't bring around a cop or anybody who would cause trouble."

At summer camp, Jones often fought a kid with dark hair and small intense eyes named Danny. They were in grade school together. Jones grew up to become a heroin addict, mugger, and convicted felon. Danny went to City College and got a degree. He is a school counselor now; sometimes he works in the projects, hanging out and talking to his old friends, helping some get into college.

He remembers that he and others teased Jones unmercifully because Jones stutters.

"We abused him. We played with him. It may have hurt him."

Danny is wary of strangers. He spends most of our brief encounter ducking my questions. He *asks* them. What kind of book am I writing? Does Jones know I am asking questions of his friends? (He does.) What do I know of his life? Danny talks and acts as though he is still in the streets. Finally, he gives, slightly.

"He's a frustrated singer. I don't know why he stopped. Maybe you should ask someone else. I can't speak for him. I don't know what the pressures in his family were." Danny stares blankly past me and adds, "Maybe that had something to do with it."

The conversation is frustrating. Of all the people I've talked to, Danny should be the most articulate, the easiest to understand.

"What about school? What was Jones like?"

Danny is impatient and answers my questions grudgingly.

"School was where we socialized. Our main worries were what to do *after* school. We didn't talk about classes or subjects."

"Did Jones fight a lot?"

"He was awkward and unsure of himself. Maybe he's gotten better."

"What about his friendships? Who was he loyal to?" *Talk to me, Danny!*

"I wouldn't use those words. People are very pragmatic here. There are pressures to contend with—social pressures, peer pressures, economic pressures. People carry these around on their backs. And they know something is working on them. But they don't know what. Things change. People move with them."

A teen-ager appears with a large, wet grocery bag. He calls out. The counselor moves over to talk to him.

"Steaks. T-bones and sirloins, right outta the A&P. Half-price for you, man!" The kid opens the bag to show the red meat inside.

Danny laughs and takes the wet, bloody bag and runs into one of the buildings.

6

Joint rolled. Feet on the coffee table. Let's talk about fantasies. Like if you could have anything you wanted . . . anything . . . what would your list be?

"Wow, I'd like to be richer than the Rockefellers! I'd have a Cadillac and a chauffeur. I would go the whole route, and get a Rolls-Royce, too. I would have a diamond ring for each day of the week. I would change clothes three times a day, and I'd have a whole lotta homes.

"I'd have a country home—I would never go there, of course, because I don't like the country. But wow, the house would increase my worth. I'd say to the dudes, I think I'm gonna send my wife out to the country this weekend. You can dig it!

"I'd have a beach house, and I'd have a boat. I'd do the same thing the rich people do, fuck it man! The world isn't ready for the changes of making everyone equal, or treating everybody like a *man*, so fuck it, I would live as well as I could. There are people so rich in this world that they have somebody to do their *worrying* for them. I would live like that.

"I would have a penthouse in the city. I would have a

couple of them, Jack! And—oh yeah—I would move out of this part of town. I would keep a few women around. I do that now, you can dig it, but this time I would really *keep* them.

"I would have the best drugs, man. Smoke you could hardly stand, it would get you off so good. And coke, wow Jack, I would have nothing but the finest crystal. I would be big and everybody would be looking to see what I was gonna do next. I'd have a penthouse for Moms, and so many clothes that I would have to get an extra penthouse just to store them."

"What about a private airplane?"

"Oh yeah, man. One of those, too."

7

It is early afternoon, another day in Jones' *real* life. The dreary, crowded apartment seems unconnected and depressing—an off-Broadway stage set.

Jones' girlfriend, Carol, kneels by the low coffee table in Levi cutoffs and a thin sweater. She wears plastic curlers and she is ironing a pair of Jones' slacks. The television is on. A bed pad serves as the ironing surface.

Jones rolls out of bed in a daze. He shuffles past her, carefully treading the narrow space between the couch and coffee table and Carol's hot iron. The television chatters at both of them: prizes, travel, cheap romance. Couples on "The Newlywed Game" laugh and compete for dishwashers and kitchen sets. Jones shuffles toward the bathroom whose plumbing smells bad.

Carol shifts from one knee to the other to keep her legs from cramping. She has a thin, medium tall, girlish body and a brooding worn face with expressive, often wistful eyes. She is twenty-one, she lives on welfare and is the mother of a three-year-old boy fathered by a high school boyfriend she no longer sees. A pot of rice simmers on a stove behind her.

Jones emerges silently from a long shower and works on

his Afro in front of the mirror. He walks into the living room in his boxer shorts and bare feet; a fragile breeze stirs the window curtains. Carol is still bent over the pants, and the steam iron hisses at her.

The television has shifted to "The Dating Game." A toothy blonde tells the audience that she plays the flute and likes "clean-cut" men. She picks a bachelor and they jet off to Acapulco for a chaperoned weekend. Carol works on the crease in Jones' pants. He flops down on the couch. He lights a cigarette and watches the television vacantly, waiting for her to finish.

8

Jones is a violent man; he knows the streets may kill him. He looks over his shoulder every moment of his life. He hates the tension of this, while knowing it comes with the life he chooses to lead. For the streets allow him to run away from himself, and from the demands and limitations of ghetto life. The alternative is a job: years of dreary work and grinding semi-poverty. The people uptown have good-paying jobs, houses and cars and good clothes.

It doesn't happen to anyone in Jones' neighborhood.

The way to get over is to stay in the street. If you stay alive, you can be *anything*—sooner or later the "big sting" comes your way and you have all the women, clothes, cars, and penthouses you need, right? In the meantime, keep moving.

"Don't ask me about my doubts. That will only hang me up. If I'm gonna survive—a motherfuckin' outlaw, man!—I have to be cool. I could die tomorrow. Can you dig that? Could you handle it? I've gotta live fast. If I make it through, I will *really* have gotten over; I'll be right up there with the Rockefellers! If I don't, nobody will say I didn't have the heart to try. I've got no time to feel pain or remorse. The coke and the music help; and I keep moving. I have to tell you, I am almost afraid to stop. I mean, the shit I got with me now—I can't hardly afford to let it catch up!"

Two

------♦------

1

"It was the first time I ever stomped a guy," Jones remembers, sinking onto Carol's couch. "I went right down on his face with the heel of my shoe."

Jones digs into a steaming plate of macaroni, washing it down with a bottle of beer. Carol is in the kitchen, and this is 3 P.M., his first meal of the day. He is talking about a Chinatown mugging; he had a partner who remains anonymous.

"The Chinks fight hard for their money. I saw this dude in the street—it was the middle of the afternoon—and I knew he had cash. I always know, don't ask me how. People just *look* like they have money. I followed him into this building but the knife flew out of my hand when I went to make my move.

"The fight got real noisy. I knocked him down, and he was making sounds and groaning and that started bringing people out of the apartment we were in front of."

Jones looks at me. "Dig it: I had to hold the door *and* stomp the guy. That's hard—try it sometime!

"My man finally got in the door and cut the dude's pockets off. He was *still* trying to fight! We got his money and ran down the stairs. Even then, the dude was trying to stop us. He fell down, and he was screaming, and the people were coming out of that door and wow, we were running! Then we see a cop car at the corner."

Jones finishes a mouthful of the pasta and looks at me in a smiling, prideful way.

"This was bad because cops stop you in this neighborhood when you are running, so I yelled at my man, 'Goddamit, you dirty old motherfucker, I'm gonna get you!' And I sort of laughed when I said it, so the cops figured we were playing. They didn't stop us."

2

"I hit the streets each day about twelve and I walk around."

This was the end of the sixties. Jones had spent nearly all of the decade trying to live with heroin and himself. He was telling me about a typical day's work during this period.

"This day I was wearing jeans and cut-off sneakers and a dark knit. It was early in November and starting to get cool. The dude I worked with then was the best crime partner I ever had. He's doin' five-to-ten for robbery now."

Jones was living at home. From that sanctuary, he moved into the larger city as a hunter might.

"We walked up First Avenue and stood in front of a supermarket. This dude came out. He had given the woman a check, and she had given him a lot of bills. You can watch people through the glass and see this.

"He lived about a block away, and we followed him into his building. It was quick; he had the bags in his arms, and I put the knife right above his heart. He said he was a working man and all that bullshit and then we took the roll; it was big, but it was only ones, like maybe thirty-five dollars. We went back to the projects to let things cool off in case he called the cops."

If the police were called, the victim would be put in a patrol car and driven around the neighborhood. The police would take a description of Jones and his accomplice. But most likely, the man would walk to his apartment and open the door with his passkey before he called the police. By the time they arrived, Jones would be blocks away.

"Then we saw this dude coming out of the building across from us. It was later in the afternoon by now, and he was between the doors. He had let the first door lock behind him, and we came in through the other way—he couldn't go in or out. I had the knife out, but I didn't even touch him, He kept on saying, 'Just take it—don't hurt me . . .' "

The man, middle-aged and wise, survived. He had the sense not to frighten or anger his assailant; so he endured fear and humiliation and theft—but not violence or death.

"He might have been around forty. Sometimes you don't remember the faces, just the things they say. He had about fifty dollars and change. We left the change. We went into another part of the projects and let things cool off again.

"We caught the next dude, who was thirty-nine or forty, the same way. He was the kind you had to show you wasn't playing. I pulled the knife and I said, 'Look, we just want your money.' He said, 'What? what?' So I hit him with the handle of the knife. That didn't faze him. I put the knife up against here"—Jones pokes his finger into my stomach—"and wow, he almost had a heart attack! He goes, 'Ah! Ahhhhh-hhhhh!' and wow, I was feelin' bad. Then he says something about how you can't leave your house any more, you get robbed, you know? My man says to check his belt. So far we had about thirty-five dollars. I pulled the belt out and it had two hundred-dollar bills behind a zipper."

As the man says, you can't leave your house any more.

"Then we saw this white dude. If you see a white dude down here, something's strange; this one had come to get dope. We said, 'Hey, man, why don't you come over here? We'd like to talk to you.' He had about seventy dollars. He said he would come back for us, and there's a lot of racketeers around that area, so we decided to cool it for a few days. We split up the cash and I laid up with my share. We had wanted to put together some money and cop a lot of dope. This wasn't enough, but I figured we should stay off the streets for a while anyway."

Not bad. Half of $337 for a day's work. Yet *not* enough. It would not sustain Jones very long, for as always the Law of Easy Money was at work. Anything above the price of a day's habit would be spent blindingly fast.

"This was in the daytime. We were downtown, and the guy I was with had a lot of heart. We saw a dude coming out of a store with a bag in his arms; he was dressed nice. We followed him to his building and got in the elevator with him; he pressed nine, so we pressed seven. Then we ran up the two flights of stairs, and got there as he got out. The elevator door had closed behind him.

"The dude was strong, and he knew what was happening. He dropped the bag and started to fight. We both went for him. I grabbed his shirt collar—you can lead a dude around that way—but my nails broke and I lost my grip. My man got scared now; he stabbed him with his K-55."

The K-55 is a smaller version of the .007. Both knives are favorite muggers' tools. The K-55 has a long metal handle, and a locking blade that is at most three or four inches long. The .007, which Jones has, is more expensive, with a hefty wooden handle and a longer blade. Neither is spring-action; a practiced thumb and forefinger action forces the blade out of the handle. A powerful wrist snap and a click! complete the movement. With practice the knife opens as fast as any switchblade.

"It was a quick thing, and that did it."

Jones' accomplice has "heart." It means that he is capable of sudden, reckless violence. Jones does not approve of this; one part of him does not. He grinds his teeth at the memory.

"He was against the wall holding himself. He was stabbed now, and he was screaming and we took his money—one hundred and fifty dollars—and split. I was scared! We ran down nine flights of stairs. I knew if I got busted, the courts would hang me."

Jones' face is tight, tense. He looks at me, and the tension reaches across the space between us. Several seconds pass before he says anything.

"I dreamed about this for three days. It was the horror of the thing; I was part of it. My man had trouble pulling the blade out of the dude. He had to pull hard, and the blood ran all down him."

Jones sits forward. "I don't know if I want to talk about it." Silence. He puts his hand under his chin, and says nothing for seconds. Then he starts again.

"The dream went almost the way it happened. It would start to happen, and I would wake up; I would go back to sleep and see him being stabbed. Moms and Pops thought I was crazy—I was punching the wall in my sleep. They asked what I was doing—I told them it was nothing. I had been down with stabbings as a kid; but then I knew the dude. He had done something to abuse me."

Jones is lost in his grim memory.

"When you don't know the person you are doing the harm to, taking his money is enough. This dude hadn't done shit to me and now he was being stabbed and I was part of it. There are dudes out there I wouldn't mind killing, but it's a bitch to stab someone you don't know.

"We ran to a park. When we stopped, I asked my man why he did it. He said he didn't know why. I didn't want to show I was afraid, so I dropped it."

4

"It isn't so safe in the streets. The cops are out; everybody is uptight. Buildings are better."

The man in the hallway might have been thirty-five years old. He was Chinese; but his face was hardly inscrutable; it showed pain and fright and humiliation. He had managed to shut the street door in time to keep one of his assailants out of the hallway. But the other was upon him. He flailed and pushed and moved as fast as he could.

"I hit him in the face a couple of times. Then I hit him again. I felt the blow crush something, something went squish. I looked at my hand and it was okay—so it had to be him."

In the darkness the man moaned and became silent. Jones

let him fall. He turned to let his partner into the building. No one had heard the fight.

"It was kinda funny. He had been up against the wall and he gas goin' uhhhhh, uhhhhhhh . . . and he didn't have any place to go. When I let go, he just dropped. I let my man in. We was in a hurry—we took the dude's money and ran, it was about twenty dollars. There was cops all over that night."

"Did the man die?" I ask, sick at the thought.

"I don't know. I never read the newspapers afterward—I don't want to feel sorry about what happened. Some dudes are different. They want everybody to know about it. Not me."

5

A neon-colored night. Jones and I walk down Houston Street, past the mute wilderness of an empty park. "I've got to get some fresh air," he'd said. "Sometimes when I've been sleeping and smoking, I get to thinking and my nerves start bothering me. I've got a lot of things on my mind."

We are talking now about women and old people—as victims. Jones is opposed to the idea.

"An old man can have a weak heart and die from the shock of the beating—that can be Murder One. It's premeditated because they say you planned the mugging. Mugging by itself is a robbery and assault charge, which is easier to beat."

This is a recurring bit of ambivalence. Jones will not mug women or old men he considers helpless. It is not just a matter of ethics; pragmatism is involved. A murder charge means a lot of prison time. And women tend to scream; you have to silence them, fast. More prison time.

A middle-aged woman hurries by, clutching her purse tightly. Jones pauses to watch her.

"Now that's a *shame*. She's alone, and she's afraid of being mugged. I see women like that, and I think of Moms. If a dude hurt her, that would bring me out in the streets like a wild man! I would *really* hurt someone. If someone hits Pops, he can take it. A woman is a different thing."

It's nice to have ideals, I am thinking. Then I ask: "Who *does* hit women?"

"Dudes afraid to face men."

He drifts for a moment as the middle-aged woman disappears.

"If a woman starts screaming, somebody, even a punk, will want to help her. Then you got two people to deal with. A woman like this can make you want to hurt her, which is a drag. I think about my mother. If someone took her off, it would hurt me; she can't really get down with a dude and win."

"If you saw a woman being mugged, would you help her?"

Jones says nothing. We pass a patrol car idling outside an all-night coffee shop. Then he nods.

"Yeah. If the woman was getting hurt, I would help her. Dudes who get down with women have no heart. I would definitely get into it."

6

Jones spreads clear polish on his thumbnail with a tiny brush to toughen the sharpened surface. We are talking about mugging techniques.

"I'm into drops now. You lay outside a bank, or a check-cashing place; you know the dudes have cash. You can be even more selective if you want. Today, like, I watched faces going in and out of this bank. Tomorrow I'll go back again. If I see those faces again, I'll know they aren't going to the bank for themselves. So I'll pick a face and follow it to its store. As a rule, stores make one drop a day. They usually make these drops between two and three o'clock. I'll time this dude for a few days. Say he's pretty close to between two and two-thirty. I make it my business to be there."

He turns to his other thumb, dipping the brush into the small jar again.

"You have to remember the faces you've taken off. You

see a dude twice, you give him a rest; because if your face becomes familiar, it's trouble. I don't walk much in the areas where I work."

"You'll mug a man twice?"

"Oh yeah. He'll be slick for a while after the first time. But he'll drop his guard again. It ain't *his* money. He isn't going to risk his life for it."

Jones is into the talk now. His hands loop and dive in the space in front of him.

"It's not worth it to fuck with people on the street. The regular dude, he's like you and me. He's working, he's got a wife and kids. He don't carry much money—and he might fight. The dude with the drop, he's got more money, and he's got insurance."

"Do you still hit people randomly?"

"Yeah, sometimes. I prefer drops, but you have to plan for them. If you need money right away, you resort to the old street thing."

"How do you spot the right person to mug?"

"You walk behind a dude. If he keeps looking around, if he's leery, you know something is up. If he's got no money, he's got nothing to worry about, right? You walk beside him, and if he's looking over his shoulder—if he's got eyes in the back of his head—you've got your man."

"What's the most you've gotten?"

"One time me and my man saw this fat dude, and I just had this feeling, you know? We followed him into this building and *wow*, he had cash everywhere! In his pockets, in his belt, in his shoes, in a case he was carrying . . . we got a thousand dollars. Sometimes a good drop is worth that much, too."

I am thinking. When Jones works regularly, he says he makes more than a hundred dollars a day. Perhaps several thousand dollars a month, perhaps $20,000 a year. It is tax free. A $1,200 paycheck has about $900 left after the government gets its bite. So he has the equivalent of a $25,000 job.

Let's assume Jones is bragging—that he makes only half that amount. Thus he is making ten thousand tax-free dollars a year. He may be short on social security and medical plans, but at ten thousand after taxes he is doing better than most of New York City's office workers, delivery men, factory people, cops, and firemen. Not to mention free-lance writers. And he pays no rent.

Twenty thousand—if he was not exaggerating—means he does as well as the middle-level executives of Madison Avenue and Wall Street. He could drink in Sardi's after the theater, shop on Fifth Avenue, attend Lincoln Center concerts, and consult the *New York Times* restaurant guide for three-star French restaurants.

Yet Jones is constantly broke. He takes money from his women, borrows from his parents, and hits me up practically every time we get together (and always pays me back). He dresses well and uses expensive drugs—but they can't possibly account for all the money he spends. Yet beyond the drugs and clothes, he lives like a welfare recipient. *Why?* There never seems to be a satisfactory answer.

One reason may be the blackly ironic economics of the ghetto. Goods and services cost more. Groceries in a bodega cost as much as gourmet foods on the fashionable Upper East Side; small stores must have a high margin to survive. Even supermarkets, as congressional studies have shown, are higher. Public transportation is usually poorer, and gypsy cabs cost plenty. Rent is cheap, but the tenants often must put money into the apartments to make them livable. Cheap furniture and household items are sold at exhorbitant prices through deceptive time payment plans. The furniture wears out before the payments are finished.

But economics is not the answer, even the largest part of it. The problem is lifestyle.

"A thousand-dollar rip-off means you can relax for a while, right?"

"Oh no! I go through it in three or four days. I buy clothes, I go out, I get high. I get shoes, or a knit, or slacks —I get a lot of things I don't need. You just live while the money's there; that's the rule of the street. That's one thing dope did—it made me live for the day. When I've got money,

I don't sleep for three or four days—you're just *buying* something all the time. If you've got the money that easy and that fast, it doesn't have any value."

Jones and money are like a lion and its latest kill. The meat is eaten now—day-old flesh is for jackals. Let the future take care of itself.

Jones doesn't entirely believe this, of course. He feels trapped by street life—somehow heroin disrupted his life in more than chemical ways. He sees cars and nice apartments and legitimate money around him, and he tells himself he should save his resources and buy things that last. But at night, when he is alone and thinking about his life, he sees two images. One reaches out, gently saying work and save, become stable.

The other shrieks that nothing matters: get it *now*. And he knows that this vision—and he hates himself for knowing it—has more strength than its cautious, thoughtful twin.

"You have a car and cash in the bank," he says to me in gloomy moments. "You *have* things. And I have a yellow sheet and a hole in my arm. Wow, what *happened?*"

It is a question I asked again and again—the question that formed with our first meeting outside the subway station on Houston Street.

Three

—————◆—————

1

It is several hours short of midnight. The corner outside the Houston Street station has no one resembling the kid I expected to find, a kid in dungarees and dirty sneakers, a kid with drugged eyes, a face reflecting the dust and venom of street life.

A man loiters near the entrance as if waiting for a date; he walks easily, smoking a cigarette. He has chosen his clothes carefully, and he has an air of confidence. In the cool night he wears tweed slacks and a brown, zippered sweater with dark leather frosting about the shoulders and neck. He stands tall in stack-heeled loafers, and his profile reveals a tiny gold pin pierced through his left earlobe. When he turns, I see a fist carved from dark wood hanging on a leather thong around his neck.

"Jones?"

He turns to look at me. Then he smiles, offering his hand. It closes around mine with the suddenness and force of a hungry reptilian mouth. I feel his fingernails; they are long and sharp, like teeth.

"Right. Good to see you, Sam." He looks directly into my eyes.

"So what's happening?" In future encounters, when I ask that, he'll invariably respond: "You, man, you."

I ask where we should talk and he suggests an apartment ten minutes away, Carol's place. We begin walking along Houston Street.

We are in an area rich and troubled in its history of immigrant struggles, bohemian life, ethnic diversity—and crime. We walk through tangled, grubby, narrow blocks of delicatessens, pizza counters, pawnshops, street corner subcultures of winos, welfare money, brown-bagged liquor bottles, rows and rows of claustrophobic tenements, through a community of Jewish, Slavic, and Italian immigrants rubbing unhappily against growing numbers of blacks, Chinese, and Puerto Ricans—a spoiling plum pudding of multiracial poverty and random violence.

"You, uh . . . have any trouble getting here?"

"I had to change trains once—no problem."

He walks with a slow swagger, eyes vaguely on the sidewalk, dragging his feet softly as if immersed in thought . . . unmindful of the street around us. He seems almost a ship's prow. His head does not move from side to side; it cuts through the darkness relentlessly, searching, always forward, shoulders hunched, watching the street.

He is medium height, though he seems taller—maybe five feet, six inches tall—and squarely built. He is twenty-four years old.

His eyes are dark and large and very liquid . . . it is impossible to know what they watch. He does not look at me. His face is locked into a a mask, tight within itself, absorbing the life and energy around it.

We walk by an asphalt park where three kids play one-on-one basketball, filling the night with high-pitched blue curses.

"The younger generation playing," he says without directly looking at them.

I am awed by his hair: an explosive Afro hovering over him like a black halo, lending a leonine appearance to the broad, muscular face. The line of the mouth is set hard, hosting a Zapata mustache and a tight half-beard that shoots down from the lower lip to the base of his chin.

He has powerful shoulders and long arms; the arms hang stiffly from his shoulders, as though he is overburdened with muscles. And the hands, square and massive and tense, hang at his hips as if he might draw a gun, cowboy-style.

36

We walk down a noisy tenement block. Woman lean out of tiny windows watching people below. Some kids play stickball against a building.

We turn into a dark hallway, pushing through a door with no lock.

The hall, lit by a single bulb, is painted moldy green and smells of rotted food and urine. The paint has acquired a skin of intertwined initials, "fuck," "shit," various threatening messages, even valentines.

A sign above some rusty mailboxes reads: "No Loitering Allowed—By Order of Police."

He seems out of place. He has more style than his surroundings. He holds the door for me. He stands politely to let me approach the stairs first. He is . . . courtly.

And he is alone. Something in the way he holds his head, his word when he turns to talk, says this unmistakably.

2

The apartment is close and crowded. He motions toward an old couch facing a wall. The room space seems barely ten feet across, one of three containers coupled together to form a railroad flat, cheap furniture throughout. He brings glasses of ginger ale without ice, then eases onto the couch so he can look at me or turn away.

I take out my notebook.

As we talk, he uses his hands to form words. His face tightens or falls into an easy smile or crinkles in laughter. But always, his hands move like gliders, floating and diving. The fingers move almost independently, spreading as his hands loop and fall, steepling as they come together in the air, diving and falling apart and dancing on the coffee table for emphasis.

"Fear is the thing," he begins, looking at me—a professional explaining his work to a novice. "I don't know what *he* knows, and he don't know what I know. It's like going into a fight. I don't like it because I don't like to fight. At heart, I don't want to hurt nobody—I don't want to be hurt myself."

He sounds like an ordinary human being talking about his work.

"The best time to mug a person is in the daytime," he says next.

He sprinkles marijuana into rolling papers and winds them carefully into a slender joint. Still talking: "That's because the people around don't want to get involved. Good things happen in the daytime; this *isn't* how things work, so they don't want to deal with it."

He brings a match flame to the tip, takes several deep drags and blows out a long thin cloud of smoke.

"Say it's two or three o'clock. You're on your lunch break and you see this dude being stabbed. You would look away—you'd say, 'Damn, look at the motherfucker, he's crazy!' In the daytime, people are always rushing somewhere. Somebody else will take care of this."

He holds out the joint. He is considerate; he shares. The man talks of mayhem, but he acts the good host.

Man? He seems younger than manhood. But he is far older than the children in the streets outside. As he talks, I nod and write in my notebook. I stop him sometimes so I can catch up with the dialogue; he likes this.

"At heart, man is a beast. He gets enjoyment from your hardships. Say you are being hassled by a mugger . . . someone might want to call the cops. But first he wants to see who wins. So by the time he calls them, you have done your bit; you are gone."

The man-boy sits on the edge of the couch, hands aloft, telling stories. He seems friendly—a boozy master plumber at a bar telling how he fits pipes together. I am hearing some of his more interesting fittings. I am writing furiously, flipping notebook pages, following him with a parallel mind-set, the journalist in me asking questions, monitoring the dialogue and struggling to transpose it into a notebook—while my Good Citizen mentality radiates fear and fascination.

I let him talk, interrupting only when he falters: questions, compliments, subtle barbs, sympathy, anything to keep it flowing.

"I dig chess. I used to play it a lot. Mugging is like that. You try to stay a few moves ahead of the dude you are going to hit; you can't let him know you are setting him up. You are deep into planning the way it will happen, and the big thought is that he might not go along with your scheme. You don't want a big scrap because that brings cops. You want to get in and get out fast."

The plumber-mugger offers me more ginger ale at this point. I say no, and he looks at me. Anything else? You comfortable?

I ask how often he "works."

"There's some weeks when I don't feel like going out at all. I'll go out once or twice. Other times, I want a suit or a pair of shoes or something. I might go out two or three times in one day."

"Alone?"

"It depends on who you go out with. It's best to work alone. You and a dude can be the closest of friends, but time [jail] scares people. Suppose he gets caught and you don't. The Man will come into his cell and says . . ."

Jones lowers his voice and wags his shoulders like a vaudeville clown.

" '. . . Well, *Goddam, Son,* there's *nuthin' we can do* unless you tell us some things . . .'

"And that's a drag. It brings a lot of worry down on you, wondering if your partner got caught. If you go out alone, it's your baby."

He is enjoying the attention. He plays to an imaginary camera, making faces, smiling, turning serious, throwing his arms toward the audience, ham hands, rubber expressions. It is hard not to laugh and enjoy the stories. I laugh, then realize I am laughing at stories of robbery and terror; and the fellow telling them is the robber and terrorist, the one mugging for the camera.

"Maybe you hang out by this bank and you see a dude roll in and bust a check. The broad behind the counter gives him bills, man, and she *keeps* giving him bills. Or a dude comes out of his store with a brown bag in his hand. It's a meat store, and you *know* the store don't make deliveries. At the end of the day, people always go to the bank. They're all so goddamned worried they'll get mugged that they look behind them, like this."

Jones swivels back and forth, his eyes darting around the room in mock fear.

"Man, they are looking *everywhere!*"

I ask about weapons. An edgy seriousness swallows the smile.

"I use a knife . . . a person feels a knife *more*. A gun is loud; the dude you have got it up against knows it would draw a crowd. But with a knife, people going by, people doing their business, they might not notice someone is being stabbed. And man, a knife is worse than a gun because . . ."—Jones reaches one long arm into the air and makes a slitting motion—"you can put the knife in a lot of places and do a lot of bad things. People know this. You know how you are walking down a street, deep in your thoughts, and a car honks at you—you say, wow! seeing a knife is like that."

Jones moves toward me. He swiftly throws his hand out, landing it lightly against my neck.

I want to back away. We are on the edge of the couch.

"Maybe you stopped the dude to ask the time, or for a dime for the telephone. You put the knife on him right then, hard, and you push him into a doorway."

Jones pauses, pondering his next statement. His hand is still against my throat.

"People are afraid of death. So if the dude's got a brain, he says fuck it man, the money's yours. If he's gonna be a hero, you've got to be deadly. Maybe he kicks you in the balls . . . but when you move that knife, *he* gets hurt, too. You can run at this point—he can't. He's got the shock of being cut coming down on him."

Jones still holds his closed hand against my throat. I pull away, saying I must write down what he is saying. I feel warm; the room is very small.

"If we are in a hallway and I've got some time, I'll probably pull the knife back and hit him with the butt. If that doesn't bring him around, I've got to cut him."

Jones has jumped to his feet, moving his hands to show how he would deal with this imagined victim, shifting his feet on the rug for balance.

The next question is obvious.

"Would you kill him if it came to that?" I am hoping he'll say no, and I feel considerable tension about this, pen stopped dead in the middle of the notebook page, waiting. He starts slowly.

"I . . . I don't want to kill him . . . if I don't have to. I'd go to jail for a long . . . long time." Pause. My writing hand pauses with him. "But if I *lose* the fight he'll take things from me that *I've* got. You have to weigh it out; but you don't have enough time . . . to think clearly."

He stops in the middle of the room, standing quietly. "I don't *think* I've ever killed anybody. I've left dudes who weren't moving. But I don't think I've killed anybody—at least I've never heard about it . . ."

Jones suddenly turns to me with a roaring fire of a smile.

"Wow, everybody who reads this book will want to hear about *that!* People are so fucked up, man! They *want* to see blood!" He stops and nods to himself. "I did some boxing once, and they would urge you on, they wanted blood, but when they got it—can you dig this?—they would say you've got no heart. You hurt someone."

He shakes his head sadly. "People are weird. They go to horror flicks, they watch the shit on television, they come around when there's a fight. *But they say they don't want blood.*"

3

Jones stutters. Words resisting him are struggling, fighting, living things inside, kicking and pushing to be born—his face contorted, eyes hot and turned into dark slits as he struggles, a scowl, almost a scream from the face as the hands move and lash out and fight to force the words out.

"Like youuuu . . . like youuuuuu . . ." The hands whirl, the face coils and tightens. "Like youuuuu. . . ." And he breaks through: "Like YOU see, street life is hard. I meeeaaannn . . ."

The hand slams down on the coffee table, fingernails clicking loudly. The thrusting hand and scowling face reach painfully for dignity, for crisp, precise words.

"I meeeaaannn . . ." The breakthrough: "I MEAN street life is watching your back, you gotta *keep* looking . . ."

Jones remembers his muggings. He remembers the time, the place, the details; he remember much of his life as precisely. He remembers once taking more than a hundred dollars from a man who fought back.

"It's not really what happens that changes, it's how they react. Thisss . . . thisss . . ." His face turns to blue ink, a relief map of the purgatory underneath. The fingers crash down on the table. "Thisss . . ." He regains control. "THIS dude wouldn't come around. I had tried to do it nice. This was when I first began mugging, and I was uptight. I had just wanted to get done and leave. But he held me. I hit him and he fell to one knee, and he still tried to be bad, you know? So I had one knee on his chest, and I was worried about getting away; so I thought, fuck it man, he can't run after me if he ain't got no clothes.

"Thaaaa . . ." The blockage again, irregular, unpredictable, often an endless interruption. Jones cuts at the space in front of him, fingers wide, choking and cursing. He regains the language: "THAT part of town was hot at the time, a lot of cops around. I pulled his pants off, then his shirt and his drawers. *Then* the dude couldn't chase me. I tried to rip off his pockets to get the money, but I couldn't do that; the pants were too good."

He pauses and pulls on the joint.

"He had old-style clothes. The new things aren't made that good."

He looks up.

"Anyway, I left him with his shoes and socks. I put the other things in a trash can. So, like, even if he found some cops he'd be excited and they'd take him for a fool. I'd be long gone."

Why—why the cruelty, why humiliate him? Phlegm is gathering in my throat. Why hurt him?

The answer is muffled. In later conversations it will involve fear and nervousness; it will involve hostility and release, pent-up aggression, undefined anger; it will involve manhood and street reputation, and most of all it will involve simple luck, how your eyes or hands move when Jones appears, what you say, what he senses about you.

A dog barks outside the window, which is half blocked by the shell of a building under construction. He turns to look for the sound. He is a bafflingly complex man; stuttering is only part of the problem, a small part.

"The dude may say, this here is cash for my wife and children. He'll say his wife is sick, and all that shit. But, like, you make it known that you *still* want the money. He has to give it up. There's times when you feel bad. He's so nice; he don't want to put you out of your way, even when you took him out of his. Other times a dude will put you through a lot of changes. He'll fight back, or give you a lot of bullshit. Then you feel like, man . . . man, you feel good! Maybe you take his pants off just to be bitchy."

4

Second joint now. And he seems . . . sharper now, picking up speed. I am relaxed, scribbling slower. It seems easier; the Good Citizen is quiet.

"You hang out a lot—so you have to look good. Levis don't make it. You want to look right. If you look like a bum, you stand out."

Jones motions toward a closet stuffed with coats and sweaters at the far end of the room.

"I might wear a two-piece suit. Knits and suits are all I

buy—people think you are waiting for a date. So they sleep on you. You look like you've got a job."

His eyes are glazed and slightly red. He is tripping on these stories, flying with the joint and the ego massage of being interviewed. And I've begun to float through this fantasyland of violence, sinking happily into the muck of it, keeping my pen barely above the waterline.

"I try to be as obvious as I can. If you sneak around, you do stupid things. Say I spot this dude in a bank. When he comes out, I walk up and say, 'Excuse me, sir, do you know the time?' He says it's two-thirty and I say, 'Wow, that broad is late again!' You keep talking and he is walking and he's half listening. He's sympathetic, you know, but he doesn't want to get involved. He sleeps on you, and you push him into a doorway."

Perhaps the psychology is elementary, yet I don't expect such detail. This isn't random violence or street hostility. He knows what he's into. Something in me is stirring. I want to know what he reads. Psychology? Novels? Mysteries? He mentioned "psyche" books earlier, and now he goes into the back room and takes a library book out of a dresser drawer.

"I been readin' this," he says, handing it to me. "It helps me get into people's heads."

It is *The Power of Positive Thinking*, by Dr. Norman Vincent Peale.

I sit for several seconds . . . struggling with the shock of seeing Peale's work touted as a mugger text.

Peale preaches the gospel of Wonderfulness. He is a conservative, homespun minister, one of Richard Nixon's Holy Men, a law-and-order man . . . certainly no friend of Jones . . . this is crazy. I can't think of anything to say.

I nod, I make noises, I squirm. I change the subject. Let's talk more about technique.

"It's best to get a person into a place where he can't move. Walls are good for that. The dude wants to get away from that wall, he wants to move. But it's hard. By the time he gets himself together, it's happened."

"What do you feel when this is happening?"

44

"I read in a book that fear is a sickness—when you fear, the other man is better than you.

"Is that from Dr. Peale?"

"Maybe. I don't remember. So you can't be like that—everybody can bleed and die. The only thing I really fear is dope. She has whipped me a thousand times . . . and I truly fear her."

He stops long enough to light a Kool, waving the hand that holds it. A thin line of tobacco smoke follows his spread fingers like skywriting.

"Fear is just another emotion. You are taught from birth you will be punished if you do something wrong. Dig it: pulling a rip is against the law, and you are taught fear of the law. But then you say, if this can help *me*, it's right."

Jones suddenly turns and looks at me squarely. His face is blankly open, vulnerable, straining for a strange innocence.

"I won't lie to you. What I do is wrong—deep, deep down I believe this. *But man, it gives me life.*" He stops quickly, looking hard at me. And I wonder what he wants me to say. That's okay, Jones?

"When I hit a dude, I feel bad for him. But I am doing a job. Dig it: I don't like my job; nobody likes to go to work. Maybe he doesn't like *his* job, either. But *my* job is more dangerous. Maybe he worked all day, and he was coming home for lunch and I grabbed him. I know it's wrong. But this gets me what I need. Life is based on survival, and self comes first. What it gets down to is that what's right for some isn't right for all."

Another delicate question, asked in some discomfort. What happens if a victim hasn't any money?

"I won't hurt a dude. I get mad, but I figure it's not his fault. Some dudes *will* hurt the guy. This is why it's hard for muggers now. These young dudes don't think how it's possible *not* to have money. This is bringing a lot of shit down—you'll do a lot of time if you get caught mugging. And people are carrying guns and learning how to box. They are going to school for the fighting arts. That's no good, man!"

He shakes his head, scowling. "If a person gets hurt, it

probably means he tried to be bad. But it could mean the mugger was fucked up. Most dudes who hurt people are 'butch kids.' They have to be bigger and badder than the rest of us. They figure, wow, if I do things hard I'll get a rep. People won't fuck with me. So they fuck it up for everybody else."

Jones crushes the cigarette in an ashtray. "One time people just got robbed; that was all. Junk had a lot to do with the changes. The junkie is sick, and he don't feel like waiting for his money. He goes to mug a dude, and the dude says, 'What!' and he bangs him. He hits him or he stabs him because he's fucked up himself, nervous and scared, you know?"

The plumber says his customers are complaining. Shoddy workmanship, high prices, the pipes don't hold water. It's hard to get decent help. Everything is going to hell. Hard times, these.

"If you are a mugger, it's really bad out there. People have gotten hurt for nothing; they are fed up. Too much has gone down . . . things have gotten out of hand."

I am feeling a little flushed. One of us is sitting upside down on this couch, because until I entered this room, I thought the public was upset about mugging, not the muggers. Is there a mirror between us? "What do you mean, nothing? People shouldn't be fed up? What if you were getting mugged, man?"

Jones' dark face registers awed surprise. "If you come up to me, Jack, and you've got the knife, it's yours." He pushes on without waiting for me to react. "Once I had to stomp a dude in a doorway and almost break his head for thirty-three dollars. Hey, wow! The dude almost gave up his life! It ain't right. If *you've* got the knife, I ain't gonna fight you, even if I've got a grand in my pocket. It's stupid, man!"

He is staring at the floor and nodding to himself. He sees his ideas vividly; I see the dusk of alienation. He lunges at me with his words, as if he is sneaking around this apartment hiding behind tables and chairs and walls . . . then jumping out to say each new, crazy thing.

A simple homily is reversed: today may be the last day of the rest of his life, not the first.

Yet he somehow sees something in this darkness. He can put his knife to your throat, take your money—and then meet his mother after work to escort her home from the bus.

"Don't worry about the neighborhood, man . . . it's okay," he said once when we planned to meet late at night. *I am talking to two men.*

"Society is built to make the rich richer and the poor man poorer," he suddenly says, looking up. "The Rockefellers were down with crime; so was the Kennedys. And wow, now they make laws so you can't get rich the way they did!"

I ask if he's heard of Watergate. It is April 1973, and while the controversy is a front-page story, it hasn't gone into televised hearings.

He hasn't heard of it. But I want to know how he sees government and law.

"Nixon is just one more crook that got over big, you know? I don't like to think about him much. He got over big, but he don't want *you* to get over big because you ain't with *his* crowd. He don't have to go according to the laws he has set, you know? He gets over two hundred thousand a year—he don't do a motherfucking thing for it. His parties are written off as a business expense; he don't have to spend a cent."

Jones lights another cigarette, nodding like a yo-yo. He likes the sound of what he is saying. I can't believe where all this is coming from: so twisted . . . so accurate.

"The best crook of all," he laughs, "was J. Edgar Hoover. He was the only dude in the world they *didn't* have a file on. He watched his back—he was a slick, slick dude!"

We are still falling through the mirror. Why not fall further? Define "criminal."

"A crook is a person who don't go according to the laws he has set. I don't feel that I'm a crook. I don't go by *their* laws, but to me I have a job the same as you."

"What laws do you go by?"

"Well, I guess you could say I make them up as I go along. That's *basically* the same as their laws. They hurt people to get where they are, too."

"They are different?"

"Yeah, I can't refer to them as part of me. I don't relate to them. They don't have to worry; they had rich parents they could get things from. Suppose their house is robbed. They can put it back together without any big loss; I can't. And you know, they talk about how they are for the poor. How can they *say* that—they've never been poor!"

Jones waves his hand around the apartment.

"This place was robbed two weeks ago; I was really fucked up about it, man. We had a stereo. It was made by the Panasonic people, really nice. They took it; they took the TV and some clothes and a glass cooking set. They came through the back window."

He falls onto the couch, settling in; his face softens.

"I do believe in things coming back to you. But I didn't think it would be *this* soon."

I have no idea where Jones' mind is moving at this moment.

"You understand, I don't think I'm above it. I can get ripped off like anybody else. I can bleed and die, too."

Pause. I'm waiting for the next U-turn.

"If a dude caught me in the streets and ripped me off, I'd be really angry the first day; I might hurt him if I saw him again."

He sinks further into the couch.

"But after a couple of weeks, I wouldn't hurt him. I was really fucked up over this apartment, but that's the way it goes, I guess. I've got a police lock now."

Four

—◆—

1

I'm driving to the Lower East Side, and the terrain as always seems startlingly like one end of a giant chessboard. Toward the East River, star-shaped orange-brick city housing projects rise, clusters of surreal rooks and smaller pawns stretching as far as I can see. At Manhattan's south end, the tall figures touch Chinatown; their northern tip reaches the middle-class brownstones and brick high-rises of Stuyvesant Town and Peter Cooper Village. Into these angular city-sponsored apartment buildings hundreds of thousands of poor people are compressed, pawns themselves in the politics of housing and urban development.

Ironically, the projects are the cutting edge of progress. For while they are poorly designed and vastly overcrowded —black leaders sometimes call them "vertical prisons"—they are a considerable improvement over the area's tenements: rickety buildings with peeling paint, roaches, diseased rats, broken plumbing, uneven heat, and precious little sunlight poking through cracked windows. The projects and the privately owned slums form a community that sweeps west from the tall chessboard figures to a broad flatland of row houses, stores, and cavernous warehouses stretching between the East River and lower Broadway

Here, wash hangs in fluttery lines outside tenement windows. The streets are exuberant with alfresco shops, noisy children, pungent bakeries, bell-ringing Softee and Sno-Cone vendors, and cranky old women in shawls and shapeless

49

black dresses. On the corners, black and Puerto Rican men strut in sky blue, plum red, and electric green clothing, drinking out of bottles wrapped in paper bags while winos sleep fitfully behind them in doorways.

It is Jones' world. He grew to manhood in the middle of this. He learned to fight in a park that fills the space between half a dozen buildings in his parents' project, and he matched skills in stickball, handball, and basketball with children of other poor families in the playing courts nearby. At home, his family life was defined by encounters around a small, crowded kitchen table. And when he wanted to be alone, he retreated to a cube-shaped bedroom with a tiny window casting its eye over the park. Beyond his parents' apartment he explored streets and stores and bus stops and subway tunnels to the rest of the world, a park near the Brooklyn Bridge where he and others built a clubhouse, Chinatown and Wall Street, which he would later terrorize as a mugger, and the East Village where he would work as a confidence man and burglar—and suffer his worst days as a heroin addict.

At night the projects blink at the city. A hundred thousand lighted window-eyes come alive as poor families relax and laugh at the passed day, argue and fight into the night. On a particular night recently, a single window stared out of the fifteenth floor of a tall group of projects near the Brooklyn Bridge; in the apartment's kitchen Jones sat at the small table pulling on a Kool and blowing smoke toward the ceiling, nodding a little, drifting.

As usual, an argument was about to begin.

2

"Want a beer, son?"
It was after midnight, and Charles Jones, a slim, soft-spoken man with straightened gray hair, had returned from his shift as a post office night clerk.

"Pops" is a tall, careful man with large eyes and boyish good looks; his face is marred only by skeins of pocked skin along his cheeks and a puffy boil on one cheekbone. He is a delicate man; his emotions rise quickly to the top of his vulnerable face: pain, dignity, anger, ego, defiance.

He has not been happy; he loves his family, he has worked hard for them, but in the long march through marriage and fatherhood he has looked behind to find they no longer follow. They do not share his values. They ask advice, but rarely take it; they visit the house as regularly as sons and daughters should—sometimes too regularly—but he and they do not inhabit the same space. The bond linking them is frayed in too many places, a rope too often knotted and kinked, sometimes oddly cut. What links them is blood, not friendship or shared goals.

That evening Jones sat at the kitchen table, listening to the night, thinking, drifting, waiting for sleep, musing about the day. Pops was behind him, pulling on the refrigerator's swinging door, hand closing around two bottles of Miller's, then moving to a bottle of Chivas Regal in a cluttered cabinet to pour as a chaser.

"He'll ask me if I want a beer," Jones explains to me. "Then I *know* we'll have this argument. Heeeee . . . Heeeee . . ." Jones' eyes are shut as he tries to tell the story. I lean back, waiting; he seems so close to explosion in these moments, and it is difficult to conceal the tension this causes in me.

"Heeeee . . ." Release—the face relaxes: "HE wants to talk. I don't want to. But I know sometimes I might want to talk to *him*. So I figure fuck it man, let's talk. I always look right at him: if I look away, I stutter."

The two are flint and stone; rub them and sparks fly. Their conflict is as deep as blood kinship and pride, as shallow as simple competition and the opposing style of generations. Begin with their service records. The older man left World War II as a staff sergeant. He served in the campaigns of North Africa, Italy, and France. The younger man is a Navy dropout; he bought hashish in Turkey, worked in a carrier's enlisted mess off Vietnam. Then he was forced out.

The older man was a hospital orderly and factory assembly

51

line worker; he returned to school on the GI Bill and passed the civil service exam. He has seen trouble; he has been out of work. But he has provided; he feels he is a man of dignity and honor in that. Yet to his deep shame, his oldest son is a common criminal and a drug addict. Two women carry the son's seed; the son does *not* support them. He loves his son, make no mistake about it. If only he could talk to him.

Divorced from his first wife during World War II, Charles Jones was assigned to Staten Island after the overseas campaigns. He had no reason to return to Dayton, where his father, an immigrant from Tahiti, practiced medicine; so he settled in New York. He had five brothers and sisters. Four survive today, and both his mother and father are dead.

The Jones kitchen is crowded. A wood and glass cabinet stuffed with beer mugs, glasses, and souvenir bric-a-brac leans against one wall; a green and white Heineken's Beer windmill stands on top of it.

The apartment is laid out in right angles, a confluence of spindly arms and legs pushing from the body of a long hallway, a dark, heavily curtained living room up front, bedrooms at the far end. In the dark living room, a large blue couch is covered with plastic; it is cast decoratively against a red rug, a plasterboard false fireplace, a stereo set, and a plastic potted plant.

An oil painting of Charles Jones hangs over the nonfunctional fireplace; and Jesus, suffering from his crown of thorns, stares with heavy eyes from a three-dimensional wall portrait near the hallway. Beyond the kitchen a long linoleum hallway leading to the bedrooms is sprinkled with throw rugs. Jones was raised in this apartment. It is the most important compass point of his life.

"You know you're not doing right, don't you, son?"

The older man settled into a chair, beer glass filled and foamy, Chivas Regal and a shot glass to one side. Jones was still smoking his cigarette, looking down at it . . . he knew the script.

"Why?"

"You know your mother is very sick—the way you live doesn't make it easier."

"Yeah. Right."

The older man spoke crisply. The words were precise, measured, almost elegant; to the younger man they were patronizing. They were clichés.

This is How We Should Live. The boy will see the Sense of It. We will Talk Sensibly. Things Will Change.

"You know she's not very well. This attack could be her last, and *goddamit,* I don't want to see her die!"

The temperature was rising, though only slightly, on both sides.

Jones turned to look at his father, jaw thrust slightly forward. "That's all you talk about. man. I believe there's times when you *want* her to die."

"No—*you* are killing her, you and your brothers and sisters."

The kitchen was heating up. The preliminary talk ranged through areas of crime, money, marijuana, harder drugs, values, family; and Charles Jones' face assumed sad-clown proportions, spectacles sliding to the end of his nose, an anger and simultaneous sense of martyrdom rising. Soon, the shoulders, and a gold chain and crucifix hanging around his neck, began to shake slightly. Almost imperceptibly, Charles Jones was shuddering.

"Check this out," his son was saying, blowing smoke at the ceiling again. "You and Moms have a savings and checking account. She puts money in savings, man, and *you* take it out . . . now . . . now you are into checking, too.

"I *put* it there," he returned heatedly.

"You go through yours, man, and you go into *hers.* You tell her this, and you tell her that, but really you are in the bar, using the money the way you want."

Charles Jones retreated momentarily, leaning back into the seat. He is the provider; his dignity is his strength. He spoke in measured tones.

"Look at you. You are young . . . and you look good . . .

and you've got brains. And *look* at you—you do nothing with it."

"Look at *you*. What are *you* doing with it? You've worked all your life and what have you got? You go to work at four and get home now; and you go to bed and get up and eat and get ready for work again. Where's *your* life?"

"When I was younger there was one way of doing things."

"Hey, Pops . . . it isn't that time. I have things I can do *now*. I wear fine clothes now, and I go out. You say I will die, or I will go to jail and stay for thirty years and come back an old man on a cane. *No way! I am living my life now.* I don't care if I die!"

Charles Jones held with his careful words. "Yes, son. But you use drugs. You won't last."

"You drink. *You* can't last."

"Yes, but I know *how*."

"Oh, yeah? So how come you get drunk every night?"

Charles Jones suddenly has lost control. His hand—absent-mindedly holding a dinner spoon—slammed against the table with a jarring clang.

"*Goddamit, motherfucker!*"

It was the breaking point, totally predictable—measured dignity gone, the face deeply flushed.

"*What are you talking about? What the hell are you saying?*"

This was the cue for other family members. Estella Jones, a small graying woman with warm, watery eyes, materialized as if she were transported through the wall. She was still tying the cord of her flannel robe, coughing from the congestion of cigarettes consumed during the day—a warm, subdued woman. She has been ill with gallbladder problems for several months.

"What's going on?"

Her voice was soft, still choked by sleep.

"Nuthin', Moms," Jones quickly volunteered.

"*I want this bastard out of my motherfucking house, now!*" Charles Jones was banging the table again.

"Okay, Pops," Jones volunteered, playing a role. "I'm leaving. . ."

He rose slowly from the table, shoulders painfully bent, and pushed back his chair, butting out the cigarette.

"*Now!*" the older man shouted again, his face nearly pink.

The tiny woman with the low voice reached out and touched her husband's arm, pulling on his sleeve. "Charles, it's late. Come on, go to bed."

"*Get him out of the house now! I want him out. If he doesn't leave, I'm leaving!*" The older man's large eyes were hot. They stared beyond his wife and son.

She tugged at his sleeve again. "Go to bed, Charles. It's late. You're tired."

"Goddamit," the older man bawled. "This is my house! If he doesn't leave, *I'm* leaving!" He paused, the face an oddly etched Siamese twin of fury and suffering. "Lord . . . if I had known I was going to have a motherfucking son like he is, I'd have *drowned him at birth!*"

He turned to his son. His voice slid into dramatic near-silence. "This is my house . . . but I'll leave—*you* can't make it out there."

"Pops, I'm leaving," Jones said in his most sorrowful voice. "You stay."

By now, Jones' younger brother, the last boy living full time at home, was awake and in the kitchen. Bruce is stocky and short, his shoulder-length curly hair parted down the middle, a friendly, strong, quiet kid who stood with his mother now and solemnly asked his older brother to forget the quarrel and stay. Finally Jones nodded and sat down again in the chair.

But Charles Jones wasn't finished. He threw back his chair, cursing loudly, and stomped into the bedroom, pulling a suitcase from the closet, stuffing clothes into it. Estella walked in, still pulling her bathrobe together. "You chose him over me!" he bellowed.

"It's late," she pleaded wearily. "Let's go to bed."

But Charles wouldn't drop it, and his doggedness was beginning to wear on her. "This is my house, and I'm leaving," he insisted. He threw another shirt into the valise.

Now the small voice rasped at him. "Then *leave*, son of a bitch! Go!"

55

"I'm going!" He picked up the valise and walked through the kitchen, slowing at the table where Jones still sat, reaching down for his unfinished beer.

He walked on, beer in one hand, suitcase in the other, stopping at the plastic-covered couch, sighing as he sank into its crinkly softness. For a while he nursed the beer, but soon he was asleep, breathing heavily, the bottle empty on the rug.

And he stayed there until Estella rose at five and left for her job. Then he crawled into the warm bed and slept peacefully through the morning. Down the hall, his son was snoring, too.

3

In the faded snapshot, Stella stands in her kitchen. She wears a frumpy housedress, and her middle son, Jerry, an amiable kid with curly hair and a Bozo smile who works in the garment district, hugs her. She smiles benignly, a plump Italian woman (she has since lost weight), warm and sweet, worshiped by her three sons.

In another picture, Jones stares alone at the camera, looking more Mediterranean than black: he has a wedge-shaped haircut trimmed close around the ears, rising to a flat-top. In another, the hair is combed Don Juan-style, oily curls pressed against his head: a Latin lover . . . a serious man, strong and silent, moody, a romantic face.

The memories are stored in an aging salt water taffy box hidden in a dresser drawer. Yet another photo shows him standing in front of a long line of barracks, a square white Navy cap balanced on his close-cropped hair. He holds the training company's flag; it shows a crossed sword and gun.

In another picture, Charles Jones thrusts an angry chin at the camera. His mouth is grim, its thin line made more stolid by a pencil mustache, eyes downcast. A color snapshot shows a happier man. He smiles broadly, one arm around his wife at a Christmas party waving at the camera, gold-rimmed glasses reflecting light from tree ornaments, a tall exuberant man.

4

Charles Jones met Stella in a Staten Island hospital. She was friendly with a nurse he'd come to visit, and soon he began to date her. They dated for two months, and one night she saw him with someone else. The ensuing fight resolved itself in marriage.

Until she met Charles, Stella's life was turbulent and often sad. Her father emigrated from Sicily after the turn of the century and found work in the oil business. He eventually bought a gas station, prospered, then bought another. And later, another. He is wealthy now, and he returns regularly to Sicily; he plans to be buried there.

Stella's mother emigrated from Naples. She met Stella's father in Brooklyn, but after several children, the marriage foundered. She left, and later remarried. Stella's father did not. The memories are bitter. Stella spent most of her childhood in a Brooklyn orphanage. Sometimes she met her father at a bar now called the Paradise Lounge to ask for money. One day when she was thirteen, he made her drop to her knees and beg for it.

She never went back.

If Stella hates her family—or parts of it—it is impossible to tell from the gentle face or the passive smile. Yet marrying a black man was more revenge than her relatives could tolerate. She had had a child out of wedlock, a girl named Billie, when she married Charles Jones.

"Let's face facts," she'll say when asked. "I'm an outcast in my family." She stirs a cigarette in the crowded ashtray. "I married someone they didn't approve of." She turns to look at me and her eyes become defiant. "I don't regret it."

Jones remembers the anger and recrimination. "We get along with Uncle Emilio on that side," he says, "but no one else. They came up one night, and there was a lot of talk. I was about nine, and they were saying things that made my mother cry. I took the fireplace poker and I told them to get the fuck out!"

Jones brings his face close to mine. The past turbulence froths in it.

"My father was coming off the eleeee . . . eleeee. . ." He is angry and he trembles, but this time the words emerge quickly. ". . . ELEVATOR. He brought them back inside— he was mad for what I had done.

"Then he found out what happened, and he got his *gun* and chased them out. My aunt called the next day, and Jerry answered the phone and told her to fuck off. We haven't talked since. My grandmother died in 1969 and we went to the funeral, and nobody spoke."

5

"I was in a bitchy mood. Pops and I had had another one of those fights. I was tired of all the hassling . . . and I decided it was time to really leave."

We are in the narrow living room of Carol's place. City welfare money pays the rent.

"It was Sunday night. Pops didn't really believe I'd go; Moms *knew*."

In his parents' apartment, Jones stood over a zippered blue suitcase, put boxer shorts and socks into it, then sleeveless undershirts and half a dozen pairs of neatly folded slacks. He lowered a dozen sweaters into the large space, placing five pairs of shoes beside them. A tiny box of earrings and a stack of 45 rpm records filled the remaining space.

He ran the zipper around the rectangular lip of the suit-case, then selected a sweater from the closet—he would leave clothes here—and a pair of slacks to match it. Slacks on, sweater with its front zipper showing the edge of a gold undershirt *just so*, he pulled on a pair of platform loafers with three-inch heels. At first, Jones had trouble walking in the shoes, fearing disaster if he had to fight or run. But they were The Fashion; and dressing well—exceptionally well—is as important to Jones as anything in his life.

He went out. He left the suitcase behind, for he must talk

to his mother before leaving officially, and he would not see her until the following morning. In the night outside he made several stops. At the basketball court, he bought a "dime" [$10] of cocaine from a teen-age dealer named Teddy; he went to another dealer for smoke. Then he walked across the street to buy a pint of wine—Boone's Farm strawberry, a constant companion. Wrapping a paper bag around the bottle, twisting the top of it around the bottle's neck, he walked through Chinatown to a stop for the B bus.

The bus would drop him on Clinton Street, a block cluttered with kids and knots of men who sit on sidewalk chairs drinking from bagged bottles and constructing endless conversations and impromptu hustles while Spanish music plays loudly from storefronts.

Walking the block one day, I made some notes.

The corner begins with a furniture "exchange"; next is a small flower shop, then an old law office, an apartment building, then a grimy red-brick tenement followed by a Chinese novelty shop and an ancient synagogue.

The synagogue is the neighborhood's past. Its Orthodox eyes have watched the block's population evolve for more than a century, a hundred years of Eastern European migrations. But now the temple's rich red coat is cracked and peeled, its front gate rusted and closed. A side door still serves the building, and members scurry in and out of it, marked apart from the neighborhood by yarmulkes and white skin.

The street is filled with black and Hispanic faces: Afros, wavy hair, Spanish mustaches. A bodega, a music store, and a photographer's studio fill out this end of the block.

I watched a young black girl across the street drawing with white chalk on the synagogue wall. She was retarded: a sad mask over a tree-stump body, balloon arms. She moved clumsily, drawing her pictures with large looping motions. An old wino leaned through the decaying iron gate and growled at her for defacing the temple. Then he moved on. After a moment of nervous pacing, she went back to the wall.

A plump man in baggy pants, yarmulke in place, walked

up and opened the side gate. He hardly noticed her, but his authoritative arrival was enough. She bolted through the open gate and didn't return.

The bus dropped Jones a block from Carol's building. He had the foil-wrapped cocaine in his pocket; the smoke was rolled in joints. He climbed the stairs and turned a key to push the police lock aside. Carol was there, but he said little to her. She soon took her child, a jumpy little boy named Ritchie with frightened eyes and a bloated tummy, into the bedroom.

Jones put half a dozen 45s on the turntable . . . the Delfonics, the Shirelles, soulful R&B standards . . . and sat quietly in the front room nursing the Boone's Farm. When Carol retreated, he brought out his works and got ready to use the cocaine. Jones shoots cocaine; he does not sniff or snort it in the manner of rock musicians, jet-propelled partygoers, or swinging secretaries. He is a former heroin addict, and though he does not enjoy putting a needle in his arm, the spike is his second nature; for cocaine shot directly into the blood stream gives the best rush. The high is intense, it is immediate.

"You give it a little chance to hit, a chance to get to your head . . . or your heart," he explained to me one night. "You want more, you want to do it fast; but if you shoot it too fast, it'll stop your heart. So you keep cool; then you shoot more in. I do it all at once, but I do it slow enough so I can feel it happening."

The apartment has dark blue walls. A curtain functions as a door separating the bedroom and living room. The room is crowded with makeshift furniture. Two tigers snarling out of tall grass stand behind the couch: dime-store paintings flanking a metal clock. In one corner, a radio balances uneasily on the back of a kitchen chair.

Jones sat on the couch. He remained awake most of the night, letting his thoughts drift and rearrange themselves.

"I was telling myself I wouldn't be back. Once I left, that was it."

Cocaine is not so speedy as pills. The high was cool and energetic; it kept his eyes open and his thoughts moving. With cocaine, he can be quick-tempered . . . but when smoke follows, he settles into easy contemplation.

"Smoke gives me broader thought . . . it keeps things in perspective. Pills make me into a bully, and coke and speed get me very quick-tempered. But smoke makes me think about getting my life together."

And he thought. And finally he went to an empty bed in the back.

Carol and Ritchie were huddled in another bed, breathing softly. He lay on his back, hands behind his head, falling freely through the warm void provided by the drugs until morning.

6

Jones rose at 5 A.M. without sleeping. The day was wet and chilly and still dark.

Wearing a black windbreaker and carrying a bent umbrella against the mist, he trudged down Carol's stairs and began a slow mile's walk to his mother's house. The street lights, still on, filled the mirrored surfaces of the pavement with pale gold as he passed them.

As he entered the apartment, he heard his mother stirring in the large bedroom. Jones lowered himself into a kitchen chair, still wearing the moist coat.

She walked into the kitchen in her starched nursing whites and flipped on the light. She was tentative; unsure whether to smile.

"Good morning."

"Hi."

She filled a coffee pot and lit a blue flame underneath it.

"Are you really leaving?"

"Yeah."

She lit a cigarette and sat down, turning to him.

"Why?"

"Because there are too many men in this house."

She poured the steaming coffee into a white cup with a small prayer written on it. "No, that's not true. It is your father's house, but it doesn't have too many men."

"Yeah, but . . . like, I'm still leaving." He avoided her eyes.

She poured powdered milk into the coffee. "You *do* have a hard head, don't you?"

"That's true."

Jones smiled . . . still a little stoned.

"Well, then, you go . . . you do what you want to."

She was not smiling, but she radiated warmth and weariness; Jones saw it as love. He took the strength he needed from her tired consent to his plans, or lack of plans. She stood with him. She is another compass point in his life.

They took the elevator down. The mist was giving way to the day. Men and women gathered at the bus and subway stops. Stella Jones turned to her son as she approached the door of a crowded bus.

"I'll see you later."

"Okay."

He walked back into the tall building, lowering himself again into the kitchen chair. Soon Bruce slouched into the kitchen. He nodded, made breakfast: four eggs, a pot of oatmeal, toast, and orange juice, rattling the dishes loudly.

"You still leavin' ?"

"Yeah."

"Don't, man, you should be *here*. You don't see Pops that much. You're out, or you are sleeping. It'll be okay."

"That's true, man. But the times *when* I see him, that's a drag. That's when I have to go all through this."

"Come *on*, man!"

The brothers have a curious relationship. Jones has little to teach Bruce; Jones' life has turned in a direction that Stella and Charles pray their youngest will avoid. Yet Jones has street stature for kicking heroin without using methadone or entering a treatment program. Bruce looks up to him, and Jones enjoys it.

Jones crushed his cigarette in the crowded ashtray.

"No, I'm leaving."

Bruce had done his part; it was time for school.

"Okay, I'll see you when you come back."

It was nearly nine o'clock, and Pops was asleep in the large bedroom. Jones took his suitcase, went downstairs, and hailed a taxi. The traffic was heavy; the meter ran to three dollars before he reached Carol's apartment. He climbed the stairs, banging the suitcase against the hallway's narrow walls, then rushed through the battered door. Finally, he walked to the bedroom and dropped the suitcase on the floor.

"I wasn't thinking about much," he remembers. "I was just leaving."

Without a word, Carol put the clothing away.

Five

1

At first glance Carol seems slow-witted—oppressed by her life to the point of giving in to it, rarely talking, even at home.

Yet the dull mask hides a more interesting human being: a decisive woman with a bulldog grip on life holding her first-born close, waiting with both fear and determination for the coming of a second, waiting for Jones to stabilize . . . or leave. She is determined to find the right man, and she is frightened that she is pregnant again because she knows the search is probably not ended.

All Jones' women are surprisingly alike. They must be both strong and weak. They must be his mother, his protector, his refuge, and they must be loyal, supportive, and fun. They must also be weak, silent, and pliable. And they must periodically support him. For although Jones maintains a brass image of street-hardened machismo, he is enormously dependent on them at nearly every level—sex, finances, self-esteem, understanding, even food and shelter.

Carol's major contribution is to provide him a place to live; also food, occasional pocket money, and companionship when it is required. Jones, in turn, sometimes shares his mugging proceeds with her; he also sleeps with her, takes her places, and half-heartedly observes certain social conventions. These involve playing a muted fatherly role with Ritchie, and sometimes an ad hoc protective role when Carol gets in trouble in the streets or with creditors.

Jones' heart is not altogether in this, as he often makes clear. On the other hand, his true love, Jo-Anne, refuses to go on welfare and take an apartment and let Jones move in. She, too, is pregnant . . . but she is smart enough to know that Jones' breadwinner potential is limited. For now, she lives with her gainfully employed father, hoping that Jones —a frequent visitor—will somehow, someday change.

I was put off at first by Carol, despite the fact that whenever Jones brought me to her home, she made every effort to be friendly, offering tea and sandwiches and soda pop. She never fed him without offering to feed me; she always asked if I needed anything, always offered a friendly—if muffled— hello or goodbye when I came and went. But still I shrank from Carol. She seemed to be doing so little about her life except hanging in there. And as my fascination with Jones' complexities grew—and his relationship with her deteriorated —I felt further distance. She seemed *so* oppressed, it was almost . . . frightening. And I was paranoid enough to assume she resented me for being white and middle-class and writing a book about her man, being privy to secrets she didn't know.

It got worse as I plunged further and further into Jones' head. For it seemed that since she resented him, she must resent me. It was only toward the end of my time with Jones —a period of considerable disenchantment—that I began to relate more to Carol; then, we had several conversations.

Carol and Jones grew up in the same projects. Her mother, Sara, is a tall buxom woman who, like Jones' parents, has made the best of the American dream. Sara's family left the South after World War II and came to New York. She married a young printer when she was seventeen, and they eventually moved into Charles and Stella's building in the projects.

"My father is in the Bronx now," Carol says. She was shy and reluctant to talk about her life during our first real conversation. "I saw him three years ago. He doesn't know I have a child now, neither does my older sister. He just left. I guess I was about five or six. I don't remember it happening."

They lived several floors below the Jones family for thirteen years. During that time, Sara returned to school and eventually found a job as a welfare aide.

"She's doing all right. She's making so much money that the welfare department wants her to move. She's got a seven-room apartment now, and she hasn't got so many kids any more—only five at home. She even might buy a house out in Queens, where my aunt has a place. My aunt has a lawn with its own flowers.

"It's nice, but I couldn't live there. It's too quiet, and after eight o'clock, everybody is sleeping. Nobody is out in the streets—the only lights are on the porches."

Carol receives $240 a month from New York City's welfare department; her mother supplements it with an occasional handout. Welfare paid for Ritchie's arrival, and it provides for his medical care, sometimes an urgent problem: he has asthma attacks in the stuffy apartment. The city also provided a lawyer when she went to court with her landlord, who is trying to evict her for nonpayment of rent.

Carol was finishing her junior year in high school when she became pregnant. "I just left. I didn't want my mother to know. I got a job—I figured when she found out it wouldn't be so bad because I would have money." Carol worked as a receptionist and switchboard operator.

Carol does not use hard drugs, and rarely smokes marijuana. Nor does she drink at home. But she flies often to her mother's apartment, there to find escape in a bottle of gin, and returns home in a defiant mood. Then she and Jones will fight, and sometimes he will hit her. She is not happy that he brings money so irregularly into the home, and she is less pleased when he asks for part of the welfare check. She is an ambiguous mix of girl and woman, most of this hidden behind a mask of dullness. Yet bold eyes sometimes peek out of the mask. She has not given up on life. Not yet.

"I quit school because people would be talking, you know? I didn't care much about school anyway. My mother didn't find out I had quit until she found out I was pregnant. Then she made a lot of fuss. I can't remember the words, but it was a *lot* of trouble."

"I didn't mean to get pregnant," she continues, shifting in

66

her seat, clearly uncomfortable when I make notes. "It just happened, I didn't plan for it." She points toward the baby dozing in the back room. "His father was a musician; he plays professionally now. He didn't want to get married—he was too young." She looks up. "*Now* he wants to get married . . . but I don't care for him any more."

"We just broke up. After Ritchie was born, he brought him clothes. I went with him about a year after that. But I had gone on welfare before the baby was born, and I just stopped caring for him. After a while, he didn't come around any more."

Carol knew Jones as a passing face. She watched him silently in the crowded elevators; she saw him on the sidewalks.

"He was on the fifteenth floor, I was on the seventh. When he was on junk, he made passes at me, but I didn't want any of that. Then he came home from jail. He was clean, and he started talking to me."

In the far room, Ritchie wakes up and throws a foot off the bed. He starts to climb down. "*You get back on that bed,*" she yells, "*or I'll hit you good!*" The baby looks up with wide, startled eyes and climbs back hurriedly.

"You just start going," she continues, "and you keep seeing each other every day. He was going with that other girl. I didn't care. Somebody had told me—'Yeah, he goes with this white chick.' She was in the projects one day and I got a look at her. We even had conversations, but she was a phony—she would talk to me, but she would hate me underneath."

Carol excuses herself and goes into the cramped kitchen to turn down the flame under some rice. I watch her over the top of my notebook: tightly styled Afro hair, a lean, awkward body. She returns quickly, shifting several times in the seat before settling in.

"He came around a lot. We would sit on the bench and talk. Or if I walked by, he'd ask me to sit down and talk with him. I moved into this apartment before I met him, but I would visit my mother in the projects a lot; that's when I would see him."

I ask why she is attracted to him, and she smiles and looks past me out the window toward the street.

"I don't know—he had a *way* about him. A lot of girls wanted him, you know? I used to always say—wow, someday I'm going to get next to him! It was his features, and the way he dressed. I thought he was *fine;* and I had to fight hard to get him. There's something about his ways, I guess. His looks really ain't got nuthin' to do with it . . . they can be deceiving anyway."

Carol points toward the sleeping baby.

"He treats this one like it is his. He loves kids. And you know"—a warmth of self-awareness brushes Carol's face—"I'm expecting. He can be a beautiful person. And he's very, very smart. He used to say things to me in the projects that I couldn't understand."

Even after an hour's conversation, Carol and I remain uneasy with each other. The talk is labored and careful. I ask what she knows of Jones' street life.

"He's always watching his back; he don't like to be crowded up. I've got to admit, I don't like some of the things he does. I'm here with the baby, you know? And suppose he comes through the door with somebody behind him, and they don't care *who* they get?"

"Would he make a good husband?"

"I don't . . . know. When it starts getting warm, he'll be hanging out a lot; he won't be here so much."

She stops suddenly, and I look up and she is smiling dreamily. "Someday . . . I always wanted to experience that thing, to get married." Her face regains its dullness.

"I don't know how it'll work out. I'll just have to see. He has a rotten personality in some ways. And in some ways it's okay. He changes a lot. I think he's got a split personality— it bothers me sometimes." She pauses. "But other times I don't even pay attention."

Carol's eyes drift away. Her child is stirring again on the bed, and she is through talking for the day.

2

Jones complains often about Carol's lack of intellect; and about her messy house, her noisy baby, and occasionally her blackness. When he is tired of coping with all this, he goes to see Jo-Anne, who is bright, bubbling, strikingly like his mother, and white.

Carol's baby is six months away. Jo-Anne, a plump, cheerful, pink-faced Polish girl with light blue eyes and strawberry blonde hair, will give him his first child shortly. She has known him nearly four years. Jones says she is the number one woman in his life . . . and as such, she has endured a great deal.

During his worst heroin days, she watched him put the needle into his arm again and again; sometimes she slapped him, applied ice packs, and gave mouth-to-mouth resuscitation as he lay on her living room floor, face purple, foaming at the mouth, close to death from overdose. She had pawned her jewelry, her father's cameras and radios, anything she could find to support his habit and keep him from further crime. Once, in her kitchen, she held a butcher knife to the throat of her small, round graying father when he refused to give her money for Jones. More than once, she was the unwitting bystander to an impulsive mugging, running as he ran, risking what he risked.

They planned once to be married; now it is an open question. Jones wants her to apply for welfare, then take an apartment for herself and the coming baby and keep house so he may come around when he pleases. Marriage, it is implied, will follow. The welfare will keep them until he finds a job.

But she is too proud for welfare. And she knows he lives with Carol . . . and that Carol is pregnant. If she moves, the result is all too predictable: Jones will feel free to move between two economically marginal households, living much of the time in the streets and taking money from his women when he is too lazy to commit crimes for it. Steady work will always be promised but it will not materialize.

Most important, Jo-Anne is safe and comfortable in her father's apartment, a two-bedroom city cooperative unit. And she is needed there. Her father, Morris, has a steady income as a tool and die worker, but her mother is gone, waiting for cancer to kill her in an Arizona rest home. It is clear the marriage has died. Morris, in effect, is a widower; his wife, Margaret, a heavyset woman with dark brown eyes and jowls, went to Arizona to be near her thirty-year-old daughter by a former marriage. She and Morris would have been married twenty-five years this fall.

And so he is a lonely man passing middle age. While he does not like the bills the baby will bring, he is glad to have his daughter near him. He has nothing to say to Jones, who returns the silence, assuming that Morris dislikes the color of his skin, knowing he disapproves of his past addiction and prison record. Jones visits and makes love to Jo-Anne in the afternoons, always with one eye on the clock. At five-thirty the shy, pot-bellied little man returns from work. He does not want to find Jones in his house, and if they pass in the hallway, Jones on his way out, Morris coming in, they will not speak.

"Jo-Anne's old man tries to clean it up when he talks about the race thing," Jones says. "He says he knows some black people, but he is really saying 'Some of my best friends are niggers'—and Jack, I don't want to hear that shit." Yet if Morris is a bigot, it is not one of his dominant traits; his face is a soft-boiled egg, feelings hidden behind shy, vulnerable eyes.

Jo-Anne has been pregnant three times, miscarrying Jones' seed twice before. She is barely twenty, yet she is a strong woman, emotionally sometimes twice her age, able to fight for things she cares about. But she can also be a silly, giggling girl, flattering Jones or turning aside his chauvinistic thrusts with warmth and laughter. It is this quality Jones likes most; he repeatedly compares her to his mother.

Jo-Anne left high school at fifteen.

"I didn't like it," she remembers with an empty shrug. "I didn't like to be told what to do. I just graduated junior high school by the skin of my teeth."

Jo-Anne is the product, ironically, of immigrant aspirations. Her grandfather left Poland after the turn of the century and settled in a cramped three-room apartment on First Avenue and 99th Street, a neighborhood more black than Polish now. He married a neighborhood girl, worked as a shoemaker, and eventually passed citizenship examinations, dying of cancer in the 1950s.

Jo-Anne remembers an "old-fashioned" stove in her grandfather's apartment. "It had metal plates for burners and the flame would come up around them." Jo-Anne's face glows at the memory. She and I talk easily, for she is open and trusting, and glad for the attention the conversation brings. "Grandma had an old fashioned sewing machine. It had a big lever on the floor. You had to push it to make it work, and I just kept pushing it. I used to pretend I was making doll dresses."

She noticed Jones because of his clothes, a notion that would please him.

"He was dressed differently than anybody else. From a distance"—she wrinkles her nose telling this—"he looked terrible. He wore knits, silk pants, and a beaver hat. Nobody down there dressed like that—I thought he looked funny. And besides, he wasn't friendly. I used to hate him when he would come up and say, 'Kiss me, so I can throw up.'"

At first, she thought Jones was gay. New to the block, she noticed a tall homosexual named Piggie who often walked with Jones and called his name aloud. Jones says he was not involved with Piggie sexually, but he enjoyed the attention. One day, Piggie asked Jo-Anne and a girlfriend to deliver a present, a sweater, to Jones' house for him: Charles and Stella Jones didn't encourage Piggie's visits. Given the taxi fare, having nothing else to do, Jo-Anne made the delivery. A few days later, Jones picked her out of a crowd of girls and thanked her.

"My mother described you perfectly," he said.

This impressed her.

Soon after that she was in Willie's Bar on 9th Street talking to friends. She jokingly called someone "tubby-wubby." For some reason this prompted a woman she knew only slightly to turn and snarl: "You're the tubby-wubby!" Jo-Anne ran from the bar.

The next day Jones threatened her tormentor; and again Jo-Anne was impressed.

At the Rosso & Nero's pizza counter on First Avenue, where Jo-Anne was spending a lot of time, Jones began writing "Will you go out with me?" on notebook paper and passing the sheets to her.

"I wrote 'no' four times," Jo-Anne laughs, "and every five minutes he'd ask me again. Finally, I said yes." She nods and looks at me. "He always seems to get what he wants. He really does."

Jo-Anne balances her chin on her hand at the kitchen table and stares out the eleventh-floor window. "Everybody was curious about him. I was curious about him, too. But when he confronted me that he wanted to *go* with me, I said I don't go with queers. The people he was with always seemed to be faggots, and that's what I took him for.

"The way he looked at me, I thought he was gonna hit me; then he laughed. He said he was going with another girl at the time. How could he be a faggot if he was going with a girl?"

Rosso & Nero's is gone. A green awning with a 7-Up sign hangs over the front door of the bodega that has replaced it. The new owner hasn't bothered to take down the Italian names. The bodega's front door is next to a tenement building's front hallway. Jo-Anne and I stand before the hallway and she points past yellow plaster walls to a dark space near a creaky stairwell.

"That's where he first kissed me."

A few days after she and Jones began going together, Piggie came to her door, slapped her, and ran. Jo-Anne told a girlfriend, the girlfriend told Jones, and he found Piggie and hit him in the face.

"Jones was the first man who ever stuck up for me," Jo-Anne says. "I fell deeply in love with him."

Jo-Anne shifts her body, heavy with pregnancy, in the chair. "I was impressed by him. He wore suede coats and pointed shoes—they were the style then—and shiny pants and he matched his clothes. He had style.

"Even when he was on dope, he was always taking showers and changing clothes. He didn't want people to see he was a dope fiend. That fascinated me. He wouldn't let himself go. When we lived together in a hotel, he only had one set of underwear—but I had to wash them out every night."

She laughs and turns to look out the window again. "He's always smelling under his arms to see if he smells bad. He can't stand to sweat."

Jones felt the likeness between his plump Italian mother and this round, giggling Polish girl deeply. "When I look at Jo-Anne, I can see my mother," he explained one day as we walked along Houston Street. "My mother is cleaner, she keeps a better house—but I'm happy with Jo-Anne because she has the warmth inside that my mother has. She sticks with her man, too. This is what I want in a wife and a mother."

We are crossing the street, Jones is barely aware that cars are moving around him. "When I came home from jail, we were going to get married, but it didn't work out. I was in the streets too much. We lived at my mother's house, but we grew apart, and I told her to leave. We would get in these arguments, you know, and my mother and father would jump in on her side. It wasn't right."

Across the street, Jones pauses and looks around and smiles. "I was doing good then. I was getting money from the girls and mugging people, too."

His mind wanders. "A job don't pay as good, but it pays off in the long run. I'll admit that. But at my age you gotta have a shot at something big. I can't wait for the job, but the way I'm fucking around, I'm probably not gonna get that shot, either."

The day is cool and windy, a spring sun working against the shadows of fast-moving clouds. I wait while Jones' mind makes the circle and returns to Jo-Anne.

"She is even built like my mother. And my mother to me is the best person in the world. It's good to have a woman who makes me think of that." He takes a long drink from the ever-

73

present Boone's Farm bottle and wipes his mouth. "Carol is trying to housebreak me, make me settle in—and I don't want to be broke. I don't feel she is the kind of woman I want to spend my life with. Jo-Anne is."

As we walk, he begins moving his hands again.

"I don't like to talk to Carol. Her vocabulary isn't very big. She says yes, yes, yes, but she don't remember anything. I don't get deep with her. With Jo-Anne, I sit up all night and talk and really get things worked out."

He looks at me, his face registering tension.

"The only two people in the world that know my deepest thoughts are Moms and Jo-Anne." He nods to himself, drifting again. "You know, when I left my mother's house it was the hardest thing I ever had to do—it was my *home*, man! Pops wants me to come back. I didn't have enough time for him as a child, he wants that now."

Back to Jo-Anne. "When she found out I was seeing other girls, you know, she just said, 'Do what you want and come around when you are done. We'll talk about it.' Wow, I really respect her for that! If it was me, I'd say, 'Fucker, get off my face!' She's really beautiful. With her, I don't mind giving. I gave Carol and her kid a stereo set, and I'm pleased that I've given it to her. But I'd have been happier if I'd gotten it for Jo-Anne."

We are in a small park filled with children bouncing on swings and teeter-totters. It occurs to me that Jones' child—children?—will soon play in this park, and I wonder if he has any idea what is really happening. No time for the question now.

"When we are out, you know, I want to get anything Jo-Anne wants. I feel bad if I don't. Jo-Anne has heart, she doesn't mind if I take the pawn ticket and get my ring instead of hers. Carol wouldn't do that."

"He had a way of talking," Jo-Anne says back in her kitchen, hamburgers for Morris' dinner hissing in the broiler pan. "He makes you hear what you want to hear. There are times when he could make you believe the sky is green. When I started going with him, I guess I heard *all* those things."

Jo-Anne rarely leaves her father's apartment now. She pads about in a worn white bathrobe; the television set in her bedroom stumbles through daytime trivia and reruns. She reads paperbacks and spends part of each day watching the world turn from her bedroom window; a pillow cushions her elbows.

"I've tried for so long to have a baby. I thought it would straighten him out. I thought he would stop running around." The pink face turns noticeably gloomy. "It settled him down a little, but not much."

"He's not giving me a penny for the baby. The doctor and the operation will cost fifteen hundred dollars and my dad is paying for it."

The gloom turns to anger. "He keeps telling me if I move out and find a place for us, everything will be okay."

Jo-Anne is talking through her teeth.

"I can't move out on a promise of *words*. He wants me to go to the welfare department to get an apartment. I don't like it. People laugh at you all day long while you sit there. It's like begging. It's a sick feeling."

She is visibly sad, eyes falling until she is contemplating her distended belly. "I don't like this, but I have no choice. I can't go to work and leave the baby at home. Sooner or later, I'll have to depend on the welfare department. I can't depend on him. *He* hasn't got a job."

3

Moms' place. Jesus watches the kitchen gin rummy game from his three-dimensional hallway portrait as though he is peering through a window. At the table, the small gray woman lights a cigarette, squinting from the smoke as she holds her cards. An old man from one of the neighboring apartments stands behind her, leaning on his cane. Ruth, who lives with Jones' brother Jerry, sits across from Moms. She is short and pretty with happy-clown features, round eyes, button nose, a wide smile. Ruth's baby boy—Jerry's son—gurgles in a bassinet behind her.

Stella Jones doesn't quite believe someone is writing a book about her son. For a moment, she avoids my eyes. I ask how she thinks her son is doing these days.

She lays the half-finished cigarette in its ashtray; her eyes flicker slightly. She turns to Jones.

"You want me to tell the *truth*?"

It is a rhetorical question, but he acknowledges it, and nods yes. She turns back to me and still says nothing. Seconds pass. Then she begins talking—to both of us.

"Actually, I think his life is a waste. I don't think he's trying to better himself—he should be doing something with his life."

"What?"

"He should go back to school. He should stop feeling sorry for himself. He has a complex about his stuttering. It stops him from looking for jobs. He's afraid people will make fun of him. Actually, he has the ability to do a lot of things, but he just *don't try* to do them."

A radio in the living room is playing muzak. The fluff spills into the kitchen; show tunes and love songs swirl around Stella Jones as she talks.

"It's the children he hangs around with. They aren't helping him. As long as he stays with them, it will be hard for him to change. They keep him down."

It is hard to imagine anyone, much less Jones, listening to this kind of criticism in front of others. His brother's common-law wife is here; I am here. I begin to squirm. Jones seems to be buried in the playing cards, his face is tight and closed, but he's listening carefully.

I ask about the stuttering.

Stella Jones sighs. "He used to go to a therapist when he was in grade school. He had to talk on records and things like that. We also gave him singing lessons."

"Did they help?"

"He still stutters, doesn't he?"

At the table's corner, Jones deals cards and keeps a stone face; his mother senses his pain. She leans on her hands now and folds them with a relaxed, dreamy look. She laughs warmly.

"As bitchy as he is, I think he's damn nice. He's got a heart of gold, when he uses it. He was always partial to me, which I guess made him outstanding to me. More so than the others really."

"Was he your smartest child?"

"Yes, I would say so. But he's just too lazy to apply himself. I guess he just feared the tests in school. He was a child who hated to admit failure. The first time he came out of jail, I pleaded with him to go back to school. But he said he was afraid of failing and being called a dummy. His father had gone back to school and bettered himself, so I guess he compared himself to that. He was afraid to fail before him— he used his father as a godhead."

I know the answer, but I ask if there is tension between father and son. The small woman turns to her son.

"How shall I answer that?"

Jones looks up from his cards and shrugs. "It's a personality thing," he says.

Stella smiles and goes on.

"Sometimes . . . I think Charles resents his son's youth. He's going to hate me for saying this. He's always hollering at him. When I was your age, and this and that and you're only a child, the things fathers say. And I think his father resents that I paid so much attention to him. Through the years I've heard him say, my parents this, my parents that. He couldn't get the attention *he* needed from his parents, so he resents me giving it to these children." She pauses to loose a cloud of tobacco smoke. "That's what I think, anyway."

Stella Jones learned of her son's first arrest when a letter arrived from the court saying that his hearing date had been changed. Possession of works; he'd told her nothing. She reacted with confusion.

"I asked myself . . . why? I didn't know about the drugs. When he was in high school, I asked him if he was on drugs, and he said no; and I didn't know much about drugs, the symptoms and all that. I tried to tell myself this wasn't really happening."

She lights another Chesterfield.

"When he went to jail, I hoped it would teach him a lesson—that he would go back to school and buckle down. Then he told me he was a Muslim. I *still* feel awful about that."

"Did jail change him?"

"No. He still hangs out with the same people."

She is by turns stern and warm, protective mother and angry critic. I ask if she thinks her racially mixed marriage caused him any problem. She reacts to this sadly.

"He resents being mixed. I think he loves me, but hanging out mostly with blacks is his way of punishing me. I'm aware of this, and I understand it. He has to prove something to himself. He knows it hurts me that he tries to be more black than Italian. Sometimes I wonder how *I* would feel about it. But I can't work up the feeling. And I didn't think about it when I got married. It's a problem . . . you don't know which side to go to."

She is forty-six, and she has lived with her husband and family in this apartment for twenty years. Jones was her first son.

"Actually, he was the only one of my children I could ever talk to. He's the only one that made sense at times"—she hesitates and glances at Jones, who seems to be concentrating on his cards—"when he wasn't full of dope. He had opinions on things and they usually made sense, at least on his level. The other kids, their minds weren't developed enough to get into serious conversations. With him, you could talk. I've often told him he was smart. He's spoiled, too. He doesn't think so, but whatever he wanted, I made it my business to get."

Stella Jones leans on her elbows, exhaling clouds of tobacco smoke. The smoke seems to be a filmy curtain parting to reveal past secrets. The corners of her mouth tremble slightly at what she sees. She turns to me.

"A lot of times when I'd come home at night—twelve, twelve-thirty—he'd be waiting up for me. Sometimes he'd meet me at the subway. He missed me, I guess. He wanted to be sure I'd be safe, or maybe"—she laughs in a small, distant voice—"that was his excuse to stay out. I don't know."

In the mid-sixties, Stella worked double shifts at the hospital: she made ten dollars for each one. Charles' factory job was gone because of a fire—he was out of work three years. She works at an uptown hospital now, which happens to have an abortion clinic. As a good Catholic, she is ashamed.

Jones continues playing cards with Ruth as his mother talks, one ear carefully cocked to the conversation.

"I think he always felt sorry for me," she is saying. "When I was out of work, he went out and shined shoes. He was nine or ten, and if he didn't make any money he would come home and feel very bad."

"Did he cry?"

"No, he wasn't a child for crying. He kept things to himself." She pauses and looks at me through slightly narrowed eyes. "I see his weaknesses, but I can't condemn him. He doesn't feel he can do things. He thinks if he went back to school, he couldn't make it through. He wants *so much*. He feels time is pressing in on him. If he goes back to school, that's another year out of his life. He realizes he's been locked up all this time, between the drugs and the jail, and to spend *more* time in school would be a waste."

Jones has left the card game. He reaches behind Ruth's chair to pick up the baby. He pokes the baby's outstretched hand and the infant gurgles happily. "Oh, you like to be beat on," he laughs. "You're a pain freak, huh?"

Jones took singing lessons in elementary school. In junior high, he sang briefly with a succession of bands, until heroin and his changing voice made it impossible.

He brings out a trophy with "Our Little Pussy" inscribed on it. (Our little *Pussy?*) It is a prize he won in singing class—sixteen inches tall with a silver trunk and an Oscar-like figure on top. Eagles rest on its marble base, spreading their wings. Stella reaches up and takes Ruth's baby gently from her son. She is smiling again.

"He's a confused boy. He's got a heart of gold; basically, I think he's a good kid. And even though he was in all this trouble, I can honestly say he was never rude to me."

She is holding the tiny baby against her cheek, rocking it gently. Jones stands behind her, listening and watching.

"I often wonder about his life. At times, I pity him. He's got so much to offer . . . and he won't use it."

For a brief moment, she bows her head. Then she reaches for the cigarettes and hands the baby back to Ruth. I lay my pen down and watch her; she is composed and warm and jovial. Then she turns to her son and lets go a strong motherly blast.

"When are you getting a haircut?"

"Not *even*," he says, turning away.

I ask why the hair bothers her.

"He's not using his looks correctly. The Afro style is not right for him. It makes him look too much like who-did-it-and-ran." She chuckles, but she is serious. "He looks like all hair and no face. That *hides* the good-lookingness."

She stops and looks at him, talking slowly.

"It symbolizes that he was once a junkie . . . and . . ." She stops again. "I don't object to the Afro itself. But he should keep it short and neat."

Jones says nothing. Within a week, the luxuriant Afro will be gone. His hair will be cut by Charles Jones in this same kitchen.

Six

1

Twenty years ago, Charles Jones returned from the factory one afternoon to find a crowd of neighbors, police cars, and fire engines outside his building. A small figure hung outside the window of a fifteenth-floor apartment; a yellow cape fluttered in the wind. It was his first-born son! Charles Jones watched as the boy struggled to climb in the window—and slipped—and tried again. The crowd groaned, and the young father dropped to his knees on the sidewalk and closed his eyes and prayed.

"Please, God, get him in that window *safely* and I swear . . . I swear it! . . . I'll never beat him *again*." Eyes closed, he listened to the sounds around him.

Another collective gasp. "Did he fall?"

Charles Jones was still on his knees.

"No, but he slipped again," someone said.

"He's safe!" someone yelled.

"I wanted to be like Superman when I was a kid," Jones remembers, sitting on Carol's couch and laughing at the story. "I thought maybe I had the power like him. I had to test it."

Jones spreads his hands wide, fingers flying.

"I figured if I hung outside the window, I would take off and fly; I even let go with one hand—I still don't know if I was gonna let go with the other or not. I would climb out wearing this yellow blanket and hang from the support bar.

I slipped a couple of times getting back in—and I looked down at the ground . . . wow!"

Forget the elevator. Charles Jones ran up fifteen flights of stairs and burst into the apartment.

"Oh, hi, Father!" squealed the little boy in the yellow blanket. Superboy was glad to see his dad.

"*Hi? . . . Hi—shit, you little motherfucker,*" yelled the older man, beside himself with love and rage. "*Come here!*"

Vows to God were forgotten. "He really beat my ass," Jones remembers. "I was sore for weeks."

Firemen had been afraid to break down the door; the noise and confusion might have made the boy slip. But if they had come to the door, they would have found a teen-age baby-sitter calmly ironing clothes in the living room—incredibly unaware of the emergency.

And if they had questioned Jones' sister Billie—who read comic books in her bedroom during the crisis—they would have found she knew. The previous day her brother had lit all the prayer candles at mass without leaving any money in the coin boxes. He'd sinned against God, she decided, and this was his punishment. He could hang out the window all afternoon for all the sense her five-year-old mind could make out of it.

2

Jones remembers a teacher named Mrs. Blackwell.

"She told me to bend over so she could hit me with a pointer. I told her not to do it hard, but she did it hard. So I grabbed it and chased her around the room. I beat her on the head and neck and legs—dig it: I tried to kill her. She was beating a lot of the other kids, and they didn't do nothing. I gave her a taste of her own medicine. Wow, I hated that old witch! She called my father and said I was crazy."

Jones was eight.

"From the age of four I lived down by the Brooklyn

Bridge. You know, near the courthouses. My childhood was ordinary. You just try to be *in*. My mother and father did the best they could. It was hard; Pops was out of work sometimes, and the nights we ate as a family, Moms and Pops gave up theirs so we could eat."

Jones has some cocaine today, but he is waiting for Carol to leave. While we talk, his eyes search the far wall. He is not used to thinking back. He likes drifting there, aided by smoke-and-coke, but today I am following each memory with questions, forcing him to stay alert. The discipline of structured memory is elusive; the talk becomes a small boat moving ahead of a reluctant breeze.

"Their pay was low. They would sit at the table and play as if they were happy. They weren't. They were happy we were eating, but they weren't happy with their lives. They got up and went to work and they got money and brought it home and put it in the house—and it was gone."

His hand begins a slow dance on the coffee table.

"Moms went to work sometimes in her slippers. It would be snowing. When Pops worked, he wore dungarees. He looked good, but he is like me, he likes to dress. He couldn't have been happy."

Jones turns to look at me. His eyes are dark.

"This is what kept Moms and Pops together, the pulling to survive. They had to depend on each other. You work as a team to raise a child—at the end you feel good. But *your* life is gone."

He holds the tiny tinfoil packet in his hand, fingering it. Then he offers me the joint he is smoking. "What the fuck, man—let's get deep.

"This is what made me take to street life. I watched my parents. Pops says you get a reward out of working. I ask him: 'How can you say this? You don't enjoy your money. You should stop working and go out and have some good times.' "

Jones picks up the Boone's Farm bottle.

"He can't enjoy a party unless he's drunk. After a party, he stays home a long time."

The day is hot and Jones is overdressed: brown tweed slacks, dark zippered sweater with big collar, the black high-heeled platform shoes he is struggling with. He hasn't shaved, and his beard stubble is shadowy, lending a fierce air to his face emphasized by thick eyebrows and a rhinestone pin in the left ear. He looks like a pirate.

"Teachers would tell me to do something and if I didn't want to, I didn't. Moms always tried to get me to go to Catholic schools—but they wouldn't accept me. My report cards said I was bad."

He takes back the joint and drags on it and laughs—a hoarse cough-and-laugh that erupts during recollections he likes.

"I would go to Sunday school and try to rap, and the kids would laugh when I stuttered. I would get mad and curse—and the nuns would smack me hard! I wanted to grab those nuns and hang them from the cross. But I said fuck it, and went home."

Stuttering often causes—but is not always caused by—emotional problems. Its origins are elusive. In Jones' case, it may have been caused by the chills and fever of measles before he could walk. Charles and Stella also theorize that he took to imitating a stuttering uncle at an early age, and the habit stuck. His family really doesn't know.

"I had an easy time with school work, but I al . . . al . . ." His eyes clamp shut, again. He swings one fist in front of him, flailing. "But I . . . ALWAYS got angry when I took tests. I would get all excited if I wrote my name sloppy. Sometimes I wouldn't hand in the paper at all. I would make a mistake and rip it up.

"I passed tests to get into the Navy and to get my high school equivalency in jail. That was all. Tests get me angry. Being on the spot fucked me up."

Jones rises from the couch to open a window. He works methodically, slowed by wine and marijuana.

"I've stuttered as long as I can remember. I get very, very angry when I do it. I used to get in fights. Now . . . now . . ." It is as if the thing eating at him must make its point.

He throws out his fist, pushing at the air: "NOW I've gotten used to it."

Carol walks by, stopping at the closet for a coat. She keeps her distance, knowing Jones will order her away if she tries to listen.

"I had dug sports when I was a kid," he continues, watching her absentmindedly. "I didn't know how tall I was going to be, but I wanted to be a pro in baseball or basketball. I wanted to sing, too. In a school contest, I wrote an article saying I wanted to be a singer. And wow, I won the contest! They put the article in the school paper."

Suddenly Jones sits up.

"Hey, don't wear that coat. That's too much print. The hot pink clashes with the purple. Pink and red and purple are hard to match."

Carol is embarrassed. She takes off the coat and looks at him sadly.

"Wear it if you want," he shrugs.

She puts it on and twirls in the tiny hallway. "Okay?"

He nods, and she leaves. He begins fooling with the foil packet again.

"I ran with mostly a mixed crowd. I didn't use a nickname much, but they called me 'Boot,' which is what you called black kids sometimes. I dug Cagney, Bogart, Edward G. Robinson, the dudes who played the hard roles. When boxing came down, I dug Sonny Liston, but he lost. I dug Mohammed Ali from the beginning. He's *still* good."

He bangs his hand on the table. "Wow, Jack, that dude put some people in their place! He turned around and said he wasn't going in the Army. I respect that dude. When the Man did things to him, he did things *back*."

Always, the radio plays in the background. If the song is right, Jones will lower his head and sing along. He has a high-pitched, melodic delivery tarnished at the edges by a slight whine. For several seconds he will slip into a sad memory.

"I used to sing the songs they teach you in school," he begins. "The teachers told Pops I could sing good; that got him started. I dug the idea of being up there in front of people—but I didn't dig the way he pushed me."

Jones goes into the bedroom to get his works. The set he keeps at Carol's apartment has a syringe minus its plunger. In the plunger's place, Jones uses a nipple from a baby's pacifier—a plunger might push the cocaine into his blood-stream too fast, causing overdose. With a nipple, which functions like an eyedropper's squeezer, he can control the flow. The other set of works stays at his mother's house in a small black pouch hidden in a dresser drawer.

There, he uses a real eyedropper; Jones inserts a hospital needle into its mouth, wrapping the needle's base with a tiny strip of cardboard to tighten the fit.

"I took singing lessons when I was six or seven. I went to 'Star Time' on 57th Street, and I won some small trophies. Then I won the Oscar for being the best singer in my class. It said, 'Broadway Will Soon Be Yours.'"

"The trophy at your mother's house?"

"Yeah."

"The one that says, 'Our Little Pussy'?" I am writing fast.

"Yeah." He laughs. "They called me that."

"Why?"

"I don't remember."

After "Star Time," Jones took more singing lessons and then dancing lessons at another studio. But soon he quit.

"I just dropped out. They put me into a dancing thing. The teacher said I had to take off my shoes and put my leg up on this pole. I walked out. I went into the singing class, but I quit that, too. The teachers were gay; I had never dug gay guys. My father hassled me for a while—he wanted me to be a rich singer or a model, and I dug the idea of being rich, you know, but I didn't want to be around all them faggots.

"My father kept pushing. He would think up names for groups, and he would talk about me being a big success. I was in my first group when I was nine or ten. We sang at church dances and shit like that."

Jones unfolds the wrinkled foil and dumps the white powder into the cap of a quart soda bottle. The bottle cap is suspended between a hairpin's legs and functions as a saucepan.

I watch Jones helplessly. I dread this ritual of self-destruction. It is more ritual than fact since he started using cocaine, which is nowhere near as abusive as heroin. But the needle, punctured flesh, and blood still make me think of dying.

He adds water to the powder and heats the mix with a match, sloshing the milky liquid around inside the bottle cap. Then he probes the inside of his elbow. Unlike many drug users, his arm has relatively few scars, or "tracks." One particularly fat vein in the soft inner-elbow flesh has served him well for years. The scar tissue forms a permanent hole.

"I wrote a song once—I was going with this girl, and I thought it was true love. We broke up, and I wanted to go back with her."

"Can you remember the song?" I'm trying to keep my eyes away from his arm. He looks up at me as if nothing is happening with the needle and screws up his face to find the memory.

> "Pretty statue in the garden,
> Help me . . .

"No, wait a minute, uh . . .

> "Pretty statue in the garden,
> Pretty statue, hear my call . . .

"Yeah . . .

> "Pretty statue in the garden,
> Help me find the one I love. . . ."

He jabs the needle into the puffy vein, blowing cool air where the tissue is now punctured to ease his pain, then pushing the spike into himself until it is nearly buried.

"Most dudes tap it in," he says to me without looking up. "But you can break the needle that way. I just push it in fast; if you do it slowly, you feel it more."

A rock group is singing "Tell Me This Is a Dream" on the radio, and like so many other afternoons in his life, Jones is bent over his arm, head bowed in a classic junkie pose. His leather belt is pulled tight around his bicep to choke back blood circulation.

"My father was pushing me," he says, holding the needle in his arm and waiting for the cocaine to hit the way he likes. "I didn't like this. Sometimes I think I lost interest in school for this reason. Too many people pushing me. And I was losing my voice; it was getting deeper, and I was smoking a lot and shooting dope and doing pills. A low voice doesn't sound as good on tape or records; so I quit—I was about fourteen."

The cocaine isn't . . . quite right. Jones eases the pressure on the nipple; tiny lines of blood creep up the needle into the milky solution. He pushes this back into his arm, and nods. Now he's got it. He leans back.

"I was in school during this time, and everybody was in gangs. I was in the Revelers for a while, then I joined the Knights. The gang I ran with the longest was the Falcons, nearly two years. I was war counselor. Me and the Prez talked to people who wanted to fight us. We'd just talk—and if they didn't dig us, we'd fight."

Jones is becoming mellow like warm, ripe cheese.

"We had chains and sticks and knives. Nobody would really get hurt bad. We didn't use the chains and knives unless things were hot."

He is deep into it.

"I remember the time Davy and I were fighting the Chinks on our lunch break. He took an antenna off a car, and he ran up to this dude and hit him. The antenna went all the way around this Chink's head and cut him in a circle."

"How often did this happen?"

"Oh, wow! By the time I got into the eighth grade, we had fought the Chinks, the Italians, and everybody else."

"How often did it happen?"

"Like, almost every day. Fighting was what you did. My first fight was with an older dude in the elevator. I was about seven, and around this time, the older dudes got on the elevator and smacked you in the head. It was the thing. This dude beat me up. I cried and I went to my father. It really upset me—I *hate* to lose."

He has loosened the belt around his bicep and pulled the needle out of his arm. He wipes the blood from his elbow with a washcloth and dips the needle into a kitchen glass.

"It's a thing with me. I was always a sore loser. If I get angry, I want to hurt someone. I don't see red, I don't see green. I don't see any colors. I just see anger. I use my fists, or the side of my hand, or my fingers"—he stiffens his forefingers and thrusts the sharpened nails at me—"it doesn't matter."

He runs water through the needle.

"There was this girl who lived in my mother's building. She was a smoker! She used to get in fights for me—I'm serious!"

Jones laughs, squirting water into the air with the eyedropper. The afternoon light is fading.

"I was eleven, and one day this big dude started to push me. I yelled, 'Vivian!' and she said, 'Come here, nigger! I'm tired of fighting for you. If you don't fight, motherfucker, I'll whup *your* ass!"

Jones doubles up with laughter.

"Wow, I was scared! I got hit in the face, and my lip was busted. I hit him, I scratched him. He had me in a hammerlock and I turned my head into him and I bit him hard! He let go of me fast. When we were done, he could hardly walk away."

He pulls the nipple off the back end of the syringe with a pop and lays each part carefully in a small cardboard box.

"Later, some older dudes who saw the fight showed me how to hold my hands, and duck and block and dodge and do things right, and after that no one fucked with me."

The works are out of sight. I am tense, almost frightened, in the aftermath of this. But Jones is as calm as if he has opened a tin to take two aspirin. The conversation casually drifts sideways.

"I went to Pope Pius the Tenth's camp one summer. I didn't dig it. I didn't like the idea of going—it was nice, but it was too quiet. I wasn't used to that.

"I'm used to noise. As long as there's noise, there's life."

Jones eyes suddenly widen like a child listening to a ghost story.

"Out at the camp, there was no noise at night except

crickets. And bugs that lit up and flew by in the dark—wow, it was *weird!*"

He settles onto the couch.

"There was too much peace. When you think of death, you think of peace. In life, it's noisy. Death is for a long, long time, and you would always think of death at this camp. There would be prayers and shit, and you would be told to pray for your Moms and Pops, and you would begin to worry."

Seven

———◆———

1

"I was thirteen when I first used junk. I was singing. The guys in the group were older, up to eighteen, and they were doing drugs. We were singing in this church, and every night they would do this in the back room, and one night they said, did I want to do some? I said, fuck it man, okay."

Jones is lying on a bed near the window as he talks and it is midafternoon. He is hung over. His eyes show red scratches, and he seems distracted.

"I snorted it first. I was shooting a couple of weeks after that, after about three or four more times. It was the thing."

A truck passes noisily outside the window and he turns to look. It was a long night; his thoughts are drifting out in thin wisps, breaking into random fragments.

"There's not much to say about dope. It brings, like, a peace. There's no high I've ever had that can match it. It's *some* high! I was in junior high school when this started."

He seems to be inside himself; the red, tired eyes signal something stirring below, but he is torpid and half-conscious. I am sitting on the edge of the bed, straining to keep the conversation going. I ask some questions twice.

"I was afraid of the needle; I'm still afraid of it. But you *will* get down, no matter how much you are afraid. I put that needle in once, twice a day . . . whatever was happening."

He turns over to reach for a pack of cigarettes.

"I was told it was bad. You try to kick it yourself—you lie to yourself. You say you can boss it. Then one day you've got a habit. My parents didn't notice, but my father found out one day through some talk. They had suspected it. I would go out for a long time and come home and sleep even longer. But they couldn't really tell."

He coughs after a long drag on the cigarette. "I had some coke last night—it felt like the top of my head was coming off." He is sniffling.

"Moms looked at my arm. She started to cry. She didn't want to believe it. I was her son, you know? But she knew I was shooting it—she had been giving me the money I needed."

Jones is almost croaking, fighting overnight phlegm and creaky mental machinery.

"Pops talked to me. He'd say, look around you. I would say I wasn't going to get high any more, and I would mean it. But I felt strange around the house—they were always talking to me. My brother would talk to me, my mother, my father. Like, I didn't want to *hear* all the talk! I'd get outside and I'd get high again."

The apartment door buzzes. Jones is suddenly alert. He watches the front door through the slit in the curtain.

Carol doesn't open the front door. She sits on the living room couch, immersed in the afternoon soap operas, ignoring the metallic buzzing. Jones rears up on the bed. "Get the door, Carol!" He settles back without waiting to see if she obeys him.

"I really got *into* dope when I was with the Night Dragons. I got out of it for a while when I went to high school, but I started again. I was by myself in high school; I got into pills and dope—Seconals and Tuinals and booze and junk."

He laughs in his gravely, hoarse way, clearing his throat.

"That kept me *fucked* up. I would be fucked up all day, and go to bed and wake up and *still* be fucked up. Pops threw cold water on me in the morning—that would blow my head, and make me want to fuck *him* up. He liked to drink beer, so when I'd go by the refrigerator on the way to school, I'd grab three of his beers and drink them and *really* get fucked up. I'd be walking around in a dream."

Twice Jones has told Carol to get the door; nothing has happened. *"Bitch, there's someone at the door!"* he barks loudly. *"Get it!"* Suddenly his voice conveys violence; the rumble is frightening. Carol moves.

He turns to me. "During a mugging, things like that make you hurt people." He points at her, nodding his finger, "You tell people to do something and they don't go along with the program—and that makes you *mad*."

Carol opens the door a crack; she talks through the small space and looks anxiously over her shoulder into the kitchen.

"Before I got down with dope, I had a paper route, and I worked in a drugstore for a while. I saved what I had. I shined shoes when I was a kid—I knew how to get jobs and keep them."

It is a recurring theme. He *can* take care of himself, and he'll take care of "his"—his women and his babies. He insists on it. It hurts that Jo-Anne will not leave her father's house. He supported her when he was a $200-a-day junkie, didn't he? He is talking and I am writing and listening. Does he think I believe this? Does *he* believe it?

I ask: could he see the changes heroin brought? Did he feel he could stop? He looks straight into my eyes, ominously, almost fiercely.

"I could . . . feel . . . the changes. But I was running too hard to think about them—like jumping off a diving board. You can't stop in midair." He grimaces and his hands twitch. *"I didn't know what the fuck I was doing, that's all."*

Carol walks into the bedroom. She has been talking to the superintendent. The plumbing again. It is an endless game. The super comes to the door to say the landlord wants his money. Hire a plumber and pay for it, he says. Her rent bill will be credited. She knows it is a trap—she should not have to pay the plumber. It is the landlord's problem. And if she pays the plumber, she has to pay her back rent, too.

Keep it in family court, Jones says. He is sitting on the edge of the bed, coughing, lighting a joint.

"I thought I could beat the truth," he is saying. "They say the truth is the light—I was blind, man."

He inhales and pushes it in my direction.

"I was shown the right way. But I didn't want to go with it. So what has happened is *my* fault—that's where it's at."

Carol is standing by, listening.

"What do you want?"

"Nothing."

"Then go in the other room."

2

"Did you like school at all?"

"Some classes. I dug science. Math came hard. I dug biology and language classes."

School had special problems for Jones. In junior high school shop class one day, he made a mistake.

"We were working on some instrument boards that teach you to wire a house. I got the wires fucked up. I'd press the button, and all the bells would ring—only one was supposed to. The teacher thought I was playing. We had words. He called me a faggot.

"The next day I wired his seat. I also short-circuited the desk boxes; he had to change all the fuses."

Jones has his Boone's Farm, apple flavor today, sitting on the coffee table. He laughs.

"I got kicked out. He jumped up from his chair with the shock and looked at me and pointed toward the door."

Jones laughs hoarsely. "I was good at electronics. If I had stayed in the Navy, I would have been an electrician's mate."

Around this time, a confluence of failed tests, poor attendance, and classroom confrontations brought Jones some official recognition. He was sent on Tuesday's to a "counselor."

"She asked about school and my parents, what I wanted in my life. I said I wanted to be a big shot. I was impressed by the Mafia; I wanted to be a member. She didn't like that.

"From the beginning, she *swore* everything would be confidential. Then I had a hearing—they wanted to send me to a school for bad boys."

His hands are spread wide, pain evident in his red eyes.

"She came to the hearing with my records and told the principal *everything* I said—she laid the file open."

He reaches for the bottle.

"I had thought she was all right, that she was in my corner. Then she did that thing—it was the last year of junior high school. I didn't want to talk to her any more."

He takes a long gurgling chug-a-lug pull, throwing back his head.

"She said it was for my own good. I said I didn't want to hear that: 'You lied to me. You said it was gonna be between you and me—and *they* ain't you and me!' I didn't come very often after that, and I didn't talk much when I came."

Jones is wearing a fat spun-gold ring today. It has a square face with nine small diamonds arranged in three rows—a gift from Moms which he prizes highly. It is also his nest egg. When he is short, he takes it to a 14th Street pawnshop and gets about fifty dollars. When times are good—or when he has to see his mother on a special occasion—he redeems the ticket. Periodically, he mugs someone specifically to avoid explaining to Moms why he isn't wearing it.

I ask about the lady headshrinker.

"She had gray hair. She was about my height—I was short and fat then. She wore glasses for reading, and she had a pointed nose. She was white but she had a lot of color in her face, like tan. It was mostly makeup. It didn't hide the wrinkles."

Jones is rummaging among bottles and containers on the dresser, looking for a place to hide the ring. We are about to go out—he doesn't want to lose the ring to a mugger.

"I carried a zip gun then; I had it in my coat. One day when I went to her office, she saw it and wanted to take it. I walked out."

Jones opens a can of talcum powder. "Nobody would think to look inside here," he smiles.

"I was always afraid of her. I guess it was because she was so old. I thought she could send me to reform school or something. After the hearing, the school told me to go back to her. I just sat in the chair. She would say, 'Talk,' and I would say, 'What about?' She'd say, 'What do you feel?' I'd say 'Nothing.' "

Jones has decided against the talcum can. He pulls a pointed-toe loafer from a pile of shoes under the dresser.

"I . . . I *was* feeling things, but she didn't deserve to know them."

"Did she know you were using heroin?"

"I didn't tell her—and she didn't figure it out. I didn't tell people until I couldn't stop it from getting out. When I really got into junk, my clothes began to fall off. I was losing weight and I was selling them. Up to then, people couldn't tell. The lady shrink was pretty dumb. I would practically go to sleep on her, and she couldn't tell what was happening."

He falls back onto the rumpled bed. A few seconds of silence.

"Anyway, I got tired of school. I tried to leave it at sixteen but Moms wouldn't sign the papers. When I was seventeen, I signed myself out. People said I wouldn't be able to get a job, but I figured I'd do okay."

3

"I got this job with Schrafft's. It was okay. I pushed a coffee wagon around the buildings on 41st Street. I robbed 'em blind."

Jones had turned another corner. School was now behind him; he'd taken a job where workers, whatever their color, are called "boy." His future had moved close enough to touch him. So had heroin.

He had become a deliberate thief.

"I'd be out late at night, copping dope and bullshitting; it would get late. I would go straight to work without going home. I would be serving coffee and taking people's money, and I would be *asleep* right on my feet."

We are in Carol's living room. The television—an aged console bought for thirty-nine dollars at a used furniture shop after the burglary—is sputtering. A soapy melodrama called "General Hospital" is jumping all over the screen and Carol complains to Jones. He ignores her.

"I would be working with my eyes *closed*, man! I'd come to a curb with the wagon, and I'd have to wait for the cars, and I'd fall asleep leaning on the cart. The light would change and I'd catch myself. I got pretty good at this.

"I'd be takin' money from the cashbox every day. With that and my check money, me and another dude would get half a load. We'd shoot it up at night. One time I told them I lost the whole box. I told them a dude had cut the pouch strings. It got by them."

A "load" of heroin, according to Jones, was then twenty-five bags. Half a load cost him forty-five dollars. He stumbled through work with little or no sleep and ran uptown on his lunch hour to find heroin; he spent the night nodding on street corners with fellow junkies.

I'm asking how heroin affected him. He tells of watching someone *else* die.

"This Rican dude named Hawk and I went down to Avenue D to get some dope; I was new to it then. We went up on a roof and he butched his way into goin' first; he was bigger."

The bloody cracks in Jones' eyes are flaring.

"He got off and suddenly his eyes were bigger than half dollars. He was gasping—ahhhhh, ahhhhh!—and he fell back on the roof and died. Just like that.

"I didn't know what to do. I ran away and left him."

He remembers another death from overdose.

"There was this dude, Mousey. Julius and I was goin' up on the roof to get off. Mousey had been there with his brother for the same thing. When I got there, I saw him lying on the roof. He was a black dude, really black, but his face was purple. You could see it, a bluish purple. He was all alone, lying on his back. His brother left him.

"Can you dig that? *He left his own brother.* I was around sixteen."

4

"I'd be taking the subway to work in the morning and the moment I'd get in the seat—wow!—I'd be asleep. I'd wake up at 42nd Street because the train would lean a certain way at that stop and I'd jump off the train. On Fridays I slept right through the weekend. I'd get up maybe once or twice and get a glass of water. By Sunday afternoon, I would be shaking and squirming in the bed; I'd tell myself it was because I'd been sleeping so long. I didn't have the money to go out and cop."

Jones and Carol will visit his family this evening. He walks to the front hall closet and reaches for a beige sweater. Holding it against brown trousers, he looks into the living room for Carol's opinion.

"On Mondays Moms gave me money. At lunch I'd take a cab up to Broadway and 71st Street; I'd cop and get off in the bathroom of one of those hotels. It went okay for a while. I was going in here"—he points to the oft-used vein on the underside of his left elbow—"and Moms would see it, so I'd change to another one. She'd see that after a while; I'd change back. She could never tell for sure.

"I was getting thin, and I was getting short-tempered. At the job, they could see this, and they would talk to me. They liked me, and they tried to help, but I was always asleep and I wouldn't hear them. I finally got fired. I went to work in a furniture factory for about a month, then I went into the Navy.

"I was feeling patriotic," Jones remembers. "This is the way you are raised. You want to help your country, fight for your home and your people. This is what my father did, and his father did. I went into the Navy at eighteen—I thought this would make me a man."

Jones takes a long pull on the Boone's Farm, finishing it. He throws his head back and laughs.

"Wow, I'd never do that again!"

We are in the streets today. Jones throws the bottle into the gutter, and we walk into Katz's Delicatessen. He orders three hot dogs and a can of orange soda.

"I was using half a bundle a day, twelve bags, and dope was easy to get. I didn't know what a 'Jones' [a habit coming down] was. I never had to be sick. I had my Schrafft's check, and the cash from the change box, and I'd go to Moms and Pops if I needed more."

Katz's is big, like a barn. It has been in the neighborhood more than fifty years; lately it has begun to recognize the area's social problems. A black man dressed in blue and holding a thick club sits by the front door. The cash register is there.

"I was high when I got on the train. I had brought my works, but I knew they would go through my things when I got there, so I threw them away. Then the Jones bullshit started—I got sick and had chills and fever. We were at Great Lakes, Illinois, and it was colder than a motherfucker. It would snow and they would ask for volunteers to shovel it —you, you, you, and you."

Navy trainees normally spend ten weeks in boot camp; Jones spent twenty.

"The physical exercise was no big thing. But the mental thing, wow! I kept fighting back."

One incident is burned into his memory.

"The company commander's aide thought he was big. He was standing on this table, and he looked down at me and said something. I said, yes? He said, yes, *what?* I said yes again, and he kicked me. I grabbed his leg and pulled him off the table."

Jones is smiling; the smile quickly dissolves.

"The company had to crawl on toes and elbows twice across the barracks. I had to put my feet on a desk and smoke a cigarette; and they would crawl up to me and turn around and crawl back."

Jones was the only black man in his company.

"It really fucked up the company. Some people threatened to get me, so I took my jackknife that night and I held it up so they could see. 'Look here, you-all,' and I put it under my pillow. Everything was cool You learn to keep people at a distance."

Jones raises his can of orange soda and swallows most of it in large gulps. He is drifting slightly. But the essential problem—his incredible loneliness—hangs over the conversation like a winter sky.

"I talk *past* people I can't be bothered with—and I move on. It fucks with you to be this way, but you learn to live with it. As long as they don't put their hands on me, I don't care. You walk by and smile—you are smiling past them—and you keep on going."

An old waiter is approaching; shoulders bent, apron dragging on the floor, smock spattered with mustard and grease.

"People talk about you until they are blue in the face," Jones is saying. "But you don't tell them what they want to know. People don't like it that I got clothes and cash and a lot of old ladies—even *their* old ladies come to me. They think I am pimping off my women; I don't tell them it isn't happening. My life is a blank to them."

The old waiter stands over us. We are in an empty section of tables. A salt-and-pepper assortment of blacks and Jews crowds the other rows.

"Is waiter service tables," he says. "You cannot be sitting here."

Jones looks at him and goes back to his hot dog.

"Is for waiter service. You wanting to order?"

Jones turns to say something to the old man—but he checks himself, as he does surprisingly often, and submits to the irritation.

"What the fuck."

And we move.

"People on the street want to pry. They think: how has he stayed alive? But they don't come out and ask. They think I'm crazy, but they look up to me because I dress good, I keep cash, I've got women, and I don't work."

Earlier, Jones gave me one of his hot dogs; he is still hungry. He goes to the counter and gets another.

"These dudes ask how I get over. I say we all have our ways. They ask if I sell drugs. I say maybe. They don't even know where I live. They think I still live with my mother."

I ask about pimping.

"I can't, man. I have a sister, you know? If a dude was to pimp on her, I'd feel bad. I keep women around because they are nice to have. I used to have four. I lost one a while back, but I still got a third one. I don't see her much, but she's there."

In Katz's, cash is handled at the doorway within reach of the guard's club.

"The hardest thing," he says as we walk toward the door, "is to keep your rep the way you want it. If I lose a fight, I'm in trouble. The dudes who won't fuck with me now—they'd come around. So if I hear something—some dude is saying something about me—I take it right to the source. If things get out of hand, it's harder to cope with them later."

5

It is easy to assume Jones missed the sixties. Hippies, psychedelia, war protest, black revolution, the Beatles, acid rock—these do not seem to be at work on him. Yet he has been through all of them. He has dropped acid dozens of times, and he ran confidence games among hippies in St. Mark's Place for six months. He has talked about, and read of, black revolution—and rejected it because of his whiteness. He is an occasional Muslim. Lastly, he has been a part of the Vietnam war.

For Jones each of these is another hustle, history viewed through the narrowest of glasses, darkly. Always, he has a supporting role: he might have been a money changer in Christ's time, a foot soldier for Caesar, selling plunder on the side, a cattle thief during America's westward tilt, a Times Square hustler in the Roaring Twenties.

After boot camp, he was flown to California and put on an aircraft carrier heading for the Gulf of Tonkin.

"I didn't get high much at first. I felt it would be wrong—you are supposed to be there for your country. I was young. I hadn't looked at life. I thought we were *supposed* to be in Nam. We couldn't do any wrong. We were the land of the free, dig it."

The carrier stayed in the Gulf about two months.

"Planes were flying off it, and they would come back. That was what I saw. They were fighters, mostly Phantoms. All they was doin' was flying—I didn't think about it much. We had practice drills, but I just did my thing, staying high on smoke, and cooking. I was a cook for the chief petty officers' mess. The air war was a different part of the ship—you just work, you know?

"I thought we were doin' right in Nam, that's all. I slept when I wasn't working."

The aircraft carrier pushed on to the Mediterranean.

"We'd get a cab driver at these ports. It was easy to find drugs because the captain gave a lecture each time you got to port telling you the words for them. If you hear this word, he would say, get up and leave. So you remember the word and go to the beach with it. The drivers were hip to what was going on."

I asked about sightseeing and Jones laughs and throws back his head.

"For what? The bars and the girls and getting high—that's what was happening. The bitches in the bars would try to get your rings. And the dudes in the street were con men. If they came to the U.S., they'd make a fortune."

He is briefly silent and looks carefully at me.

"Of course there'd be a language barrier."

He drifts on.

"I took a cab and went into Sicily for a couple of hours. I didn't like it much but it was where my mother's people came from."

We are walking toward Chinatown. A line of Puerto Rican teen-agers sweeps down the sidewalk. Jones nudges me and we move to the curb.

"I did opium in Turkey. It came in little balls, and you could mix it into a cigarette. The seeds looked like smoke seeds, only they were white. Just before I got kicked out, the ship was hitting all the big drug ports—Marseilles, Barcelona, Sicily, Turkey. We were getting so much hash that I was getting sick of it."

He nudges me again. "When you see dudes walking down the street in a line like that, be cool. If they want to fuck with you, they will be all over before you know what is happening."

The Navy again.

"The hash came in five-dollar blocks. We stored it in the ship's vents. They don't clean the vents at sea so everything was cool. I sold it and made money, too.

"I was really digging the Navy. I dug it so much I had my blues and whites done by a tailor. It was beautiful! You'd go places and the people would be changing all the time. Sometimes I think about going back in."

It is, at best, an unrealistic notion. Jones has a felony record now.

"One night they put me in the hold. The hold man has to be down there with all the powder and shells, and that's a drag. I told the captain I felt things were closing in on me, and I was put out on the watches. But they kept me out there too long one night. This dude I worked for came out and started fucking with me."

We are walking down Mott Street, past markets with butchered birds hanging in the windows. We walk past a wino in a sailor's stocking cap. He is sprawled in a doorway, red-eyed and unshaven, holding a half bottle of muscatel.

"That's a cop. He ain't dirty enough, and he's too young."

I look back. Jones is right. The man's eyes dart in and out of the passing crowd. He is too alert to be a wino.

"One thing led to another," Jones continues, "and I hit this dude. He pulled a knife. I grabbed this flare and popped the cork on it and burned him. Later I was sent to see the ship's headshrinker. The shrink said I should have got on the phones and called the bridge; the ship's cops would have come down. No way! By the time they got there I would have been dead."

A middle-aged Chinese man in a gray suit passes us. "There's money," Jones says without turning his head.

"I told the shrink I would do it again. He said I was criminally insane." Jones' mouth curls in distaste, as if he is about to spit. "I was really pissed. The chief said they would leave me my E-one rank. Man, if you want it, I said, take it. I ripped it right off my arm and gave it to him. Two weeks later I was out of the Navy."

We are sitting on a bench, and Jones is watching a bent old Chinese man. The old man walks stiffly, as though his legs hurt. He wears a rumpled suit and a drooping hat, and keeps his eyes on the sidewalk, leaning on a gnarled wooden cane. But he has an unmistakable air of dignity.

"Those Chinks are really something," Jones says. "They've got the family thing together. They pull a lot of cash together, and they've got their own schools and hospitals. And if you fuck with one of them, you've got to deal with all of them."

The old man passes from sight.

"The shrink asked me about putting a square peg in a round hole. I said I'd take a knife, cut up the peg, and make it fit. He asked if I ever saw my mother in a bra. I said yeah. He asked if I got hard. I thought the questions were stupid; so I asked him if *he* ever saw *his* mother in a bra, and did *he* get hard.

"He asked if I ever felt like I wanted to be a woman. I was feeling smart-ass. I said, 'No, dear.' He looked at me and went back to writing. He asked if I had sex with my father. I said I loved my father—but not that much. It was all bullshit; I had been asked a lot of this by the woman counselor. Then he sent me to the XO [executive officer]. He said I was being smart."

Jones lights a cigarette and hunches over it.

"The XO said, this is a man's Navy. And I said, then I wish I had some men to talk to. We were right off of Naples. I got flown into there, and then into Spain. Then I was flown into McGuire [Air Force Base] in Jersey, and then to the Naval Station in Philly. I was out. A month after I got home, I was arrested for carrying works."

That would be the first entry on his yellow sheet: he got six months' probation.

Eight

1

The momentum of Jones' descent quickened.

"The first day I got home, I went into a nod on a bench and somebody got my watch. They slit my pockets, too, and got about thirty dollars. That made me so mad I didn't cop for another month."

He laughs oddly and looks at me.

"Not mad enough. I had my first OD that January. My father had a birthday party; he had it in a bar, and we all came home. I was high on alcohol, and I had popped some pills; I left and went to this woman's house and copped, and I OD'ed. I was really out."

What Ever Happened to Baby Jane? is bouncing on the television screen.

"You don't remember an OD. But as soon as you shoot it, your body *knows*. I was suddenly outside this woman's house; that's all I know. I don't know how I got to my parents' building. I went into a dream. Some kids found me the next morning on the stairway. My mother and father came to get me, and when I woke up, they said the things any parent would say. This is your life. You are messing it up. I won't do it no more, I said. That was my second or third week home."

The women in the movie are fighting, and Jones is laughing and shaking his fist: "Go get 'em, bitch!

"I had cash when I got home, so everything was cool for a while. I had four hundred dollars from the Navy, and a few thousand I'd sent home in bonds from playing craps and selling hash. I had thirty-two dollars a week unemployment money, too. By February, I'd spent it all on clothes and dope.

"I started selling things—my rings and my clothes went; I was broke. I was going to radio and TV repair school, and Moms picked up the fees, but I had to get more money."

One of the women in *Baby Jane* swings at the other, and Jones punches at the air. "Wow," he is grinning. "The old bitch has got a lot of shit!

"The last two months before I dropped out of electronics school, I would stay out of classes, or come in half a day. This teacher said it had to stop. He said he'd give me another chance because he dug the way I worked. I would fall asleep in theory class, but I would work hard in the shop. The teacher didn't dig me personally, but he dug this. But I was too into myself to look at him. I think of him sometimes now."

Jones lets out a slow breath of air and turns away from the television set.

"I dropped out of school on June first. I was busted for burglary four weeks later."

He continued to live at home, but he used the needle more and more, and stole more and more. Charles Jones returned from work one day and saw his son spread-eagled against the downstairs hallway wall. Housing police were searching him for heroin. And Charles Jones turned away. His boy was hanging out of a window again, but he couldn't help.

"I started taking off apartments. I dug burglaries. My man and I would knock on a door to see if anyone was there. If they were, we'd ask for John, or maybe Jean; girls' names worked the best. If no one answered the door, we'd go through it. We worked fast and looked for money or things to sell."

"Who bought them?"

"People in the streets. TVs and stereo sets sold really good. Off 14th Street there's some co-op apartments, and we'd walk through and people would come up and ask about the stuff. They knew they'd get a good price. We were doing this every day—every day *and* night. I was going with Jo-Anne and I was spending a lot of money. You can ask her. Figure about two hundred a day in loose bags, plus clothes and going out."

The memories are scandalously good; Jones' face warms with an easy smile.

"We were workin' seven days a week, gettin' typewriters, radios, TVs. Those were the best times. We did the burglaries before five o'clock. Then at night we had all the money and it was too late to buy clothes, so we'd get high."

Jones' face begins to boil suddenly with bad memories.

"You've got money, you don't stop to think of the next day. You think of now. Your habit really comes down. One day you have bad luck; you've got no money and you are sicker than you should be. It's *bad!* I would use Jo-Anne's radio. I'd take it to the pawnshop in the morning and get thirty or forty for it; I'd get my first fix, and pull some rips and bring it back in the evening. She got uptight because it belonged to her father, but I always brought it back before he came home."

Carol walks into the living room. She has gone to the furniture store to complain about the television. A clerk said the shop would buy it back for eighteen dollars. He snorts and watches the movie to its end, ignoring her.

Jones' burglary phase lasted four months. It ended in the brownstone apartments of Stuyvesant Town.

"This pill freak comes by and says, 'Let's go out.' I say no, but he says, come on, man, and he has his tools and I say okay. We go to this house, but some private guards come by and they see him going in. I was halfway up the stairs, and he was too high on pills to know enough to split. We got busted for the tools: attempted burglary. We hadn't opened the door yet, so they couldn't put an actual burglary charge on us."

Jones turns back to Carol. "The motherfuckers ain't gettin' no television set they sold for thirty-nine dollars *back* for eighteen. I'll get an antenna and it'll be all right." She says nothing.

"Getting busted like this scared me. I decided to stop doing burglaries—too many things against it. The cops had been following our jobs. In the precinct, they had a whole *string* of locks to put on us. But our tools didn't fit the bites because we had bought a new set that week."

It was Jones' first time in jail. He did two weeks in Manhattan's Tombs before his mother made bail, then additional time when he angered the judge by failing to hire a lawyer and then arriving late at his hearing.

2

Jones was lucky. The case never went fully to trial.

"The DA wanted me so bad he forgot what he was doing. One cop and one guard were the witnesses, but the guard couldn't remember who had the tools. My lawyer was like Perry Mason; he asked the guard if he could remember what we had on. The guard said I had on a white shirt and white shoes, and that was wrong. I had on blue Navy dungarees, a blue shirt, and black shoes. The lawyer asked the guard who had the knife. I did—but the guard couldn't remember. The cop had a good memory, but the guard blew it for him."

It was a pretrial hearing, lasting one day.

"They had taken some of my keys, and they said these were burglar tools. Jo-Anne came to the hearing and said they were keys to her house, which was true. The judge said there wasn't enough evidence, and he dropped the case."

While he was on bail between the arrest and the hearing, Jones robbed two liquor stores and burglarized half a dozen apartments.

"But when I beat the case, we split up. That was a turning point. I got to thinking more about mugging. It seemed safer."

A month after his acquittal, he knocked on the door of a "shooting gallery" and found police inside. The junkies using the apartment didn't live in it; he was cited for "illegal trespass."

In 1970, he and Jo-Anne were caught in Macy's stealing

sweaters. He ate the drugs he was carrying, hid his works in a phone booth, and copped a plea for petty larceny. He got thirty days. Jo-Anne was let off.

3

After he gave up burglary, Jones worked in a nursing home; his father made the connection. And Jones worked diligently, though he remained fully addicted to heroin and had to scramble constantly for money.

He was twenty at the time. He remembers the patients as weak, dying, malodorous scarecrows, trapped in wheelchairs and lying in hospital beds. They received small amounts of spending money on Fridays. Assigned to the four to midnight shift, Jones was talking one day to a wizened little man when the man sat bolt upright in his chair.

"You know *what*, Mr. Jones?"

"No . . ."

"Tomorrow is check day. I don't want my money!"

"Why?"

"The man who works here at night will take it—and if you don't give it to him, he hurts you."

Jones was shocked. He didn't believe this, and he continued his rounds. Then an old woman said she'd been robbed, too. The older patients often hoarded their allowances in closets and drawers. The night man apparently had discovered this.

Jones went to his immediate boss, a supervising nurse. She was skeptical. More than one patient has complained, he said. She said she'd check it out.

"Things will be different," he told the old man.

The next day he saw the old man again.

"Mr. Jones, you lied to me!"

Jones listened.

"He came around. He wanted my money. I said no, and *he beat my ass!*" The old man was practically in tears.

Jones checked with other patients. They'd also been robbed, and they were angry.

Jones went to his father's friend, an assistant administrator. A trap was laid, and the night man was caught and fired. Jones' reward? A transfer to the man's shift. "I hated that shift," Jones remembers. "I can't work at night."

Jones *had* thought of robbing the patients himself. "I didn't do it because I could go to Pop's friend. He was my godfather. He knew I was on drugs and he gave me money because he knew I would get it anyway; I always paid it back. It crossed my mind to rip off the old people, but the only time they got money was when I got paid, so I didn't need it."

"So why did you stop someone else from doing it?"

Jones' face assumes a righteous, square-jawed look. He leans forward, crossing easily to the other side of his personality.

"Most of those people were old and senile." His hands develop a palsied shake to make his point. "Some of them got three dollars a week. They had been there for years—it was the only money they had! I feel sorry for old people. They have to put up with a lot of shit. My mother and father will never go to a nursing home!"

We are riding a bus today. Jones watches an elderly man climb in. The old man falters; his hands shake badly. Jones goes to help him to his seat.

"I got a thing about old people. An old dude had an apartment once that junkies used to go to. He was all fucked up. He would spit on the floor, and he didn't take baths and he didn't eat right. The neighborhood junkies used his place to get off in, and they would wreck it and beat him up. It wasn't right. Me and my man stopped this. We made the junkies pay him for using the place, and stop beating on him."

4

It is a shadowy afternoon in the projects, and Jones sits on a park bench waiting for a smoke connection. I am asking about his worst times. A few months after the incident with the night man, he was fired. He had worked six months at the home.

"I was coming back from taking lab tests downtown and I heard this big bang when I was climbing the stairs. Some old dude wanted to pee and got up to get his bedpan and fell. I helped him back into bed. But I ran into the owner going back upstairs. He asked why I was off my floor. I was running this errand, I said. But I'd been back a while already, he said, what was I doing? I couldn't say anything—I don't know why, I just couldn't. He told me to punch out and I said, fine, I'll do it."

Then came the terrible time. Jones turned twenty-one in the Tombs. When Stella made his bail, he learned that his grandmother had died. Then his family life fell completely apart.

"Most dudes' parents turn them loose when they go on drugs," Jones remembers. "Mine hung on a long time—then bam! They turned me loose. I had to learn how to survive in the streets, fast."

He became known as a junkie. His clothes suddenly seemed baggy, showing the beginnings of a bony, degraded body. Police stopped him. He was hunted, spied upon.

"You get nervous. The cops stop you all the time; you don't know what they know. You might have a joint in your pocket you forgot about. They search you on any pretext. I was clean most of the time . . . not exactly clean, but I didn't get in trouble."

The night Charles Jones saw his son against the wall, a cop demanded to know where Jones carried his "spike" [needle]. It was in his mouth, hidden between his jaw and the flesh of his cheek. He said he didn't have one—and the cop slugged him in the mouth, cutting him badly.

Jones left home. Jo-Anne ran with him; they moved into a drifter's hotel on Sixth Street off St. Mark's Place. The room had a bed, dresser, and sink; the toilet was outside in the hall. It was Christmastime, 1970, and they went without heat several days a week. Jones paid an astonishing ten dollars a day for the room.

The hotel was filled with prostitutes, winos, and junkies. An old wooden door on Sixth Street led up a long flight of stairs to the front desk. A mirror hanging out of a second-floor window allowed the clerk to see who was ringing the door buzzer; it might be the vice squad.

"I used to sit and watch him," Jo-Anne remembers. "He'd put the needle in his vein, and I knew he was taking his life piece by piece. Each needle was taking something . . . how could you know what was left?"

They stayed six weeks. After that, they stayed with friends. Jo-Anne coped often with overdose emergencies. At one hospital, a doctor calmly told her he would die. Another time, he collapsed in her apartment just as Morris was due home. She brought him out of it minutes before he arrived. During one collapse, she could not feel his heartbeat.

"I was hysterical! We tried everything. My girlfriend's boyfriend beat him so hard he knocked out a tooth. We gave him milk. We put ice between his legs. We blew into his mouth. He turned purple and he was gasping for breath. All kinds of white stuff came out of his mouth . . ."

Jones was in the streets full time. He was running con among hippies and weekend tourists in the East Village. Occasionally, he mugged his victims. His days were devoted, like those of a foraging animal, to hunting. Heroin, the hotel bill, hamburgers: money had to be found for these—in that order—each day.

"I got pretty good at running con. I'd break up a six-inch piece of opiated incense and sell it as black hash; I'd get rid of it in one day. I sold sleeping capsule powder as dope. I got vitamin B-12 tablets at the drugstore and sold them as acid trips. I'd get catnip; I'd mix it with seasoning and sell it as smoke. If you take the powder of a Darvon pill and put it on your tongue, it numbs it; you can sell this as coke. I was doin' okay."

In a manner of speaking. Jo-Anne soon had to return to her father. "His habit got too heavy. I wasn't eating well. He was worried about that, and he sent me home. Jo-Anne went to Arizona after that and stayed with her mother. She hoped it would be the end of the relationship.

"He was out hustling and robbing and mugging people, and I couldn't take that life. I wanted to forget him."

Jones worked occasionally in other nursing homes. His biggest job lasted a week ("I went in high and they fired me"), and others came sporadically after he signed with a referral service. Just how well he did depends on who tells the story. Jo-Anne remembers the tension of mornings he pawned her father's radio. She remembers when he begged her for Morris' money. She remembers when *she* threatened to cut Morris with a kitchen knife. She was seventeen.

Listen to Jones:

"I was cleaning up. I was out of the house, and Jo-Anne and I stayed at this hotel. Each night she ate and I ate, and I got high, and I paid for the hotel, and I was puttin' my clothes in the cleaners and taking them out."

The truth lies somewhere in their shared memories. Sometimes, he did well. He says he used a steam iron one day to press a carton of incense sticks into a black "brick." He sold the resulting "hash" for six hundred dollars.

"Didn't the customers object?"

"Everything I sold gives you a high or a nod. It ain't big, but a trip is a thing of the mind. Some dudes got off on this stuff. There was no way they could *really* come back at me."

Jones made a fragile peace with his parents and returned home. He also changed careers; he became a full-time mugger. He'd mugged people before: "A dude says he wants to buy something. You get it. Then he says he doesn't want it. So you take him off because he's playing with you."

At home again, he was closer geographically to Wall Street and Chinatown than to St. Mark's Place. The former is mugging territory; the latter a place to run con. Equally important, the intricacies of con games had grown irritating.

"Dudes wanted different things and I would have to get them. I had to wait for my money. My habit was getting worse, and after a while, I couldn't wait."

5

A year later, Jones mugged a man too close to his home; he feared recognition. So he went to the housing police and complained that the man had picked a fight with him—an irrational, doped-up bit of logic.

Shortly after that, he met his second victim of the day in an elevator, a middle-aged father of four.

"He was carrying some bags, and I put the knife up against his throat; he had about forty dollars. He didn't try to fight, but he gave me a real *mean* look when I went through his pockets."

Jones used the money to make a heroin connection.

"I was with this girl. We ran down the stairs and went to the gym to get off. I wanted to get away from the projects until things cooled off, but we went outside and she started talking to some girls. I sat down on a bench and went into a nod. Six or seven cops walked up; they were all around me."

After years of mugging, burglaries, confidence games, and armed robberies—easily totaling more than a thousand criminal acts—Jones was going to prison. He drew a "bullet"—one year.

"A cop kicked me. I came out of my nod and said, 'What the fuck you want with me?' but they didn't waste no time. They hustled me down to the projects' police office; both the dudes I had hit up were waiting."

He spent the night in a precinct jailhouse.

"The cop said, 'You know what?' I said, 'What?'

"He went to his file cabinet and showed me a knife. It was big enough to cut a cow in half; the second dude had been coming after me! So in a way I was lucky to be caught." Jones grimaces. "But dig this: it's fucked up in the jailhouse. You sleep on a bench, and they take your shoes, your belt, anything you can hurt yourself with; the bench is two wooden slats. No blanket, no pillows."

For two years, Jones' life had been a pinwheel of street

violence, risk, tension, sickness, and relentless scrambling for heroin. Jo-Anne had left him. His parents were pressuring him to enter a rehabilitation clinic. Charles Jones had promised him a car if he would enroll. One of his friends had taken him to New Jersey, even put him in the Hilton hotel one night to keep him clean. Nothing had worked.

"Pops and everybody was down to earth. But I wanted to take care of myself. I was out in Jersey for a while; one morning I was in the bathroom and I was getting off, and they started banging on the door. I had been inside a long time. My arm was bloody and there was blood on the floor, and on the way out I threw the bag at the toilet and missed."

"I came back that night, and they were waiting. They said, come on man, we know what you are doing; and I said, hey man, I ain't doin' nothing. I went back to the city."

And back to the streets.

In jail, Jones had to kick cold turkey; ironically, he now had the will power to do what was necessary with little fuss.

"It takes about a month before you sleep and eat right. But it was no big thing because I didn't have any choice."

Arraigned and charged with two counts of felony robbery —backed up by a rap-sheet containing burglary, shoplifting, and heroin-related arrests—Jones knew he was in trouble. But it was convenient trouble. Prison would be a refuge from his street entanglements.

"I had been running like a madman. One of the dudes I'd taken dope off had put out a contract on me. The contract meant that any dude who wanted to take me off could do it and get money from this dude.

"So here I was in jail; I figured, fuck it man, I'm gonna cop out."

It was just a question of how much time.

"It's like 'Let's Make a Deal.' You bargain. The aide comes to the bullpen, and he reads what the people say you've done. It's wrote up big, so they can scare you. You know from the way they wrote it up, if you can beat it. If it's wrote up good, and no one had to tell a lie, you can't beat it."

Jones' street-sharpened senses of self-preservation were at work.

"The aide is using words you don't understand. You say, hey, I'm not a lawyer, and he *still* uses those words, and so you gotta keep after him and get him to break it down . . . like, how does this apply to *me?* Otherwise you go through the whole thing without knowing what is happening. That's a waste of time; and man, you got no time to *give.* The aide, he is hurt, he says look, I'm your lawyer, you've got to trust me. But man, you can't do that, you can't trust *anyone.* You've got to keep askin' what does this talk *mean?*

"You tell the aide, you say talk to those people and see what you can do. And he comes back and he says he has been talking to the DA and there is no hope for me. The dude passes his hand by you to show how bad it is. This is the moment. Nine times out of ten, you come out okay if you keep your wits about you. The aide says the DA wants five years and wow, I am thinking I gotta do at *least* two of this with good behavior, and I gotta go to a bigger court for trial because the most this court can give you is one year, so I say ask him if he'll give you two A's [misdemeanor counts] and I'll do them back to back."

Manhattan's clogged courts are dinosaurs overwhelmed by their environment. They cannot keep pace with urban crime. To survive—to retain the appearance of efficiency and justice —they will reach acress galaxies to compromise with Jones, who faces two airtight armed robbery indictments. He could go to jail for a decade. Yet they will let him plead guilty to a misdemeanor robbery charge to avoid the delay of a jury trial. One count is even dropped to make the package neater.

"The aide comes back and he says, hey, I really had to twist the DA's arm. I had to really get him to do me a favor, you know? He said he'll take the time."

And Jones drew his bullet. The judge leaned over the tall bench in his black robes, adjusted his spectacles, looked briefly at one of a score of street punks before him that day, and passed sentence.

"I had been on heroin. I figured maybe he would send me to a house. But he said, 'Son, you get a house all right—the House of Correction,' and so I went upstate."

Nine

1

"State time is *all* fucked up, man."

Jones did not adapt easily to jail. He kept to himself, maintaining silently whatever individualism and dignity he could muster in the ancient state prison. He did not relate easily to authority figures, so the guards were a problem. He was intensely proud of his manhood, so he had problems with the prison's homosexuals. He was stubborn and opinionated; arguments with other inmates were difficult to avoid.

"Lots of trouble. Trouble with the hacks, trouble with the faggots, other trouble, you know? It must be the hack's job to fuck with you; right away you are supposed to think he is God. But God don't bleed, and you know the hacks can bleed and die just like anyone else. I was supposed to give them respect—and wow, how long can you keep *that* up?"

The prison sweltered in summer and froze in winter. It was a world unto itself, riven with racial tension and driven to near-rebellion by the dictatorial power of rural-raised white guards and administrators.

"They would beat a guy bloody; then take him to sick call and wrap him in bandages; then bring him back and beat the bandages *off*. I saw this happen. They'd try to break your spirit—they couldn't break mine. Moms and Pops came to see me every month. That meant the hacks couldn't beat on me; it would show. Without my parents, I wouldn't have got out of there.

"Jail is always the same, you know? Only the days change.

My cell had a bed, a cabinet, a sink, and a toilet. I had pictures of my family, some candy they brought me and canned fish and bread from the store. I had notebooks from my classes, too. That was it. The cell was a little bigger than the one in the Tombs."

For a moment, silence. He is thinking back. "Compared to the Tombs, you know, it was okay. The Tombs is *really* fucked up. Everytime I went there dudes in the receiving line would be sick. They are barfing on the floor, they are moaning. There was so many dudes in the 'A' pen once that I couldn't sit down. Some of them getting sick on the floor; the dude next to me was moaning about his bust. The hack came to the bars and called out my name. I was supposed to hurry over to him—but I couldn't because I had to get over all those bodies. He fucked with me for that."

Jones' mind is still in the Tombs.

"You are coming off the street, and they take your keys and money, and you stand naked in line. The hack says get up on the bench and run your hands through your hair. You do that. Open your mouth. You do that. Lift up your balls. He looks underneath them. Turn around. You do that. Spread your legs. You do that. Lift your feet, you do that. Bend over and spread your cheeks wide. You feel like a pig being sold. Then you see the doctor. This is a hard-to-take dude. He feels you are trash. He doesn't want to touch you.

"By the time I got to my cellblock, it was about two in the morning. The hack was asleep—hacks *always* sleep at night—and he got mad because I woke him up. He looked at his clipboard. He walked around. He gave me a card. It said U-A-5. That meant the top tier—up, you know?—'A' cellblock, cell five. I didn't know this, so he fucked with me. He finally gave me blankets and he cracked the cell. All night, dudes in the other cells were sick. One guy was so sick he had the whole tier fucked up. Nobody could sleep. I had to get up at five, and I was laying there thinking how did this guy get past the doctor? The doctor had to be blind!

"And each night when the lights went out it was like they flew in troops of mice. They'd come in the cell in the dark, and I would get up to take a pee and step on them. They'd go 'wheeeeee'—wow, it was really bad!"

Upstate, the days began in darkness.

"A bell wakes you up. You come out in the corridor and you are still half asleep. Sometimes you are cold and shaking. The bell was like a fucking fire alarm; now you line up when the hack bangs his club against the wall. The sound of it echoes up and down the hall—it always sent chills up my spine.

"In the line, they'd fuck with you if you walked slow or out of step. We'd go to chow. It would be cereal, a cup of coffee, jelly, and bread. We'd go back in line again. I always tried for the end of it. Dudes would be fucking around and hit each other; all kinds of shit would start. I could get away from this at the end. At eight-thirty another bell rang and I went to school."

Jones took high school equivalency courses. School was the easiest of his alternatives.

"I had been in the streets so I wouldn't have to work—I didn't want to work in prison, either. I got out of school at eleven-thirty for chow, then again at three o'clock for the yard. I was punished a lot, so I had usually to go to my cell. Small shit: I didn't run into the lineup fast enough, or I was talking with some other guys after the last bell."

Night.

"You went to your cells after supper. That was it; you were locked up until morning. I would read my mail or study or write letters. Sometimes I'd get high. I went to the doctor once and said I had a toothache. The pain pills weren't much of a high, but I had to make do.

"Sometimes I got high with bananas. I'm serious. If my parents brought them, I kept the skin and dried it out and mixed it with the tobacco they gave me. The tobacco was strong; you just about got high on it alone."

Jones preferred to be alone, but it was difficult.

"I tried to get down with books and stay to myself. I had a small group of dudes I was close to, and I always kept my cigarettes and food with them so I didn't have to go to other people. If somebody outside the group gave you food or cigarettes, he'd want some ass. And if he gets your behind, everybody *else* wants it. Dig it: I didn't go into jail a faggot, and I wasn't *even* coming out one! I knew dudes would try, so I wasn't shocked; but it *kept* happening. Once I was gonna take a shower, and this dude who had been looking at me in the mess hall came in.

" 'How come you're watching me?' I said.

" 'Because I think you are fine, man,' is what he said.

" 'You ain't so bad yourself, you fine old motherfucker,' I said back. Then we came to blows. Somebody stopped it before we was finished. He walked away with his cherry unbusted, and that was cool."

He sealed himself off from others, and got into his class-work, which had an ideological spinoff.

"I got into the idea of revolution. I thought about jail, and the system I was in; I got as far as the black thing, but I couldn't relate to prejudice because I hadn't been done wrong *that* much, except in the Navy, and a few times when I was a child. I decided there should be changes made—but they didn't have to be from white to black because both do the same things. But there should be something for everybody, you know? The best way would be for people to go to bed and wake up and be ready for change. But this can't happen; people have got to be shaken. War shakes them."

And mugging? What does that do?

"I don't know, man. I have to survive, that's all. If everybody had an equal share of things, maybe I wouldn't be into mugging." Jones pauses, as he often does, to contradict himself. "But I can't really say that. I had chances to do okay."

Back to jail.

"The revolutionary dudes said that life outside was jail, too. I didn't dig that. Jails *aren't* real life. You don't deal with real people here; the hacks deal with *you*. In a revolution, I figure black dudes would fuck things up just as badly as the white ones; so the best thing would be, like, if you had a board of ten people ruling things, five would be black. That would be worth something."

Jones was interested in the ideas he encountered, but his

habits of drift and self-indulgence were strong. He did not keep reading. And he lacked the discipline to confront the ideas he found.

"They had a black class. I read a lot of Nikki Giovanni and Sonia Sanchez, and that dude, uh . . . the dude who called himself LeRoi Jones. I liked his work. I liked Nikki's work, too. She was more of a revolutionary; I didn't dig that, but I liked her spunk. Sonia Sanchez is the best. She speaks from the streets and gets down with drugs."

2

In the cold light of his cell, Jones worked carefully through his life. He decided to quit heroin.

"I was tired. I had run for a long time. Everything I had was gone. I didn't know anything except the streets, and I had *nothing* to show for this. I had a talk with myself, and in this talk, I thought about what I had been through. I drew a blank on my life. I couldn't lie no more . . . I couldn't *think* of any more lies."

He did not snap his fingers or announce his decision. It was a feeling, something he finds hard to explain.

"Kicking dope is like breaking up. You love someone, but you take only so much shit. Like if she cheats on you, and she keeps on doing it. You can handle just so much. And dope is one bad downfall after another. You are in a dream, you are in your own world, and for a while things are easier to accept. But all you *really* do is chase the bag and get more and more fucked up. For a while in prison, all I was thinkin' about was my next cop. Then I read this poem called 'King Heroin'; the dude knew what was goin' down. He was talking about how the King *has* you. I decided that was it—I would go back to school and not use dope any more. It took a lot of thought."

A few weeks later, Jones was released.

"I was brought down to the Rock [Riker's Island] and cut loose. Bruce and my father were at home; Moms was at work. Pops was shocked! He thought I wouldn't be home until June. He thought I had escaped. I told him, no, man, I was home."

Jo-Anne had returned from Arizona; she was invited to the fifteenth-floor apartment without knowing he was home. Jones thought about heroin while he waited for her.

"I was scared I wouldn't be able to kick. Jo-Anne cried and all that shit when she saw me, and we went to the Chelsea Hotel for the night. I talked with my father and I got high on booze first. Later that night I wanted to get high on dope . . . so I just kept on drinking. We went up to the Bronx the next day and slept on Jerry's couch for a month. I didn't come back downtown until I knew I could handle it."

Narcotics experts talk of something called "multi-addiction." Heroin has become scarce, and addicts turn to other drugs to compensate for this. Medically this is mystifying. Heroin is a depressant; cocaine, a favorite substitute, is a stimulant. Pills can take you either way. It was always assumed that addicts used a particular drug because they liked—or needed—the high it produced. The new trend belies this theory. In the Bronx, Jones rejected heroin and moved almost effortlessly to other drugs.

"I got to liking smoke again. That helped a lot. I took some acid trips; then I got into bams [pills], and then into coke. Smoke and coke were the main things. I didn't get into dope again . . . no sir! I am still afraid of it. I do mostly smoke now, sometimes acid trips or bams or coke. But smoke is the big thing."

3

"I don't believe," he is saying, "that I think differently than anybody else." He says it often.

"Most people would argue with that," I answer, upset with this idea. "They think rip-offs are wrong."

He is suddenly on his feet, his right hand angrily thrashing the air.

"People think a mugger doesn't think or feel. It's not true! You do feel! You know it is wrong. I wouldn't want a dude to take *my* cash."

He stops to catch his breath while his mind works through a labyrinthine rationale.

"No one in the world is happy all the time. When a mugging happens—when I take someone off—it is their time to feel sorry. It was *meant* to happen."

"Destiny, right?" I am being sarcastic, but he doesn't notice.

"Yeah, that's it. You know you will die. You know you must love and you must feel sorrow. It's all planned."

"Who plans it?"

Jones smiles, almost shyly.

"I believe in God. I guess when things are planned . . . He plans them. I was Catholic, you know? I went to church every Sunday. Moms said I had to go or I couldn't go out for the rest of the week."

Jones sees religion as an elaborate hustle.

"The Pope is a rich, rich man, you know? And the church isn't charged any taxes. It says in the Koran, which I dig, that a messenger of God doesn't need anything; he lives down with the people. But these evangelist dudes live *better* than the people. I saw a dude who had a Cadillac, and rings and mink coats. People carried him on their shoulders and he had this big white mink coat on *his* shoulders."

We are at Carol's. Roland has dropped by. Jones laughs and puts his hand on Roland's head. He stiffens his back in a mock oratory pose and motions toward the ceiling.

"Ahhhhhh, now this dude will throw away his crutches, right? And then you-all will give me money, dig it?"

Jones doubles up in laughter at this and falls back onto the couch.

He stops and looks at me. "If God is so strong, how come he needs three people, this Trinity thing? And when you pray, you are supposed to pray to the saints. Why do this? Why not go right to the top?"

Jones raps the table with his outstretched fingers.

"Church has got a lot of shit with it, man. It's the place where poor people get poorer. The minister'll say, 'We are now having a collection for some shit, and a dollar or more *will be appreciated.*' And people cough it up. My old man sends money to the Reverend Ike. He has these ads in the paper that say you can write down the things that trouble you on the back of the coupon and send it in with your money—wow!"

Jones' prison experiences pushed him out of the church. His mother became sick; the family had written him, but the letter went to Riker's Island after he was transferred and took several weeks to get upstate. He was shocked and upset to find out that his mother had glaucoma and kidney stones.

"I put in a slip to see the chaplin, and the hacks talked to me like it was nuthin' and *I* was nuthin'. I said, look, I'm in a bad situation. I hope *you* are never in this situation. They let me see him.

"This chaplain was crazy. My mother's sicknesses are a slow death, dig it? I wanted to speak on this; she is a beautiful, beautiful woman; she had done no wrong in her life. How could God *do* this to her?"

Jones' face is black and brooding.

"The chaplain wouldn't talk to me. He said I shouldn't have wrote up the note like I did. Wow! Can you *dig* that? I had said that my mother was sick, and that I hoped it never happened to him, and that I had to talk to someone. This motherfucker was pissed off because I wrote the note wrong!"

Jones learned the Muslim teachings in prison, and he liked them. The Koran says, more or less, that Moses stuttered. Jones was enthralled. He keeps the quotation underlined— Surah 10, lines 26–28—Moses is praying for help in communicating with his followers. "Loose a knot from my tongue . . . that they may understand me saying . . ."

"All my life I was ashamed to rap with people. I didn't feel bad after that."

But his interest in Muslim teaching wasn't related to race.

"Some of Elijah Mohammed's teachings are well thought

out. He tells you the white man is all fucked up; he's a devil, like he was made in a test tube or something. I don't believe this. White dudes can be good and bad; black dudes are the same way. So are Chinks and Ricans. It don't work like Elijah Mohammed says."

Jones' hand is moving spider-like over the coffee table.

"I don't feel that I fit into a racial thing. If there was a racial war, I'd be all fucked up. I can't be white and I can't be black. I'd just have to stand there."

4

Jones left prison in May, and he returned triumphantly clean from his brother's Bronx apartment at the end of June. It was a good time. He was ready for a new life. Then he ran afoul of City Hall.

"I was getting money from Moms, and I was looking for jobs. It was all right. I got on the welfare—but that was *unreal;* they treat you like you are nothing. I finally stopped going. . . I would have hurt someone down there. I'm serious."

I'd read about this problem a few days before Jones and I happened to talk about it. The Fortune Society had complained in a *Village Voice* article that newly released convicts almost always find the city welfare department hostile and confusing. Paperwork and bureaucracy keep them from getting even minimal money for weeks, sometimes months. Broke and burdened with readjustment problems, they soon become angry and all too often return to crime. Some re-enter prison *before* the first welfare checks arrive.

"Dig it!" Jones exclaims. "The lady in charge of my group was some bitch . . . like it was *her* money, you know? She was a taxpayer, right? She *knew* she was on top. She could tell people how to do theirs. I had to go uptown to fill out papers; then I had to come downtown and stand in line. Then I had to come back and stand in line again. I had thirty-nine dollars from prison. They must have thought I was one of the Rockefellers, and I had lots of time."

Jones is dragging on his cigarette furiously.

"They laugh at you. They make you wait while they fuck around behind those desks and drink coffee. One day I got called, but then the lady said I had to come back the next day. It was five minutes to four. I got *really* angry."

This is utterly serious, but it seems to be coming out of a strange Chaplin film.

"I looked at her and I talked slow. 'Lady, I have never mugged a woman in my life,' I said. 'But if I don't get that check today, don't come outside. I'm gonna mug *you—today.*' She said, Oh, oh, oh! and she called the guard. He said I was wrong to do this. I said THIS WHOLE PLACE IS WRONG!"

Jones grins.

"But you know, I got the check."

Pause.

"It cost me. She fucked with my checks after that. Finally I didn't want to go back—too much bullshit. I went back out in the streets."

And back to mugging.

"I needed money. It was three months after I got out of prison; I started again. I don't do it as much as I used to because I don't have to buy dope, and I'm into drops as much as possible. But I do it when I need to; I guess I'll be doing it for a while longer."

Ten

————◆————

1

A gusty spring day. Sun and wind chase each other along First Avenue under the cover of fast-moving clouds. A burst of gold fills the avenue; gray wind quickly pushes it away.

Jones wears a windbreaker and the dark platform shoes. As we turn the corner of Third Street, he pulls a bent, ragged cigarette from his pocket.

He holds it up with both hands and tries to smooth out the paper and tobacco—a difficult bit of maneuvering for a man with thick fingers and pointed nails.

A whooshing wind lifts it out of his struggling fingers, and it sails into the street.

Jones leaps after it. The wind pushes the errant cigarette further into the street. It rolls like a greased pencil and moves so fast that Jones, yelling curses after it, is forced to run with a noisy clacking of platform heels to catch up.

"Come 'ere, you motherfucker!" he shouts angrily.

Borne by the racing wind, the cigarette careens fully across the street with Jones in hot pursuit, arms flailing. Three feet short of the curb, the wind suddenly dies. The cigarette rests —Jones has won.

But then his passion dies as suddenly as the wind. Jones just stands over the cigarette. He will not bend down and reach for it. He looks back at me, then raises his hands in an exaggerated shrug.

"Fuck it!" he growls, and he drops his hands and walks back to the curb. We continue down the street. He says nothing more about the cigarette. And he does not reach into his pocket for another.

2

The day threatens rain. Jones pulls a windbreaker out of the closet and picks up a bent umbrella.

Halfway down the block, the skies explode in a violent thunderstorm. We run for a shallow doorway, but its shelter is no help. Jones hastily raises the crippled umbrella; it is no more help than the doorway.

I am suddenly struck—and irrationally shaken—by the fact that I am crouched in this doorway with a *mugger*. The rain blows angrily at us; I am in a foxhole with a terrorist. A thunderstorm, a doorway, a tattered umbrella: props for an absurdist play starring Sam and Jones, unlikely actors from separate and unequal drama schools. What am I *doing* here?

Jones shifts the umbrella, and I am caught in the face by the windspray.

"Wow," I am saying. "What a *trip* this storm is!" And then I catch myself: I even think like him now!

There is more.

A day earlier I watched an elderly man cash a large check. He stood at the teller's counter and counted the handful of bills; they totaled more than two hundred dollars.

"Wow!" I thought. "What a rip this guy would be!"

3

As suddenly as it began, the storm is over. We walk toward Jo-Anne's through a light drizzle, and Jones stops at a drugstore to call ahead. Then we walk along wet sidewalks toward the middle-income apartment complexes.

Jones is upset.

"I hate the rain—it fucks with my mind. Maybe I'll have to change to my dungarees, and that messes with my head, because dungarees are not my best clothes. And I want to shoot some coke, but I don't *even* want to get it in this rain."

Jo-Anne, plump and happy, stands at the door. She is all energy, bouncing around as we talk, hovering as we sit. She'll leave us soon and go into the bedroom—but Jones will not ask her to go as he would Carol. He has little to hide from her, though he attempts to keep some things quiet.

As we walk in, he whispers: "Don't mention Carol, okay? Jo-Anne knows about her, but it's best not to bring it up."

Jones pulls a joint from his pocket; it is soggy. He turns fiercely toward the window.

"Fucking rain!"

He hands it to Jo-Anne. "Put it in the oven." She pulls nervously on her ponytail and dances around the table. It is late in her pregnancy, and she is very big.

"You gonna have a boy or a girl?" he asks.

"A girl."

"You're gonna have a *boy*," he growls, somehow both friendly and gruff, "nothin' else."

"I'll have what I want," she pouts.

She dances out of his reach, giggling.

Jones plays with the window curtain next to the table, then turns and asks Jo-Anne if she has any money.

She pulls back, wary, a trusting mutt confronted with a leash. Jones wants her to go to the dry cleaners and pick up his slacks. He wants Jo-Anne to pay for them.

"Jo-Annnnnnnnnne," Jones calls with a seductive whine. "Jo-Annnnnnnnnne, come here. I want to taaaaaaaaalk to you."

She stays out of reach. He finally takes several small bills out of his pocket. She moves close enough to take them and dances away again.

She leaves.

"She's just like my mother," Jones says proudly. "She even gets mad like my mother. I'll show you something."

We walk to the bedroom, and Jones pulls a magazine cutout of teen idol David Cassidy off the plywood door. A jagged, fist-sized hole is hidden behind it. A year earlier, he and Jo-Anne had an argument; she threatened him with a knife.

"I took a swing at her," Jones chuckles, "but I hit the door." He walks back into the kitchen and reaches for a drawer. "I'll show you the knife."

He pulls a fat kitchen knife out of the drawer.

I try to picture chubby, giggling Jo-Anne red-faced and crying and waving a kitchen knife—would she have stabbed him?

Jones remembers her refusal to give him money and he walks again into the bedroom. He suddenly begins searching her clothing; then he goes to her closet and examines the bottles and boxes on its shelves. He is flushed; he is excited.

"If I find any," he says loudly as David Cassidy and I watch from the doorway, "she ain't *never* gonna get it back!"

Watching him steal spare change from the woman carrying his child gets under my journalistic armor. I want to say something. I have listened to him talk again and again of Jo-Anne's ability to give, her warmth and intelligence, how she stood with him during his worst days. He says she reminds him of his mother. *Now he is emptying her pockets.* I feel sick; I turn away and walk back to the kitchen.

Finding nothing, Jones returns and takes the joint out of the oven.

Back to journalism.

I ask about the coming baby. He looks at me silently and blinks. I wait. This is serious stuff.

"I don't know . . . I guess I'm enthusiastic. But I don't want to face it—I don't feel I can teach a child anything."

The man who rifles his woman's purse now appraises himself with a cold honesty few Boy Scouts could match.

"I can raise him," Jones continues, "but what do I teach him? Mugging? That will put him in jail, or I could teach him to deal drugs and rob people; he'll go to jail for that, too."

Jones is neither shy nor sorrowful. He looks straight into my eyes.

"The things that you preach, you must do. I can't preach to him about working if I am out on the corner."

The flatness of the statement is unnerving. Jones has been

pushed—or has pushed himself—so far down into a canyon of his mind that he has nowhere to fall.

Then he adds: "I can go out and get a job and live the way I want him to live."

"Will you do that?"

"I don't know. It will be a hard change to make. I don't know if I can."

I see a man crawling and reaching, one hand straight out. He is screaming and begging silently for help. A mob advances—his victims?

Jones pushes the joint toward me. He will soon be the father to two children. He cannot marry both women—besides, the welfare laws encourage him not to marry. Without him, Jo-Anne and Carol are eligible for assistance.

We've left the table, and we are leaning out of Jo-Anne's bedroom window, The view stretches across city rooftops. Jones watches a green-roofed tavern. Morris usually stops there on his way home and when Jones sees this, he will leave.

He is drifting. He is depressed. He shifts on his elbows.

"I don't like the thought of two babies in two homes, but there's not much I can do now."

He lights a cigarette and blows the smoke into the wet afternoon.

"If I have a baby girl, I'll be lost. You can't teach her the things you teach a boy. You take a boy out to games and boxing matches, but a girl, she wouldn't fit into a boxing match."

He sees Morris walk into the bar. Jo-Anne hasn't returned from the errand.

"As a child I used to get afraid. I'd cry and go to my parents. How come you have to die? How come you can't keep on living? It was *meant* to be—that's all they would say. I dug what they said, but I still thought, goddam, *how come you are here to die?*"

We stand in front of the elevator waiting to go down. I am silent, trying to fit spiritualism into my fast-changing image of street criminals; it won't go.

"It doesn't make sense, really it doesn't. All you can do is accept it. You have got to figure that things are meant to be, and that's all."

We reach the ground floor, and Morris stands with a small crowd of people waiting to go up. He lowers his eyes as we pass; Jones returns the silence. A light rain is falling outside. Jones looks up and scowls.

"It's all a circle," he says. "The bullshit is all a circle." He smiles in a thin line. "But things will work out. They have to."

I wonder.

4

I am riding the subway home late at night after seeing Jones. A blue subway cop laden down with guns, club, walkie-talkie, handcuffs, notebook, and flashlight walks into the car. He seems menacing, an adversary. I watch him stand at the car's door, hand on his gun handle, pushing at it idly. I feel tension. What if he approaches me? I feel oddly vulnerable for being close to Jones. Sensing someone's eyes, the cop turns—and I turn away for fear of discovery.

Of what? The cop walks past me and into the next car.

Jones is an outlaw. I am close to him now. He travels in a world within a world, and I am briefly in it. Yet I am clearly a stranger. We are very different people.

But how? I am thinking suddenly that I tend to see society and my life as linear: patterns of lines, not altogether orderly or consistent, nonetheless lines. They form paths that I am comfortable with. They help me focus—and limit—my life; they are concepts, objectives, laws . . . *laws!*

In Jones' world, the lines form no pattern I recognize. Patterns do exist. He sees them. He has his laws. "I make up the rules as I go along," he says in utter seriousness. But even this requires a structure.

How to define it?

My assumptions about him sometimes begin with insanity. Why else would he live this way? Then I remember how insane his world is. What *is* rational in it? At times, I am filled with an odd respect for him; then I feel sadness. He is intelligent, gentle (with me), and shockingly truthful. He is articulate; he has ideas. And he is incredibly stoic about his life.

He touches me. *It is so goddam sad!*

But there are two of him; two engines running on parallel tracks heading . . . over a cliff? He is crazy, I insist. Then I wonder if I am so filled with tension and fear during our encounters that I transfer my craziness to him? No, I have seen contrasting parts of him that seem . . . well . . . out of balance. Disturbed? Psychotic?

Now, tonight, making notes in a subway car, I do not understand the structure beneath his words. Or whether my assumptions about his pathology are more than parapsychiatric prattle. He leads me across the lines and patterns of his world, explaining its parts. I am lost. Repeat this, I ask; explain this. He is impatient. It is all so *clear*.

Well, one of us is crazy, I smile to myself. That is all for now. I settle back into the subway seat and wonder if the cop will pass by again.

5

Darkness. Jones walked beside a faceless woman. He was in a small alley, and he sensed that he was watched.

He turned and suddenly saw rats as big as rabbits—one was stalking him. He turned again; he was cornered in a crowded doorway. The woman had disappeared. He banged against packing crates and garbage cans trying to escape. But the rat, large and menacing, lunged at him; he was helpless. It came closer, snapping yellow teeth.

Suddenly it began to glow. The rat moved even closer and became brighter . . .

"I don't know why, I just couldn't move." Jones remembers. "Fear, I guess. It was like a horror flick, you know? I have weird dreams like that a lot of the time."

We are walking down Houston Street, past a display room of gravestones, when Jones remembers the dream. I look at the tombstones again and ask what he wants written on *his*.

"Nuthin'. I don't like to think about death. I figure the way I'm living, I'm pushing it."

But in other conversations, he will say a great deal more, for his mind is steeped in death's mystique. He remembers a dream two weeks earlier.

"I was dead. But I was also out of my body. I saw my body in a box. I don't know how I died, but this was the whole show. I was dressed up, and there were flowers around and it was all quiet. Wow, I woke up and I was sweating! I sat up for a while. I couldn't figure out why I had dreamed this."

He turns and his face is nearly ashen.

"I can sense things sometimes, like when the day is going to go bad, but I don't think I can sense death. I am told that people can sense things coming . . . but I don't know how true it is."

He shrugs and his face shifts to blankness.

"What the fuck, I can't do anything about it."

"You remember any other dreams?"

"Sometimes I wake up swinging and knock Carol out of the bed. She gets scared—but I can't remember what was happening.

"I have good dreams, too. Once I dreamed I had enough money so that I was really big. I was one of the ruling people —up there with the big powers, the five Mafia families. I was doin' good. I had cars and a home—then I woke up." Jones lights a cigarette, chuckling.

"Just today, I dreamed I was pretty big. This was in drugs. If you could name it, I had it to deal." He laughs again. "I don't know why, but I always wake up when it's getting good."

6

Tonight, I am deeply frightened. I've gotten off the subway. I need coffee. I am almost shaking, and I have walked the distance from the subway to a favorite coffeehouse twisting the pocket clip of a ballpoint pen around its body as if it were an engine's rotary unit.

I must keep it running.

The fear carries me through crowds of people and across streets, but it is elusive when I try to confront it. I began to feel it while we talked. There was a sense, slight, then growing, that I was too close to something.

His eyes, so often bright, were dull and angry as the talk went into its second hour. He'd been into drugs, heavy ones. I hadn't asked about it. But there was tension, and as my notebook grew full, I began wishing fervently that the day would end. I was tired. My hand was cramped from writing. My back hurt from leaning over him to hear his mumbling as he lay on his bed. A radio next to us blared and squawked.

I'd ask him to repeat something, and he would grunt and scowl; the silence between us became a dark chasm, and I felt myself on the edge of it.

Finally it was time to leave. He reached behind his bed to pull out a lead pipe wrapped in tape. He would walk with me. He wanted air.

Out on the street he turned to me in a low, angry voice.

"I want to give you a warning."

I stiffened, genuinely frightened.

"Don't get platform shoes, man. They're bullshit. They hurt your feet."

What! I walked close to him, feeling terribly silly, realizing his anger (or fear) had nothing to do with me. He looked behind him once, twice . . . again . . . and we walked further down the block. He held the pipe tightly, poised. We walked past two men looking into a store window. One turned and looked at us . . . oddly, I thought. A dog growled as we passed some men playing checkers; he skirted it widely.

All day his eyes had been dull holes in the granite of his face. I became frightened again. I had looked too deeply into him; something was out of control . . . *I had seen it* . . . and I would be caught in it. It would touch me and destroy me.

I asked where he was going. He moved his shoulders in a dull, slow shrug—"I just have to get out and walk." He looked over his shoulder again and banged the pipe against his palm. "My nerves are bad. I need the air."

Down another block. Through a foggy park. Under ghostly streetlamps. He was bent over as we walked, almost crouched. He was leading me toward an unfamiliar subway stop; the fear was gathering me in its arms. Half a dozen junkies nodded on a corner near a smelly pizza parlor—two cops cruised by in a patrol car. I began to fear them as much as the force beside me . . . and finally we reached the subway stop, and as if nothing was happening in my head and heart, we shook hands and promised to meet in two days.

I went down the dark stairs and got on the train.

I am in the coffeehouse, writing these notes. The Italian waiter brings capuccino, and a young couple holding hands laughs at a table behind me. They are miles away. The pen with the rotary pocket clip is quiet and all this is written in blue scribbling on the back pages of my notebook and I look at it and the letters forming the words seem cold and bloodless.

But I can do no more, Nothing really happened—except in my head. I had seen his fire and felt its heat; that was all. I signal the man and pay the check and walk back into the street to find the subway.

7

Jones reaches out and draws back the window curtain.

"What do you see?" I ask.

"Suckers . . . everybody thinks they can make it, and they are living a lie. The working man don't make it; he has got nothing to show for his work. Suckers, man. That's what I see."

He is still turned away from me.

"On a job, you are a paid slave. I am a slave sometimes, but not a paid slave. The things I've got, I've taken."

"But is it right?"

"Self comes first, man. This life gets me what I need.

What is right for some *ain't* right for all. Life is based on survival."

"How does your color affect this?"

His flat, sluggish voice is heavy with sadness. "In my case, things that are . . . *really* wrong, I did myself. Dig it, I've got a record—I can't get a good job. I could say, yeah, prejudice is the thing; but it's not. *I* did it. I've had plenty of chances to make it . . . but I fucked them up."

His head droops, and he doodles with his cigarette in the ashtray. I shudder suddenly at the pathos of this man whose heart insists one moment that he confront his worst truths— then supplies truckloads of lies to smother them. Today, his heart bleeds; tomorrow, the wounds are hidden to fester again.

"My life is my fault," he is saying. "Moms and Pops gave me plenty of shots. They showed me the best—you couldn't get it any better. My teachers put their necks out on a limb. They'd pull me off to the side and try to break things down. I would always chop those necks off."

He reaches further into himself.

"I could have done better with my life. I had jobs when I was young; I worked, I saved. But the dope thing really took me down. I was even a Boy Scout once."

He turns suddenly and looks at me. This is when he first says it, when he lets me look at everything.

"*You* have things. You can see what you've done. Except for some changes I've been through, I can't say I've done this or gotten that. You've got a car. You've got cash in the bank, too. I should have that."

He looks at the veins in his elbow.

"I've got a hole in my arm. That's what *my* life is all about."

I want to cry, . . . *anything* to get rid of the pain Jones is putting out. Twenty-four was a beginning in my life, I couldn't count the possibilities. Here is a man at that age beaten and degraded by his life, choking back in his half-focused rage with cocaine, alcohol, and elaborate excuses. *I've got a hole in my arm. That is my life.*

"Sometimes . . . I'm glad I went into the streets," he is

saying, brightening a little. "I've seen things. I've been with different people—dudes who run con, girls who sell their bodies, working dudes, people who mug. I've walked a lot of roads, you know? I know life."

"This is what you enjoy?"

He stops. He grimaces and scratches his chin.

"I don't like some of the bullshit. But I enjoy the money—no point in lyin' about that."

It is the moment to ask a key—and tremendously difficult—question. Slowly.

"I won't lie to you." I pause. "You . . . are the person who disrupts society. You are . . . the terror . . . for the rest of us. Do you . . . understand that?"

He looks up. No words; then he begins.

"Yeah . . . I dig . . . what you are saying." He spreads his hands on the arms of his chair. His face is tight and dark. "I . . . don't always . . . feel like goin' out there, you know?" Another pause. Two parts of him are fighting hard.

"But this . . . is the only choice . . . I've left myself. It is too late for me to change." Another moment of quiet. Then a faint smile—his defense mechanisms are forming. "Let's say I went back to school. Let's say I became a lawyer, you know, and I went to one of those big law firms for a job . . ."

Jones leans forward quickly, almost as if he has jumped the space between us. His eyes are huge; they are deep and jet black. I see lines and circles underneath them. Whatever is coming will be dredged from the bottom of wherever he is.

The stutter cuts into his voice and he falters, but only briefly; his need to communicate is more urgent. "Do . . . do you think they'd accept me?"

He sinks back into his seat, relieved, relaxed. I am left to grapple with this. I fumble badly.

"If . . . if you got through law school . . . something would happen. Maybe they would hire you—they'd be impressed."

"*No man!* They'd be lookin' at my background. When I was around, they'd keep the safe locked. This is how it is. If I go for a job, the man says, hey, have you ever been arrested? I say yes, and he looks at me and he says, we'll call you. And if I lie—they find out anyway. I looked for a job the whole goddam summer after I got out of prison. I like electrical work. I learned it in school and in the Navy. I could get up each day, I could do all that shit. But I haven't got the papers for electronics work, and when the dude gets to the part about my arrest, wow!"

Jones has his story together now; he lights another cigarette and relaxes into a moody, fatalistic acceptance of himself, his best defense mechanism.

"The dudes look at me"—he lowers his voice to a dramatic baritone—"and they say, 'Oh!' They read the newspapers; maybe they have a son who got mugged. They hate the people who do this. And they get back at them by turning me away. You dig it? They are worried that I would be mugging people in the office—and who wants to live in fear of that?"

8

"I don't know why I'm here," Jones is saying as we walk down Delancey Street. "I just know why I'm here, and someday I'll die—and dig it, man—the thought of dying freaks me because I don't know what's there."

He is depressed again, hunching his shoulders slightly forward.

"One thing I'm sure of, I don't believe in hell. . ."

He throws back his head.

". . . Cuz, man, *this* is hell. *Earth is hell.* So if you die and go to a place that's said to be hell, it's got to be better than this. It can't be . . . no worse!"

"It's that bad?" I feel his darkness touching me again.

"Wow. Yeah. Everything is fucked up in life. You deal with sickness, you deal with fools, everybody is trying to get slick. People will say they are your friends, but they hurt you. They think they know everything, too. What a drag."

He pauses and drifts, and I am bracing myself for more.

"The laws are okay . . . but they aren't applied right. And

there's fear all the time. Anything can happen to you; your life can be fucked up in a moment."

He's right, I am thinking, suddenly jumping into my Good Citizen bag. A person can get mugged any time.

He nods to himself, defense mechanisms again moving quickly into place.

"I can't be thinking about all that shit, of course . . . my life would get worse. If I'm facing down a dude, I can't be thinking about the things he might do to me. I just think about what I'm gonna do to him. If it's meant for you to lose, you'll lose, that's all. You can't predict life, because life can end in the next second. You have to enjoy it."

Eleven

1

Sometimes in the middle of an afternoon, I forget who he is. We are talking, arguing, drinking wine, and I am wrapped up in this kid with the sad-clown way of talking about himself. He is joking, contradicting himself, laying his crazy street logic on me, and I laugh and marvel at him . . . and suddenly realize that I could easily be one of his victims. Give me ten years. He likes his victims to be fortyish, old enough to let go of their money without a fight, a little slow. My turn is coming. I am frightened.

Long before we met, his face was a silhouette I saw regularly. My apartment building, like thousands on Manhattan's West Side, has no doorman. It is a tall, somber structure, built before World War II. At night as I approach it, the street outside is cut by shafts of light from tall city lamps, and brightened by flickering neon lights from a business district around the corner. There is an old Irish tavern next door; light and loud arguments spill out of it.

It is a night I walk into at the end of each day, and its darkness is often a time of fear. Not open, stomach-jerking fright; I tell myself I am too sophisticated for that. The fear is vague, suppressed, subtle. If I walk to the corner newsstand or a neighborhood restaurant—and I refuse not to—I walk in the middle of the sidewalk, away from parked cars and the sides of buildings. Hearing footsteps, I look for their source. I watch shadows, and I carry carefully calculated amounts of money, no more than I am willing to lose, but enough to avoid angering an assailant.

Returning, I separate the nickel-plated door key from others on the chain long before I reach the unlocked glass and wood street doors which open onto a cavernous foyer.

The foyer's walls are yellow. An ancient carriage lamp hangs from a domed ceiling. The foyer's space is empty, almost echoing. Beyond it lies a set of locked glass doors, answerable now to my nickel key; answerable, that is, in the manner of an old building. The lock rarely opens at the first turn, for it and the new key are generations apart. For precious seconds, I must turn the lock until it catches.

Each night I saw him during those seconds.

The details of his face were always unclear. I remember that he was massive, dark, and threatening; yes, dark. Fear of the unknown, racial tension, urban terror, random violence —describe the inkblot they form. Politically and emotionally, I am liberal and humanist. I am also a son of the white middle class; my subconscious is filled with suppressed racism, and the man I saw was invariably black.

It was not a logical reaction. For my experience now shows that Jones' street friends are white, black, and Latin; race is rarely a factor in what they do. They carry knives for economic reasons; add alienation, emotional problems, perhaps heroin. Jones, in fact, belongs to no particular ethnic group at all except an amorphous subculture known as "poor people."

My subconscious assumed further that I would meet an irrational man. And some of Jones' friends are quite irrational. Some are emotionally disturbed; others are heroin addicts whose habits are coming down, fast. They are sick and nervous and close to exploding from their own pain. The sadists among them also feel a sense of power and grandeur during these acts. And they know violence will enhance their street reputation. They will be less vulnerable to people *they* fear.

Yet my assumptions were mostly wrong. Muggers, given a choice, prefer nonviolent robbery to anything beyond it.

Violence involves noise, movement, and risk. Unless a mugger is a sadist, it is distasteful. Mugging victims—Jones' victims—are bloodied because they resist. The mugger sees the encounter as a matter of survival. He becomes frightened, then angry. The terror in him surfaces. And then it is a massive, staggering force, for if Jones is a fair example, the mugger has been fighting—in gangs or for self-defense—since grade school.

Jones has probably fought with his hands more than a thousand times. If you choose to resist him, the odds are overwhelmingly against you.

In New York City, about a hundred muggings are reported every day; at least twice that number occur. The city dweller, rightly or wrongly, has no greater fear, and none more poorly defined for him, than the fear of being mugged. Jones is the darkness of his mind.

This man with no face hasn't come into my foyer. Not yet. But I see him. I—and the city I live in—cower before our vision of him as unhappily as if we were waiting in our basements for wartime air strikes. We keep huge dogs in our small apartments; we install double locks; we carry weapons. On two occasions in this city, friends visiting me have been mugged as they entered my building—trapped in the hallway and threatened with a knife; one of them refused for weeks afterward to walk alone at night. Other friends have told me of this experience. One, a man in his late forties, now takes taxicabs door to door. Two men seized him one night on a dark block and held a knife so tightly against his throat that he could barely breathe. A writer friend was caught in his own building one night by two men, robbed, and pistol-whipped; his head wound required more than twenty stitches. He is convinced that he would have been killed if a dog in a nearby apartment had not begun barking. A woman I know was mugged and then raped on the ground floor of her building; she began sessions again with a therapist she'd happily quit a year earlier.

A mugging can be a simple street robbery—or a moment of bloody terror. If no one is hurt, it still leaves psychic wounds. For the victim is not simply the man or woman relieved violently of property, but also a vision of the rest of us who fear we will be next. It is hardly surprising that we relegate muggers to the darker parts of our minds, keeping them faceless and without form except for that outline defined by our fears. We fear we diminish ourselves by admitting them to our species. We call for Law and Order campaigns, for better police protection and stiffer prison sentences. We go to great lengths to create distance, psychic and physical, between "them" and "us."

Yet Mr. Jones, as we have seen, is pathetically human. He has neighbors, debts, relatives, a doting mother, a drinking problem, children on the way, an argumentative father. He takes firecrackers to Coney Island on the Fourth of July. He worries that people will think badly of him. He is also extraordinary, of course. His life is filled with extremes. He has been a street fighter, heroin addict, burglar, confidence man, drug dealer, prison inmate, and possibly a murderer as well. He'll soon have two children out of wedlock—by two different women.

What to do about him—put him in jail?

But police work alone cannot stop street crime. By my estimate, Jones has committed thousands of crimes. They've cost him one year in jail; and his sentence was drastically reduced through plea-bargaining. There is no *forceful* way to change his behavior.

The real answer is counseling and job training. Yet he has had both; he still commits crimes. More counseling and job training? I think the larger problem lies within the fixed images people have of each other. Jones is a mugger; he is a junkie. Other people are bankers, businessmen, legislators, shopkeepers, or bus drivers. One corrective—and I realize it is only a beginning—is to view him more as a human being.

For if the larger society saw him in human terms, it might have reason to approach questions of crime and rehabilitation differently, perhaps with better results. A naïve view? Maybe. But the thought keeps me going as I ride the frightening subways each week to see him.

2

"Life is a big game," Jones is saying as we begin walking. "I don't know all the rules and answers, but the ones I know, I'm sure of. Rule number one is that everything's okay as long as you don't get caught."

The game we are playing today is rather serious. Jones and I are pretending to be muggers. It is a guided tour through victim-land, and Jones is pointing out areas of interest along the way. You and your wallet, for example.

Two black men walk by, jive-talking, finger-popping, carrying a wine bottle. One says something about "banging that bitch," and they laugh. Jones does not look at them, but he reacts strongly to what he hears.

"It's dudes like that who fuck things up," he says in disgust.

He assumes the "bitch" who got "banged" is a mugging victim who was roughed up, maybe even raped. It gives the profession a bad name.

I see a jowly, middle-aged man with wavy hair carrying a grocery bag toward a car. He is about fifty yards away.

"Him?"

Jones sees the man but does not turn. His eyes seem to be aimed at the pavement.

"Yeah, he'd be good. He's got his hands full. You let him get in the car and you get with him before he can close the door. You are right on top of him, and you show him the knife. He'll slide over and go along with it."

"After that?"

"If you think he's gonna chase you, you can put him in the trunk."

We turn toward a cluster of buildings. I see a man in a black suburban coat. He is taller and younger.

"Not him," Jones says, again without looking directly at him. "He looks hard. You could take him off in a hallway, but he would give you trouble in the street." The tall man glances at us casually as he crosses the street. His face is pocked and angry.

On to bigger things. We walk through one of the project parks. I have a *sense* of us. As a kid I tried to look tough walking with friends—chest out, dour expression. Watch out. I might *do* something. Any moment now.

I have this sense today. I am thinking about violence, and I assume it shows. Jones keeps a steady, clicking heel-and-toe rhythm, head down, hands hanging loose, eyes alert, saying nothing. Nothing new to him. But I am drawn as tight as piano wire. I am concentrating so much that my thoughts seem written on my back.

An elderly woman sees us. She abruptly takes a side path; my paranoia index jumps.

"Did she do that because of us?"

"It doesn't matter. You either hit her or you don't."

We walk to Second Avenue, moving among crowds of shoppers—sad faces, tired arms filled with packages, coats, purses, fat hip-pocket wallets in the sunny afternoon . . . so much *money* in this speckled fools-gold afternoon.

Suddenly I am seeing with Jones' vision. All these people, they are nothing to me. They have jobs and money and security, and they flaunt it, buying things, wearing nice clothes, carrying packages. They do not know suffering; they have not bled from the veins of their arms, walked the streets, doubled up with the pains that bring your guts rushing into your throat. They have not passed out from poison and gone into dreams of darkness and death. They know nothing.

The street is filled with these ignorant people; chickens and turkeys, fat, feathered birds with stiff necks and pompous ways who gobble of law and morality and sit in their henhouses cackling and counting money. They would peck out your eyes if you could not defend yourself. We are in their barnyard; they walk by, smug in expensive clothes, on streets they think are defended by their soldier-policemen. *They are waiting to be plucked*—and they deserve it. It is as though you could walk through this barnyard with a bucket and gather all the money in.

We are inside a bank. A dozen people stand in line before the paying/receiving window. Jones takes a withdrawal slip at a back counter and begins writing on it. I look around nervously, scanning people in the line, wondering if the bank guard sees anything funny about us. Again, Jones seems to be watching no one. He writes $48 on the slip.

"What do you see?" I whisper.

"That dude in the striped pants."

I see a short, nervous man in his mid-fifties who waits while the cashier helps the person ahead of him in line. He wears a full-length coat and blue pin-striped slacks.

Middle-class money.

He gives the teller some small slips and a check; the teller gives him a big bill, a few smaller ones, and several pieces of paper.

"He's making a drop," Jones says without looking up from the bank slip. "You saw the receipts. If I wanted to do a thing, I would follow him to his store. Then I'd watch for a few days to see the times he goes to the bank. I'd get him on a Monday. Then you get the money he made on Friday night, Saturday, and Monday. Maybe Sunday, too, depending on the type of store."

The man counts his money. He glances over his shoulder—at us?—and starts toward the door.

Now I see a tall man in suede boots and a raincoat in the line; he holds a paycheck and seems to be irritated at the delay.

"Him?"

"Uh-*uh*—he don't look right. Today's Friday. There's a precinct house a couple of blocks away—cops get paid today."

I look again—I can't tell a thing. The man is tall and his face is hard.

"Let's go out," Jones say, "I'll show you something else."

We stand before a bakery display window, pretending to look at strawberry cake. Jones nods toward the first man, who is half a black away, walking north.

"You can watch him in the reflection and let him get a little ahead; then you follow him.

"How do you watch him so closely in the bank?"

"You learn how to look like you are doing something else. There's a line on the withdrawal paper, you know? You can keep writing on it and look around without being conspicuous."

Jones moves his hand slightly as if he were writing and swivels his head. As I watch him, my eyes fall naturally to his hand.

"You look around. Then you put your head down and think about what you've seen. Then you look up, but your hand is still writing so it looks like you are doing business. You have to blend in, be another face. The better that you look, the less they think about you. You want to look like a workingman—like, my gold ring is a good thing to play on; it looks like I have money, so nobody thinks I am a mugger."

He chuckles at the wordplay he is about to make.

"Or that they will be a *muggee*. You get careful like this, because you are doing wrong, and you know people are out to get you for it."

He looks across the street.

"There's a precinct house on that block. The check cashing place near it is a good place to pull rips. Nobody thinks a dude would have the heart to do it so close to a cop station; so nobody watches it very closely."

He nods as we cross the street.

"There'll be a lot of cops around. Are you clean?"

". . . Uh, yes."

"Good."

We walk into a grimy side street between First and Second Avenues and stop across from a storefront. The red and blue sign—Checks Cashed/Money Orders Filled—is ringed with light bulbs, and the windows are covered with wire and protective devices. Half a block away, the precinct house has patrol cars clustered in front. Brawny plainclothes detectives pass by every few minutes.

Jones looks at my watch and sees that it is two-fifteen.

"It's a little early now. Pretty soon, this place will be doin' business." We lean against a store window and wait.

A black street hustler in his mid-twenties, lean and quick, wearing a blue hat and leather jacket, walks up to the front door with his arm around a pudgy Levi-clad white girlfriend. He stops short of it, kisses her and moves over to lean against a brick wall; she goes in.

"Why is he waiting outside?"

"It's probably a bad check. The chick will have an easier time with it."

The woman emerges smiling as though she had won a pie-eating contest. The man breaks into a grin, too, and throws his arm around her as they walk away.

"She got over, man," Jones chuckles.

We wait a few more minutes; I am drifting, watching the policemen get out of a car down the street. Jones nudges me.

"That dude's got cash. Watch him."

Across the street, I see a tall man with snow-white hair. He walks confidently, head erect, wearing a black cashmere coat; in profile he bears a striking resemblance to former Chief Justice Earl Warren, the same bright eyes, broad nose, and prominent cheekbones. I mention this to Jones, who laughs, only vaguely familiar with the Warren court.

Jones' street sense is astounding. The man as yet hasn't moved directly toward the store. He has stepped off the curb, but for now he could be headed anywhere on the block.

Jones says he will cash a check.

The Chief Justice passes the storefront. Then he stops, steps backward, and disappears into the door.

"He is being careful. That means he's got cash."

"A good victim?"

"Yeah."

Three minutes later, the man emerges and continues walking down the block.

"From the way he walks, I think he lives on this block."

"Why?"

"The way he moves. He looks like he knows where he's going. He's afraid to move too fast, but he looks like he knows where he wants to get to."

As Jones finishes the sentence, the tall old man turns on one foot and walks into a brownstone apartment building.

"When would you move?"

"I'd wait until he gets through the door. The building is old, so the second door won't lock fast. If you time it right, the lock won't stop you."

Jones drags on the cigarette he is holding.

"I'd be in there now. I'd let him start climbing the stairs. Then I'd take him."

And the old man, who looks like a statesman but lives on a bad block, would lose something. His social security check? A stock dividend? His life? I have this crazy vision of Earl Warren scurrying along this grimy block, flowing robes trailing in the gutter, clutching his law books and stealing glances behind him. He is followed by a mob of street people who don't know how his court affected their lives. They will follow him into the doorway now and beat him, stepping all over his robes, searching his law books for dollar bills between the pages, screaming and kicking at him when he tries to talk. What are you to *me*, they are yelling—another rich bastard who thinks he knows about poor people!

Two detectives drive by. The look at us carefully.

"Let's move," Jones says.

We walk further down the block, past the cavernous precinct building. Its flag juts out like an arm in a plaster cast.

"These cops think they are slick," Jones is saying in low tones. "There used to be a guy dealing a lot of dope in this building here"—he points to a tenement next to the precinct house—"and they think I don't know there are three of them behind me now."

Suddenly I am aware of three men in step with us. They seem to be walking aimlessly. One mentions a card game, another says something about an "easy mark." But they don't look like cops, and they abruptly turn away and walk across the street. Is Jones paranoid?

" 'Mark' is an old word," Jones is saying. "Cops give themselves away by their language. Nobody in the streets uses that word any more. They probably wondered what we were doing hanging around."

We turn at the next block and walk toward a group of projects several blocks away. The tour is over.

3

Friday night. A big excursion is planned . . . Jones, Jo-Anne, and I are going uptown to see the relatives. It is about 7 P.M. now. Carol is at her mother's, and we are in the apartment, nearly ready to go: colors coordinated, shoes buffed, Afro fluffed . . . the buzzer rings.

It is Jeff, Jones' best friend, looking fly. Flared pants, stack heels, broad-brimmed hat. "Hey man, what's happening?" Slap . . . pop . . . pull . . . the clenched fist, and everything is cool with the flesh pressing.

"We're goin' to the Bronx," Jones says.

"Oh, wooooooowwww. . . . You're takin' Sam to the Bronx, but how come you never take your man to the Bronx? You dig it?"

"Hey . . . hey, man . . . hey, I'll take you up to that place any time you want to go. You know that, man.

"Right on, my man, everything is cool here. I just came by thinkin' maybe you wanted to rap, chug a little of that wine, smoke some of that good weed, you know?"

"Hey . . . hey . . . hey, right, we'll do that, I got time; I'll call Jo-Anne when we go down to the corner to get the bottle, you know."

Into the liquor store. A short fat man with white hair takes the crumpled dollar bills of blacks and Puerto Ricans clustered around the counter and passes quarts of Boone's Farm, Italian Swiss Colony, and other cheap wines across it.

Back upstairs. Jeff pulls two thick joints rolled in yellow paper out of his pocket. Jones is already into the Boone's Farm. The network news has a report about militant Indians at Wounded Knee, South Dakota.

"They'll . . . they'll suffer for it," Jones is saying, toking on the reefer Jeff had lit and pushing the bottle at him. "But wow . . . wow . . . wow, the government will *know* that somebody really tried to change things. Those people are doin' it right, you know? Right now, the government is too used to that black thing, where there's just all this talk."

Everybody nods.

"Wow, I dig what the fuck they are doin'—they are get-tin' together as one and gettin' a thing done, you know? But they'll pay for it, mo-th-er-fu-ck-er, they'll suffer for doin' this jive-ass thing."

The smoke is curling about the room; various topics are discussed.

Fifteen minutes is given to determining whether or not Jones is "known" to the mechanics at a garage on Mott Street.

Now: consider Boone's Farm strawberry. Jones alleges that his father once claimed it would cause sterility. Scotch is okay; that's what *Charles* Jones drinks.

There follows the question of World War II. For open-ers, which came first? D-Day or Pearl Harbor? Jones allows as how he wasn't born yet, he isn't sure. And Jeff points out that as a result of the war, "Russia is up our ass." Jones is confused as to whether "our" refers to the U.S. Navy or the whole country, because he read somewhere that the Rus-sian Navy was getting big.

Somebody notices that clouds of marijuana smoke—and wow, this *is* good weed—are shaped like . . . mushrooms? Like . . . atom bomb . . . mushrooms? Yeah . . . like mush-room clouds. Which naturally brings up the question of Dr. Strangelove . . . wait a minute, Jack, he was the dude who invented the bomb, right? No. . . no . . . man . . . he was in a movie . . . and he . . .

"Well, what the fuck, then . . . who *did* invent the bomb? I dunno, man, he mighta been like, you know st-ra-nge . . . But *Dr.* Strangelove was the dude in the movie . . . the one who brought up his hand like Hitler, you know? And then he—wow!—couldn't get it back down . . . I mean what a trip . . . and you remember the dude who rode the bomb down from his plane, waving his hat . . ."

"Dig it, and you know that dude, Hitler?" Jones goes on. "Wow, if *that* dude was in town, now, he'd really clean up, you know? This man was *heavy*, you know. He'd have all the powers on his side now—he was ahead of his time, you know?"

"Ahead? What the fuck you talkin' about?"

"Well . . . well . . . well, you know . . . you know, he wanted to start things a new way. He would do well today with all the shit that's goin' down. Russia and China and all them big powers would have to listen to him . . . you dig it?"

"Oh yeah, wow!"

The bottle is nearly gone and the second reefer is halfway down, and it is time to move on to other subjects: Ho Chi Minh, Mao Tse-tung, Bobby Seale, Eldridge Cleaver, revolution.

"Wow . . . you . . . you know these revolutionaries, these *black* revolutionaries, they . . . they . . . are getting *over* on the blacks. They got that gift of gab, you know, and they are talking and helping some people get over . . . yeah, they are doing' that . . . but wow, Jack, what the people don't know is that they are helping *themselves* get over *more* . . . you dig it? . . . Yeah, can you dig the crib that the dude Huey P. Newton's got out on the West Coast? That ain't no hole in the motherfuckin' ground, Jack!"

It's getting late, time to go down those stairs again and get Jo-Anne and start for the Bronx. There follows discussion about the F train, as opposed to the D, and you gotta switch over to the A, you know, and then catch the IRT and change at 72nd Street to the one which goes to the South Bronx, one goes past Jerry's house, and the other stops before it, but one is an easier walk than the other, you know? And in the South Bronx, you can dig it, you want the *easiest* walk possible, because there's a whole lotta shit goin' down in them streets!

Jeff leaves, and we walk to Jo-Anne's apartment. She is bouncy and giggly again, and the walk to the subway is consumed with games of tag and happy put-downs, you . . . you . . . you know, Jo-Anne, our-love-is-real.

"Talk is cheap," she pouts.

"So's your sister."

The train rolls into an elevated wooden platform at 179th Street, and we walk down the creaky stairs into an area that may be the nation's foulest and worst slum. Each block looks as though a bomb fell. Carpets of glass and trash, broken concrete, and parts of junked cars cover whole streets and sidewalks. Passing cars make crunching, gritty sounds as their tires run over broken glass. It is impossible to walk without stepping on garbage and broken bottles. Bands of teen-agers move swiftly among the blocks as we walk—pushing over trash cans, throwing bottles, picking fights—kids with death-mask faces in T-shirts and tennis shoes.

We round a corner and one group pushes past us. One kid is carrying a jagged piece of sidewalk concrete the size of a dinner plate, and he looks as if he is going to throw it at something.

Crash!

"Don't you look *back*," Jones rasps to both of us. "Don't look back and show fear—don't show *fear*."

We round another corner, past broken doors and jagged glass on the fronts of buildings, and finally reach Jerry's apartment building. The hallway, again, is locker-room green, dark and sickening; writing and dirt and garbage befoul the peeling smudgy plaster walls. The doors in the hallway are bent and broken and chipped; smells of garbage and urine roll down.

Jones' brother Jerry has heard us coming and is standing at the door with Ruth; Billie, Jones' sister who lives nearby, is inside, and a big black dog is tied to a stovepipe in the kitchen. Jerry is into a six-pack of beer; eight-track tapes of the Delfonics and Gladys Knight and Smokey Robinson are stacked by a tape deck.

"I thought you wasn't goin' to make it," Jerry smiles. Jones visits his younger brother every Friday, a precious family link since Jerry went north to get away from the Lower East Side's heroin action.

Jerry packs dresses in Manhattan's garment district to pay the rent, and as a sideline, he sells some of them in the neighborhood. His son, Roger, age eight months, is sleeping in the bedroom. Jerry breaks out more beer—Jones already has his Boone's Farm—and the joints come out. It is time to . . . drift . . . and dance . . . and rap . . . and get mellow.

Jo-Anne takes a seat in one corner, happy and pregnant;

Ruth is over by the tape deck. Jerry is happily stoned and dancing to the music in the middle of the floor—by himself—dancing and rapping with whoever passes by. Everything is cool, he's got his gun in his belt, and a beer in his hand; and a joint is being passed around.

Jones is on the couch. Ruth's little sister sits on his lap, a thin, quiet, sad-eyed kid of eight or so, who spends most of the night watching the festivities quietly, sitting with Jones. He takes her hands in his and beats patty-cake time to the music between pulls on the joint and Boone's Farm. Halfway through the night, the mugger asks the shy little girl for a dance. "I'll wait until nobody is looking," he says in a big-uncle voice, "and *then* I'll have that dance . . . and if you say no, well . . . I'll be very angry." And they dance, and Jones struts on the floor, breathing heavily from the wine and drugs, and the little girl looks up at him with big, shy eyes until the song is ended.

Jerry and Ruth met in the eighth grade. He was already fooling around with heroin; eventually he dropped out of school. After that he went to the Bronx to get away from his schoolboy friends who had begun to use the drug heavily.

Jerry is tall and curly-headed with an easygoing manner and a wide smile on a boyish face. He is eighteen now, neither smart nor crafty like his older brother. But he is relatively honest, and he works hard. He conforms far more than his brother to the stereotype of law-abiding citizen. The neighborhood dress business is a minor hustle; Jerry has held the packer's job for more than a year—and shows no signs of quitting. He has a baby and a woman who cooks and keeps his household together and they hope to have more children. At eighteen, he seems as much a boy as a man, yet he has supported a family and dealt with problems of rent, medical and grocery bills for several years; and all things considered, he is doing reasonably well.

"When I first met him," Ruth remembers, "I didn't like him. I thought he was a bully; but he turned out to have a good personality. I guess at that age boys have got to show who they are. Maybe that's why he acted like that." She is eighteen as well.

Jerry is dancing happily in the middle of the rugless living room. A dingy shelf filled with cheap bric-a-brac hangs on the wall behind him. A picture of Charles Jones in military dress stares at us from the other wall. The room is tacky, dark, and depressing—yet that is a visitor's impression; and it is changing. Somehow amid the music, wine, marijuana, and talk, it seems a gay, lively place. And the drunken clown with the gun in his Levis dancing alone in the middle of the floor seems to be behaving in an entirely appropriate fashion. *What else should he be doing?* It is Friday night—3 A.M. by now—he is having a helleva good time. He can't afford opera tickets, and besides, the seats at the Met might get lint on his Levis.

As a young teen-ager, Jerry had misshapen teeth. He was nicknamed "Wolfman."

"I was afraid to kiss him," Ruth remembers. "I thought he would bite me."

Across the room, Wolfman, flashing a big smile, is dancing out of the bedroom holding his baby. Little Roger needs a change. Jerry lays him quietly on the couch and, like any good father taking his turn at night duty, pulls off his diapers and proceeds to work; the pistol handle protrudes ever so slightly from the rim of his jeans.

"Hey man," says Jones, looking up from his game of pat-tycake, "When I get a baby, I'll feed it and stuff, but wow, I'll never change it. No way!"

Jerry looks up from his wiggly son and addresses his big brother with considerable fatherly dignity.

"I figure it this way. It's my son, and I figure I should do everything for him that I can."

"No . . . no . . . man, I'll never change the baby's diapers. That can't happen."

The argument is unresolved. Jerry dances back to the bedroom with the washed and powdered baby. Throughout this discussion, Jo-Anne sits silently in the far corner. She will stay that way all night, as though she knows more than the others in the room, except perhaps Ruth; the life growing inside her is all she needs for entertainment and solace.

Jerry sits down on the couch. He doesn't know—precisely —that his brother still mugs.

"My brother just wants to get over the hump," he begins. "He grew up in clubs and gangs like everybody else. I can't blame him for what he does—*everybody* wants to get over."

We come to a recurring theme.

"One thing: I could always count on him when I got into trouble. I hope my baby has a brother like him. He was as good a brother as you could have. Whatever else he has done, *he's been a good brother to me.*"

My Good Citizen self is thinking about mobsters who support Sicilian orphanages, or movieland tough guys who are cupcakes around their mothers. You need to be soft, vulnerable with *someone*—with Moms, with your brother, with the sad-eyed eight-year-old sitting on your lap. You must take part of your life—whoever you are—and say . . . and insist . . . that it is good and that in some way at least, you set an example of love and warmth. If you can establish this, and reach out and touch it when you feel the need to prove it exists, then whatever you do beyond it is permissible. For your humanity—however incomplete it may seem to others—is proven. You have feelings. You sniffle at sad movies, you love puppydogs and little children, you remember your mother's birthday.

Then why—I am still talking to myself—are you different?

Because you compartmentalize your emotions far more than most of the people you prey on. You treat the parts of your life separately. The social or moral fabric that binds most individual lives is broken in your case. Here, it applies; there, it does not. In one sense, you are very much in control of your life—you can adjust the rules to meet *your* needs. But whatever is in you also brings pain and guilt. Your pain is transferred to your victims.

"He has these dreams," Jerry is saying. "He does what he's gotta do. But I figure he's gotta give up the street life sooner or later. The baby is coming. I'm not saying he's wrong now, but sooner or later he'll have to find a more steady way of getting over. What he's doin' now is not a life, you know?"

Jerry thinks his brother is a "hustler." Or something.

Will Jones get a job?

"If that's what he wants. He may not be at work every day at first—but he'll show. When the baby comes, he'll try to better himself; he'll get into a settled-down thing—like me. *He* says he ain't never goin' to change, but I know he has to. There's no other way out . . . unless he tries something stupid, something big, you know. But I don't think he's gonna do that."

Jones is out on the floor dancing with the eight-year-old again; strutting and cutting a mean figure while Jo-Anne watches dreamily from the corner.

"Oh yeah, he's very smart. He tries to get into things, and when he was in school he studied a lot. He jived a lot, too; but he reads a lot of things, and he keeps at it. Sometimes I wonder . . . I really do wonder why he's doin' the things he's doin' with the mind he's got."

I ask about Jones' legendary temper.

"Oh, wow, when he gets mad, nobody can say nothing! He's my brother, so he won't hurt me, but he can be *mean*. He believes he can kill the world if he has to, and you know, that's really the problem. The world just ain't like that."

Jerry waves his beer bottle in one hand as he talks. He is really into it; for in a sense, he is justifying *his* existence as well as explaining his brother's.

"He's trying to get next to the world; and really, it's not going to work like that. I can't argue with him because he is my brother, but he has got to get off that high horse sooner or later. If the world can be beat, I hope he can do it—but what's really happening is that he has to give some ground."

I look at my watch; it is four in the morning. I have somewhere to go in a few hours, and I tell Jones and Jerry that I must get back to the subway. Everybody objects; the party is just beginning and it will continue until sunrise. But I have to go, and once this is established, the next problem is tactics and strategy for the six-block walk to the elevated platform.

Jerry assumes that his gun will be needed. The problem is that it lacks registration; he could be stopped for it. Without the gun, it is assumed that someone should at least carry a club. What about the dog? Yeah. That will be good protection. There will be three of us, plus a dog and a club. That is reasonably safe, though dicey. And worse, the eight-year-old wants to come along. She's okay, though, because no one will hurt her, and she can run. Jones is also wearing his gold ring tonight.

"Why don't you leave that here?" Jerry suggests.

"Nigger, I'd die before I'd lose this!"

But Jo-Anne intervenes, pleading with Jones to leave it behind, reaching out and pulling it from his finger. He fights briefly—"No motherfucker will get this ring; no way!"—but he gives in. We are planning long-range reconnaissance. The war outside is raging. The patrol is now armed and ready to go.

The mission, as it happens, is uneventful. The dog gets a welcome chance to pee. We pass an all-night hot dog stand, and cargoes of corn dogs and french-fried onion rings are loaded for the return journey. Finally we wait on the elevated platform and talk in the darkness as the train rumbles into the station.

"He don't know what he wants in life," Jerry is saying, "and he's got to change his way of thinkin' soon. But I've got to say one thing. He's tried to help *me* in a lot of ways. I always knew that I could come to him if I needed help; and you know, he's the only one in the family who comes up to the Bronx regular. He comes every Friday night, man, and it means a lot to me."

Twelve

1

Davy's apartment. Curtains are drawn in the narrow, low-ceilinged space. The shadows mix with crude drawings of voodoo masks, pictures of naked women, and a snapshot of Davy taken during his tour in Vietnam; he is smiling. The dresser top is crowded with black magic books. Clothing and comic books are scattered about.

Davy deals smoke, coke, and guns . . . anything conveniently marketable. He is a thin, slit-eyed hustler who ran with Jones in teen-age street gangs. They have also been a mugging and burglary team. Among Jones' friends, he is Moms' and Pops' least favorite; Jo-Anne also dislikes him. Davy still uses heroin; even among street corner people, he has a cheapness about him, a sense that he will sell anything, that his values are so thin, so close to the most primitive notions of survival, that they are transparent, perhaps altogether gone.

Next to him, Jones is a pillar of integrity.

Even so, they are closely linked. Davy is Jones' tight pair of shoes. He says he has taught Davy how to hustle women, how to fight, how to be fly. The last lesson failed. Davy is junkie-thin; his Levis hang perilously on bony hips. He looks as though he is starving—not altogether out of the question since, like many drug users, Davy is far more concerned about the chemicals he shoots into his arm than what he puts into his stomach. Jones sees Davy as something of a little brother, someone beneath him, and Davy admits that Jones has saved him in more than one street fight.

In the matter of street commerce, however, the relationship is reversed. Davy leads. Jones needs a rifle for a bank robbery he and Jeff are vaguely contemplating. Davy will supply it. Jones periodically buys marijuana and cocaine from Davy—and just as regularly gets bad quality. When this happens, he will carry a grudge briefly and complain loudly to other friends. Yet he does nothing. Somehow he and Davy are too intertwined to run afoul over this.

A few days earlier, Jones and I were on a bus and he recognized someone through the window.

"Wow! That's the dude Davy said he killed with a pistol!"

Jones is suddenly explosively angry.

"That motherfuckin' liar—wow, Sam, I am tired of this! Davy is fuckin' with me! There ain't a motherfucker *out there* who isn't lyin'. I've got five for him, man! Fuck him!"

Jones swings at the air, smashing the invisible Davy to the floor of the bus.

"I have taken him under my wing and showed him how to fight. I got him the broad he is with now. I lend him clothes. He wants to be a pimp; I'm teaching him how to do that. Wow! He don't even take care of the clothes. Sometimes he doesn't even bring 'em back—wow, the thing that hurts me is that this is a dude I didn't have to help. I lend him clothes, and now he is buying his own and trying to get fly on me. I I still have him beat, but wow, this bullshit has got to stop. He and I are gonna have a *thing* about this!"

In the room, Davy digs into a dresser drawer for cocaine. Jones sits on the bed. Suddenly he growls at the skinny hustler.

"Hey . . . remember that dude you said you iced . . . with a *pistol?*"

Davy looks up in surprise. Jones' voice is low and threatening. Davy does not look at him directly.

"What the fuck you talkin' about? I never said that."

Davy is defiant; the argument is thrown back to Jones, who can't handle it.

"Aw, fuck it," he says. The subject is dropped.

Davy is coming into some cocaine—he needs money to make the buy, and Jones may decide to help. Today's portion of Happy Dust, therefore, is a wholesaler's sample. The room is aglow with anticipation. Jones and Davy and a kid I don't know named Freddy strap belts around their arms. Then Davy holds out his arm to me.

"Are you finicky?"

"Uh . . . I guess not."

"Then put your finger right here, man. I need some help with this vein."

Davy's arm, like his body, is ravaged and bony. His veins are scratched and marked, yet bloated and full of blood. And as I press my forefinger on the biggest of them he pushes the needle into it. Then he pulls up on the plunger and brings his blood into the milky solution inside—he scowls and lifts the needle out.

"Ain't gettin' it right."

And he pushes the needle into his liquid vein again. The spot where he is working is messy and red, and this time he gets it and relaxes, and the room is warm and dark with the windows closed, and I look at Davy's pocked teeth and skeletal flesh. And I think about the distance between us. Is it only the needle, the idea of puncturing myself, that separates us? I wonder if *I* could become like that? Could I *learn* to cut myself for the rush which junkies say is a mood and a trip beyond imagination, beyond orgasm, beyond anything else that matters? What stops me? A sense that I do not want to be punctured? It is a protective mechanism that could be overcome.

"It's coke all right," Jones is saying. "It's not the best coke I've had, but it'll sell."

With the needle still inside him, its syringe cradled in his elbow threatening to tear his flesh if it slips, he reaches for the half-finished cigarette he lit before starting. He is at once smiling and serious.

"I didn't know how to get high like this on coke when I got out of the Navy. I'm sorry I found out. I shouldn't be shooting coke so much. But you can never get enough of it, you know?"

Jones has untied his belt; he pulls the needle from his arm and a drop of dark blood is left on his skin. He goes to the bathroom for a piece of toilet paper and sponges off his arm. Needles and glasswear go back into small black boxes and everyone is agreed that the coke will sell, though it should not be advertised as too good.

The room is dark and warm and mellow; the high has settled in.

"When you gonna have that gun?" Jones asks.

"Next week."

"That's cool."

They shuffle out of the room, dreamy and buzzing on small wheels and ready to face the rest of the day.

2

Easter weekend, and Moms is cooking a big dinner. Jones is ready: shoes shined, clothes cleaned and pressed, gold ring redeemed. A few days earlier he and Davy had robbed a dope dealer in the restroom of a First Avenue bar. That covered the cleaning bills, the pawnshop ticket, and a few extras.

"Christmas and New Year's and Easter is meant to be a family thing," he observes. "It's good to get together."

Jerry and Ruth and their baby will be there. Billie is coming down from the Bronx. Bruce will be there, and Jones will bring Carol and little Ritchie. Jones also plans to help Pops color eggs on Saturday night.

On Saturday, Ritchie has an asthma attack.

"The baby was asleep. Then he jumps up and starts crying and says his chest hurts. He wants me to help him, but I can't do nuthin'. I had to take him to the hospital and call Moms and say we would be late. We was supposed to go to church after coloring the eggs."

A hospital emergency ward on Saturday night is all tears and blood and pain—made worse by maddeningly slow clerks who take your name, your parents' names, your health insurance or welfare identification, your address, telephone, religious preference, age authorization for doctors to probe the patient, medical history, and on and on . . . until your pain is psychic as well as physical.

"I get angry, man! I was worried about him, you know? The only time they move fast is if you are cut up or broke up."

And Jones waited to confront Ritchie's father.

"Sometimes I look at Ritchie and I *see* him. For a while that night, he didn't exist; then he came to the hospital. I got angry."

I ask him to explain.

"He put me in jail once. It started when he said things about me that I had to straighten out. But he wouldn't fight me. I got angrier and angrier about this. I got him up to the apartment and robbed him and took his pants off. He still didn't fight; he went to the cops instead. In court, we almost had a fight. After that, he didn't show up, and they dropped the case."

Jones' hatred for Carol's old boyfriend is complex. Jealousy? He clearly feels threatened by Carol's past. But he is also concerned about his street reputation.

"He told Carol's mother that Carol was my whore . . . that she was on the street and that I had her on drugs. He even came up to the apartment once while I was there. She told him to leave, and he said. 'I don't care about that fucking punk!' He didn't think I heard him. A few days later, I passed him on the street and he smiled at me. Wow, I had to get that motherfucker!"

Jones looks down at his hands; even now, the memory upsets him.

"I left the hospital. When I got to Moms', I wanted to talk to someone. She fell asleep. So I talked to my father. I asked how he felt when he first got down with my mother. I asked him if my sister, who is not his child, got sick a lot, and he said no.

"All Pops said was to watch Ritchie carefully, but I already knew that. He wanted me to help with the eggs, but I was still depressed."

As usual, Jones stayed up most of the night; equally typically, he endured his crisis alone.

"We went to see the baby Sunday and stayed with him about two hours. He was breathing better, so I felt better. I took him a big chocolate rabbit. I have a weakness for kids."

"What about the hospital expenses?"

"The welfare takes care of him being there. I pay for all the extras, toys and things like that."

Toys? Don't you see what is happening? a voice inside me explodes. The hospital expenses will run to a hundreds and hundreds of dollars; Carol's pregnancy, Jo-Anne's pregnancy, and the coming babies will cost thousands of dollars. Your family, Jo-Anne's family, and the city taxpayers will pay the bills, not you. Toys will be courtesy of some terrified people in dark doorways, holding their grocery bags. *Can't you see this, Jones?*

But I say nothing. I am not his adviser or his conscience. When he *asks*—which will be soon—I'll talk.

"The dinner was all right," Jones is saying. "We had baked lasagna and meat balls and stuffed beef and eggplant, and sweet potatoes and salad and spinach, and ham, too. I was puttin' down everybody at the table. It added some spice to the dinner. I can't really rap with my brothers too well, so I don't try to talk to them. I just keep 'em laughing. There was a lot of eggs, too. I wore my brown pantsuit and I went outside before dinner and smoked a few joints. Moms was glad to see my ring."

3

We are sitting in Carol's apartment. She is eating a slice of watermelon.

"Hey, girl," Jones mocks, "you showing your color?" Tension fills the room like fog. Carol says nothing. On the television, white suburban housewives arrive for a bridge game.

"Did you have fish last night?" one asks the hostess. "I see John still smokes cigars," says another.

The unhappy housewife is told to use a particular brand of air freshener. It solves everything.

Carol moves into the kitchen. Jones follows her. She has welfare money, and he wants part of it.

"How come you're takin' twenty dollars. That ain't right!"

"Yeah, it is . . . I'll show you what I can take."

She shouts something and walks hurriedly past the television set into the bedroom.

"You got to keep 'em angry," Jones says as he sits down. "You got to keep 'em thinking."

On the television, a black man stands in a hospital beside his child, who seems to have survived an emergency. "Every little boy should have a father like you," chirps a white nurse.

"Wow," Jones laughs loudly, "don't that break your heart?" Carol returns and takes a wicker chair by the window.

"Caarrroool, Caarrroool . . .I want to talk to you," Jones holds out his arms mockingly.

"Bastard—you're slick!" She runs into the bedroom, and he follows her. The voices behind the curtain are angry, yet tinged with laughter.

"Don't play with me—don't you play with me!" She is yelling and then laughing. The argument dissolves into taunting.

"I got a trick up my sleeve for you," she says defiantly.

"It's not gonna *compare* with the fire I got for you."

Jones has been picking tiny fights like this for weeks. He wants out of the relationship; but he wants to be kicked out rather than be accused of desertion. Carol waits; she is not happy, but she is not ready to let go. She nags Jones about bringing more money into the house. Jones becomes irritated and angry. He views Carol as a temporary convenience— yet she is pregnant. And Jo-Anne won't leave her father's apartment. It is all too complicated; he is becoming restless and depressed.

One of Jerry's dogs, a large, mixed-breed collie, has moved into the apartment.

"My brother beats on it," Jones says. "I figure I can take care of it better." It is strange reasoning for a man who normally fears dogs. The animal is chained in the tiny bathroom each day, yipping and pulling pathetically against the pipes. It is fed irregularly and beaten without warning; it raids the garbage can whenever it can stretch its chain far enough, messing the floor around it.

Carol is not pleased.

"You like dogs?" she says one day when I arrive. "You like dogs in the house?"

Pause. Silence.

"WELL, I DON'T! They smell . . . you can tell they are around, the house has THAT SMELL! I didn't want the dog in the house!"

She stalks into the kitchen angrily. Then she returns.

"I got to ask you a question, Sam."

I'm hoping to stay out of this.

"Dogs eat lots of food, don't they?"

"Well . . . yes."

"Do you think a dog will be hard to feed in a house with three people and hardly no money comin' in?"

I plead neutrality. And I feel worse than the dog for doing it. She is right; Jones is being an ass. My journalistic armor feels as thin as my notebook. The fight will soon grow violent.

4

Little Ritchie is still in the hospital. A story is going around that a nurse hit him with a ruler the previous night when he wouldn't stop crying.

"I figured I'd better check it out," Jones tells me later. "I went down about three o'clock in the morning—it shocked the shit out of the nurse. Nobody usually goes at those hours."

The nurse said she hadn't worked the previous night. He

went to her supervisor; the older woman said no one on her staff would ever hit a child.

"That was bullshit. I had worked in hospitals, and I had seen people beaten, old people and everything. This was an old jive bitch; and I wasn't gonna let her get over on me."

Jones returned to the night nurse, a young black woman. He asked Ritchie if the nurse had hit him. The baby nodded and pointed to his leg.

Still, the nurse denied it. She turned to Ritchie and asked if Jones had beaten him. The baby also nodded yes.

"You see," the nurse said, "the baby doesn't know who beat him."

"That don't change anything," Jones shot back. "Maybe a child can't remember *when* he was beaten, but he knows the people who did it . . . and he says you beat him, right?"

Still, the nurse denied it. But now she admitted she had worked the previous night.

Jones looked at the young woman heatedly.

"Well . . . if it *was* you . . . I *wish* you would stop."

Then he stalked out of the hospital.

5

Ritchie is home. He runs happily around the apartment, hitting things with a plastic baseball bat. He bangs Jones on the knee—plonk!

Jones reaches out with a long arm and grabs the little boy by his shirt collar. He pulls him close, talking into his wide eyes with a low threatening voice.

We are walking down Houston Street now. "What did you say to Ritchie?" I ask.

"I said, 'You hit me again, Ritchie, and I'll break your motherfucking jaw.' "

"Those *exact* words?"

"It's the way my father talked to me."

Jones is very attached to children—but he is still troubled about Ritchie.

"The baby is beginning to call me his father, and I don't like that. Carol is pushing him to do that. She wants me to act like I am her man. And I don't dig that. I want to be with Jo-Anne, and I'm worried that I'm getting too used to living at Carol's."

Jones is wearing a dashiki of hot pink and royal blue patterns. The afternoon breeze ruffles it as he walks.

"I can't believe that Jo-Anne won't move out. Like, she doesn't think I can take care of her. I did it when I was on drugs, didn't I? I hope she don't wait until I'm too involved with Carol." He stops in a drugstore to call Jo-Anne; she isn't home.

"What will happen to Carol?"

"I don't know. She knows I'm gonna leave; she talks about it. But she doesn't *really* think it's gonna happen. Carol knows the things I like, and she will do them that way, or better than I like, and then I get soft and she can see this. I have to get that straightened out. I didn't give her any cigarettes today. That will start things going."

"What about the baby coming?"

"I want it. But it doesn't mean I have to stay. I want to be with Jo-Anne."

We are back in the apartment. A blonde with piano-key teeth tells three clean-scrubbed California college boys— "Dating Game" again—that she is part Polish and part Rumanian. Which part would they like?

The door buzzes. Carol goes into the living room to answer it and closes the curtain behind her. It is a sister of Ritchie's father, angry about something. Jones jumps up.

"Wow, I got to meet this bitch! I've heard about her!"

Jones puts together a carefully coordinated outfit: gray slacks, black platform shoes, a blood-orange satin tank top. He works carefully on his hair.

"Wow, she is rappin' about the baby's father! Just *think* how they will talk when I leave." He laughs and lowers his voice to mimic the future conversation. "He ain't noooooo good. He was a dirty dog. Wow!"

He never meets Ritchie's aunt. He walks through the living

room once . . . twice . . . pretending to be on his way to the kitchen or bathroom. The women ignore him. He returns to the bedroom and a joint he has been rolling, laughing at a private joke. It seems time to ask something I've been curious about.

"What do you think of women's liberation?"

"WOW! I can't believe you askd that question!"

Jones is coughing hoarsely and laughing and nearly choking on the joint. He slaps his legs and rolls on the bed.

"No, man . . . no, man, I don't *even* think about that. They are right where they belong. They don't need to get any higher *at all*." He pulls on the joint and chokes and chuckles again. "Wow, that was *some* question . . ."

"Why?"

"Because I feel that woman is a slave. Her place is to serve a man—that's all she should do. I talk to these women, you know, and it gets pretty hot. They talk about having kids, and man, they can't have one without a man. I used to go with this ex-butch. She tries to pop some game on me from time to time, but it don't work."

He raises up on the bed and calls loudly for Carol, who jumps quickly through the curtain.

"Get my jacket!"

She nods and returns and stands by the bed to see if he wants anything else. Ritchie's aunt leaves soon after that. The apartment is quiet.

A few weeks later, Jones and I are sitting in a delicatessen. Three prep schools girls walk by our table. They are pushing bicycles they parked in the back of the restaurant while eating. One bike has a package tied to its fender rack; the binding is loose.

Jones touches the girl on the arm. "Sweetheart, your package is slipping."

She turns on him coldly.

"First of all, I am not your sweetheart!"

"Secondly"—she softens her delivery slightly—"thank you for telling me about the package." She smiles mock-sweetly and walks away with her bike.

Jones is stunned. And embarrassed. "Wow, I can't believe it," he is saying, nearly blushing. "I can't believe what she said. Maybe I shoulda smacked her."

Now a soap opera is playing on the television, and a woman is crying and yelling at her lover.

"He should knock that lamb out," Jones observes. "She is takin' him through too many changes."

He is drifting and thinking about women in his life. He remembers a baby-sitter.

"I used to make fun of her because her ass would shake when she walked. I was standing on this cabinet and she walked by and I said, "Wow, your ass shakes!"—she smacked me good! She almost knocked me off it. She was seventeen and I was six."

He lights another joint.

"I was about ten or eleven when I first had sex. It was on the stairway up to the roof. We had gotten together, a few guys and a few girls, and it just happened. It was beautiful. Then I went to my father, and I asked about sex. I didn't tell him I had already had it—and wow, he lied to me; he said your dick will swell up as big as you are. He said to stay away from it."

Jones' mind is moving sideways again.

"My father liked to give parties. There was this one woman. My father's friends said she liked to fuck a lot. She was in the kitchen, and she wanted to use the bathroom. But someone was in it, so she pissed in a flowerpot. I just watched her; this was the way she was.

"When I was around eleven, she had a daughter who would come around. My father caught us making it, but he didn't say nothin'. She lived at the house for a while because the lady was in the hospital. We made it a few more times, but I didn't get caught any more."

Jones drifts further.

"I have both Moms' *and* Pops' tempers. Pops gets mad fast, and then it is gone. Moms takes a long time. It builds and builds and builds—and then it's *hell*."

Jones finishes the joint and puts the butt into a small pill bottle. When the bottle is full, he'll roll the roaches into a large reefer and smoke them all again.

"I'm that way, too. If you hurt me, I'll get you in a way that you'll always remember. Moms really lets go. She threw a meatcutter at me once when I got kicked out of school. I was twelve—it missed me by that much." He holds his thumb and forefinger two inches apart. "It took a big chunk out of the wall."

Jones leans back against the wall. His facial expressions flicker like movie projector light.

"I'd get beat sometimes. My father would come home from work, and he'd catch me comin' up the stairs. He'd have talked to my mother on the phone—and wow, he'd spank the hell out of me!" Jones face is suddenly solemn.

"Then he'd cry. He didn't like to do it, I guess. But he'd still beat me—and every time he did it, he'd cry."

He laughs abruptly.

"He was beating me once, and I told him to knock it off or I'd beat *him*. He beat on me more. He had this long, thin belt—and he did a number on me! I'd have parties with Moms, too. She'd throw things: cans, bottles, whatever was ·handy. I got beat almost every day."

Ritchie is asleep, rolling around and sucking his thumb in the midst of toddler dreams. Jones motions toward him.

"I beat kids if they need it. But nobody likes to beat children."

The baby rolls off the edge of the bed and lands on his head with an echoing clunk. He is stupified first at what has happened. Then he bursts into bawling tears.

Jones scoops him off the floor. The mugger holds the baby's head and carries him back to the bed. He talks in a soft, fatherly voice.

"Easy, Jack—take it easy now. It's okay, take it easy . . . easy."

He cradles Carol's baby on his lap until Ritchie breathes easier and the fear and pain subside into sniffling; then he puts him back into the bed.

6

Jones opens the door—we are nearly overpowered by the odors of dog excrement and rancid garbage.

The cause of it all cowers in the bathroom, rattling its chain, climbing further behind the sink pipes as we approach. Melon rinds, chicken bones, globs of rotting rice, paper napkins, and odd-lot bits of food are scattered across the floor. Urine and runny excrement add stomach-churning color to the sad collage.

Jones stands over the dog, which slinks even further into the gloomy bathroom.

"I ought to beat your ass, motherfucker. You better hope Carol doesn't come home to see this."

But he does not hit her. He reaches instead for the kitchen mop. When he is finished, he strokes the animal's head.

"Easy, girl . . . easy. Everything is cool."

"I should have fed her. The whole thing is my fault. I can't beat her for that."

Fifteen minutes later, Carol comes through the door. She is worried about Ritchie, and notices nothing.

"The welfare people want to put the baby in a camp," she begins. "They say it'll be good for his asthma. I don't know . . ."

Carol is oddly talkative.

"They say he should stay in a foster home until I get an apartment in the projects. That really means they want to take him away. I'm trying to get into the projects now, but it could take time."

She is plainly distressed. All her world is threatened. Men come and go, but Ritchie is evidence that Carol matters. She has a household; she is more than one of nine sisters, more than a child of a fractured marriage. She is a family.

"He's better now, but I have to give him medicine; I've got it with me. I don't like this camp thing; I had to tell the welfare people I was living with my mother just to get out of the other hassles. They say I can't keep him alone."

Jones says nothing. Won't the city's summer air be bad for Ritchie, I ask?

"Yeah. I can understand it; the camp would be good. One of my sisters was sick all the time until they took her to a camp in Arizona. She stayed a year, and she wasn't sick any more when she came back."

Carol sits on the edge of the chair, confronted with further problems she doesn't care to share with Jones or me. Like Jones, she is essentially alone.

"Maybe it would be good . . . maybe I should let him go. I don't know . . . I just don't know."

7

A gray, drizzling day . . . dark and depressing. The sky is falling upon the city's streets, and the corner where we meet is nearly flooded. Jones is hunched over in the drizzle, sucking sullenly on a wet cigarette. We turn and walk south. He wants cocaine before we do anything else. He wants it so badly he does not mind walking through the rain.

"I've got to get out of Carol's apartment. It's goin' too fast with her. She's makin' too many demands. I just can't deal with it. This is on my mind all the time . . . it's getting hard to live."

"Maybe it's the rain."

He brightens. "Yeah"—but the smile folds—"no . . . I went to bed feeling like this. *Everything* is fucked up. I'm gettin' high too much—but I have to. I can be an expressionless dummy . . . I don't show happiness or disappointment."

He turns in his black raincoat and looks at me savagely.

"And I *know* where that leads. When I am buying coke rather than clothes . . . when I put a quarter down on coke first, then dig it, something is happening. I'm not goin' back to dope, but this is how it could happen."

A bus pulls up, splashing water at us. We go inside. In the seats, Jones talks in a low, angry whine.

"I don't know . . . if . . . I should . . . talk . . . about this . . . maybe it's too deep." He plays with his hands in his lap.

"But . . . when that baby is born . . . I hope it is . . . *dead*."

The air is still. The bus rumbles noisily through the traffic. There is nothing to say.

"I don't want her to have it—she wants it to keep me." The chunky hands start to move.

"Wow . . . I don't even know if it's *mine*. Carol is hot-blooded; and she was seeing some other dudes when we started up. I don't . . . *want* that baby."

He falls into the seat, relieved at having said it.

"When I was in school, I'd get excited about things, then I would tire of them. It's this way with Carol. Jo-Anne is the only one who doesn't make me tired."

We are walking toward the projects. The drizzle beats against our faces, and Jones turns to me. His mouth is set hard; his eyes are jet black. There are lines cutting through his face, as if a dark etching is bleeding its ink. He throws one hand out, clawing at the gloomy afternoon.

"Wow, Sam . . . sometimes it would be easiest to die. Maybe I'm asking to die the way I play in the streets. I think how easy it was on dope. Everything worked out because I didn't care how things worked out. If it didn't go my way, fuck it!"

He sighs deeply and thrusts the hand back into his pocket. He is ominously silent.

"What are you thinking now?" I am becoming frightened.

"How dull all this is . . . how dull life is, dig it? Jeff talks to me. He says things aren't as bad as they seem. Wow, things are *worse!*"

Even for drug dealers, the day is gloomy. Davy leans out his window and spreads his hands, palms out. At the basketball courts, Pinky is dry. He suggests Eddie, a skinny kid in glasses standing by one of the buildings. Still, no coke. We catch a bus for Broome Street.

This is pushing it, a lot; my fear is rising. We are riding into an area of skeletal buildings. Junkies huddle on the corners like packs of starved rats; the streets are deserted in midday, stores closed, windows boarded up. I remember the eerie silence in Vietnam before battles began—birds stopped trilling, people ran away, suddenly I would look around and see no life, only fear . . . and death . . . there is very little time to run.

We step off the bus and walk toward a windowless drugstore on the ground floor of a grimy brownstone . . . junkies all around it. The city here is diseased, dying all around me.

The junkies scatter. They probably think I am a cop. Jones recognizes one of them, a Puerto Rican with swept-back hair.

"We'll go talk to that nigger," Jones says.

He adds:

"A nigger around here don't mean a black dude, you dig? It's a low-class dude who ain't going' nowhere—that's the true meaning of the word."

I dig. Today's nigger is Andrew—and he does seem like a low-class dude. He's thirty, maybe. I see a bloody cut on his left jawbone; and the bandage is slipping, blotched with dirt and dried blood. I look at his right hand. It has a large bloody bruise on the middle knuckle. Andrew doesn't talk so good, either—his teeth are rotted like grave markers in an old New England cemetery. He wears a cheap windbreaker of brown vinyl and imitation fur. His hair is combed into a greasy ducktail.

Andrew is friendly. He knows Jones will reward him if he makes a connection. I'm already wondering how long Andrews will be alive after today.

Jones asks about coke.

Andrew shakes his head. I look around nervously.

"Hey, man, there ain't nothin' good around here. There's dynamite stuff on Avenue A. I'll take you down."

Jones glowers. He doesn't like strange neighborhoods.

"No, man, I ain't goin' to Avenue A. You got some stuff here, show it to me. I don't care what it's like as long as it's coke, you dig it?"

"Yeah, man, but it's not good stuff."

"Fuck it . . . let's get it."

Down a long block of deserted tenements, across another one, down one more. A stray cat moves in a garbage pile halfway down the second block. In one dark doorway, three neighborhood junkies wait for a connection.

"There's some good dope [heroin] around," Andrew says hopefully. "We had some stuff last night that put my head between my knees!" Where it still is, I am thinking.

Jones isn't interested. The junkie tells us to wait, and he takes the money and walks into an old tenement building.

We wait.

It is too long. Jones worries that the junkie has run out. He crosses the street and disappears into the building after him. This leaves me alone. Nothing to do . . . except wait. I glance fearfully at the far doorway.

At this moment I feel closer to disaster than I've ever felt since knowing Jones. Somehow I feel *all* the pain around me. Minutes pass. I shrink further into the doorway. A creaky door or a spitting cat could send me halfway to Brooklyn on a dead run.

Jones and Andrew walk out of the tenement, arguing. They have the powder, but Andrew's manhood has been affronted by Jones' lack of trust.

"Hey, man," the junkie whines. "I've run for you before. It was wrong to come into the house, it fucked things up. I ain't never beat you before . . . my word has always been good."

"That don't mean shit," Jones growls.

"Hey man, let's get off right now," Andrew urges. "I got works. We can go over to this empty lot on the next block."

"No . . . no, man, this ain't the place for me." Jones is still angry and depressed. He wants to return to Carol's apartment.

Andrew whines, but Jones has the coke, Jones is in control. We walk six blocks to Delancey Street, finally leaving the neighborhood's wailing silence behind. Even as we flag a cab, the feeling of it sticks like coagulated blood.

In Carol's apartment, we are safe—but the mood does not improve. Belts tightened, works out, the spike is fitted into the syringe. Jones pushes the milky liquid into his arm and waits . . . and waits . . . and he scowls darkly at Andrew.

"It's *weak*. It's a waste of fuckin' money!"

Andrew had predicted this, but he is still to blame. Pulling the needle out of his pocked arm and wiping away the blood, he agrees, yes, it is weak powder. He beats a hasty retreat to the door, heading for the street corner again . . . so long, man, see you . . .

"FUCK IT!" Jones bellows to no one in particular after the junkie leaves. Silence chokes the room.

"I feel trapped," he says again. "Everything is fucked up. *I don't want Carol to have my baby.*"

More silence.

"The tears, man, the tears are a bitch. A man is raised to think that a woman is softer; she can get hurt easier. It ain't true . . . but I'm still a sucker for them tears. Moms and Pops used to fight; Pops would say he was leaving. I got tired of hearing it. I asked him once why he always said that—and never left. He looked at me and said when you get someone, and you want to leave, you will know."

Jones looks up.

"*Now* I dig what he was saying. It's no easy thing to pack up. I didn't plan to get this . . . this . . . this . . ." He checks the stuttering by angrily throwing back his head "THIS involved."

Jones begins to drift. I look at him . . . for a moment; the conversation has disappeared. Then he leans toward me.

"Hey . . . can you loan me ten dollars until next time?"

I've done this many times. But I have nine dollars plus change in my pocket today. I'm set to go to the movies in a few hours: a double Bogart bill. I can't help him.

"Okay . . . dig it . . . I'll get over some other way."

More silence. He is depressed and still drifting. I'm struggling for ways to make the conversation move. An obvious, if crude, question occurs to me.

"Made any hits lately?"

"Naw . . . but from the looks of things, I'm gonna have to get back into it . . . and I hate to do it at night. Too many things can go wrong."

"Why at night?"

"There ain't no more daylight today, man."

"Tonight?"

"Yeah."

I am suddenly on the edge of my seat. "Tonight! Wait a minute . . . maybe we can go downstairs. I'll call my date . . . maybe she has some money for the movies. I mean . . . Christ! I don't want to be watching Bogart and thinking about you mugging someone because I didn't loan you ten bucks . . .wow!"

"No man, you need your money. Keep it."

"No, let's go down to the telephone. What if I give you seven and keep two? That be enough?"

"Yeah. I just want some smoke so I can go over to Jo-Anne's and get high."

I call, and she has money. We arrange to meet at the theater. Then I begin thinking—is this some kind of con?

"Tell me straight . . . would you really have taken someone off tonight?"

He looks at me oddly, genuinely surprised.

"Oh yeah. Like, you get in the mood, you know? Like, all kinds of things are coming down on me . . . it's not like when I was on drugs and I *had* to do something. It's more serious than that. It's my happiness, dig it? My life is going to be short enough without having to fuck with this. So I'll go out and do that thing, and fuck it, if something goes wrong, at least I'll go happy."

And so while Bogart unhappily puts Ingrid Bergman on the plane and kills bad Germans in the foggy Casablanca airport, I confess I am relating to his anti-hero status more than usual. Someone out there owes me a favor.

8

The glass protective wall is shattered. The old television set's exposed picture tube stares blankly into the room.

"I was mad. *Wow* . . . was I mad! She kept runnin' her mouth, and I slapped her. But she kept talkin' shit. Things were getting hot . . . I told her I was leaving, and she said leave—take your shit with you! And I said I was leavin' but I would come back later for it. She said take it now—I said *later*. I took this pill bottle . . . I was seeing red . . . and I threw it at the TV set."

Jones looks down at his hands. One has a puffy red scratch between the thumb and forefinger.

"I was *really* mad. I grabbed her by the throat and I was choking her. I wanted to kill her. Billie was there—she saved Carol's life. I had my hands on her throat and I was watching her eyes bug out. She scratched me, but that was all she could do. Billie stopped me, and I decided right then I was leaving for good. I went home that night and slept at my mother's."

The fighting has been escalating for some time. Carol has sensed his ambivalence and has resisted him. But she has become angrier and angrier at his continued willingness to live off her. She also knows he is picking some of the fights purposely.

One friction point is the clock. Though Jones drifts through most of his days with little regard for passing time, he expects others to be punctual—especially his women.

One night a few weeks earlier, he'd expected Carol home at 11 P.M. She arrived past midnight. She had been drinking at her mother's, and she met his peevishness with defiance.

"Is *this* eleven o'clock, Carol?"

"It's only a few minutes after . . ."

"A few minutes—my fucking ass! You say you're comin' home at eleven o'clock, you be here, bitch!"

"I come home when I want, motherfucker!"

In a swift, sweeping motion Jones hit her in the face with the flat of his hand. She cursed at him again. His hand moved again across the space between them with the gathering force of a huge winged bird. She was knocked across the room and down.

"You don't like it," Jones said mockingly, "You can leave."
Carol was sprawled on the floor and crying.

"FUCK YOU, YOU CAN LEAVE, BASTARD!"

He shrugged: "All right . . . what the fuck . . . I will."

He didn't.

"I'm setting it up," he told me after the incident. "This way I can leave when I'm ready without any bullshit."

The television was broken after that when Carol asked to accompany him to the Bronx. Jones told her to meet him at his parents' apartment precisely at ten-twenty. She didn't arrive in time and he returned to their apartment with Billie to shower and change clothes. And wait. Carol arrived at twelve-thirty. She had been drinking again, and this time *she* was angry.

"You didn't wait for me!"

"You was supposed to be downstairs at ten-twenty."

"I *was* there. *You* weren't there—you're lying."

"Don't you tell *me* I'm lyin' or I'll bust you up. You hear me, bitch?"

"Go to hell, you faggoty motherfucker. You're lyin' *all* the time, lyin' about this and takin' money and lyin' about that. You go over and get that white bitch, and you take her to the Bronx, you hear?"

Again, someone was calling Jones a homosexual. He reacted with blinding rage, breaking the television set, then trying to choke Carol. She screamed and Billie intervened.

A few days later Carol called and apologized. Jones was glad to return to her apartment. In the intervening time, he had another fight with his father.

"Pops and me got to talking about the thing with Carol. He don't like her, and he wants me to come home; I told him no. He wants me to come home so he can say I tried to make it on my own but failed. Fuck it, I'll sleep on a bench first."

He will sleep at Carol's.

"We had to settle some things. The beef was that she wasn't around often enough, and we talked about it. This . . . this is her home, you know? I was angry about the baby, too. She dresses him wrong. She dresses him like it's still really cold outside, and it's not. It's hot enough now so that I have to crack the windows when I come inside, or the *walls* will start to sweat. Being dressed like that isn't good for the baby."

We are walking, and Jones flicks his cigarette into the gutter, exhaling a melancholy cloud of smoke.

"Wow . . . I feel better getting that done. I *had* to get down with it sooner or later. I still dig Jo-Anne the most, but she don't want to leave her father's place. So fuck it, I'll stay with Carol until she's ready."

9

"It was really stupid . . . I didn't have a knife or a pistol or nuthin' "

Jones had gone to the bank where Jeff works and committed an impulsive mugging. He bangs his steepled fingers on the half-naked television set repeatedly as he talks about it.

"It was funny, really. I saw this dude come to the window with a check; the teller handed him a lot of bills. He kept counting them, and I let him finish. He was dressed well—he had on a gray suit . . ."

Jones walks to his closet and pulls out a silk suit.

". . . cut about like this, you know? Except it was darker. I was writing on a withdrawal slip, and I saw the teller hit the sponge with his thumb four times—he was really working —and after that the dude counted the bills himself."

Jones' nails are clacking loudly and nervously against the surface of the television as he talks.

"So I followed him out. I pushed him into the back doorway to the bank, and I put my hand in my coat pocket as if I had a weapon. Wow, the dude bought it!"

Jones slaps the top of the television set again—and again— to make his point. He is extremely embarrassed.

"I put the roll in my pocket. I told the dude to stay there— or I would shoot him, dig it? I called a cab, and I got in the back seat. *Then* I looked at the roll. I was thinking it would be fives and tens. And I got to the bottom and it is twenty-nine one-dollar bills!"

One more loud thump on the television set.

"*Wow, I could have gone to jail for ten fuckin' years behind twenty-nine dollars!*"

Now the story's true climax. Papa Jones, erstwhile provider, blows the roll on his surrogate kid.

"I ran into Carol. She saw the money, and she said the baby needed clothes. So I bought him some shirts—that cost twenty dollars, ten shirts at two dollars apiece. Then I bought him a truck . . . you know the kind that goes whirrrr . . . whirrrr when you push it and the wheels spin? I'm a sucker for kids. Whatever they want from me, they get. That truck cost eight-fifty, man!"

Thirteen

1

Tomorrow and tomorrow and tomorrow . . . Jones has three. In one he sees a void. "You live for the day in the streets," he says. "No point in looking for more." But he contemplates other futures.

One, after a fashion, is law-abiding. It is a variant of the big sting fantasy common to most small-time criminals and street people. One big hit, followed by retirement. Jones adds a personal twist or two.

"It would be about twenty thousand dollars, I figure—a bank job, or a really good drop. I'd jut the money into drugs next. Drugs turn over fast. I'd have a hundred thousand pretty soon. Then I'd put the money into stocks. I'd have a big portfolio, and I would use my earnings to buy a store. It would be my place, and I would run it. That's where I would end up. I'd have my store and a lot of bread, and I would settle down. I'm looking for that sting now."

Jones comes close in this fantasy to integrating the separate, combative parts of his personality. He seems to hope genuinely for a more stable, settled life. He talks, for example, of going back to school, either for electronics training or college. He also talks about taking a counseling job in a drug clinic; his experience with heroin, he assumes, would set a good example. A half-imagined federal grant also figures into this.

"The counseling job would get me back into the time thing. I'd be getting up at seven-thirty again and that would make me able to go back to school. Then I would get a grant, and when I got out of school—and I had been teaching besides—they would have to let me in the electricians' union. I could be like Roland, and be a contractor; I would work for myself—that's the best way."

Every time we talk about this future, Jones becomes excited. It is all too pathetic a fantasy in some ways, yet each time I listen seriously as his hands move and his eyes become bright. It is a moment of hope, however fragile.

"When you work for somebody, he tells you this or that and if you don't do it he beefs with you. I don't want to work for *nobody*. That way, I got no beefs, and I can keep my own hours."

He shifts his vision slightly, and I follow hopefully along.

"I've lost a lot of time, you know? Roland and Jeff were on drugs. Roland went through a program and got trained; Jeff has money from his wound . . . pretty soon he'll be a printer. They both had time to get what they need."

Jones whirls and looks at me. The late afternoon light is fading.

"There are so many things I want. I've *got* to get them. Something has got to change in my life. I've got to go *all* the way, one way or the other—soon."

2

"The "other way"—the third tomorrow—is dealing. Jones is wildly ambivalent here.

We pass a newsstand one day and see boldface headlines describing the arrest of more than a dozen heroin smugglers. At Carol's apartment, Jones reads the story with large-eyed fascination, following his thumb carefully through the news columns.

"Wow . . . one of these dudes had a house worth eighty-two thousand dollars—a Mafia dude. That ain't right, you know? These white dudes bring it in, but it goes to the black families. They ought to be killed . . . the motherfuckers ought to be axed!"

He bangs the newspaper angrily with his thumbnail, tearing it.

"One of these dudes had a son who was a dope fiend—at least he knew somethin' about it. Wow . . . I hope they send these dudes up *forever*."

"I thought you wanted to be one of them."

Jones looks up. He chuckles and nods to himself. He'll have to go some distance to get his rationale together, and he knows it.

"Yeah . . . I would be putting my money into drugs," he begins slowly. "That would have to be . . . dope or coke . . . yeah."

"If it's wrong for them, what about you?"

"I've put a lot of dope into me. A lot of my life has gone that way." He's getting it together.

"That makes it right?"

"No . . . but that's what I'm gonna do. It's time that I got paid back. Dig it, it means somebody's life gets hurt. Maybe it'll be my brother or someone else, but fuck it, that's too bad."

He's hoping this tough-guy bluff will work—he knows it won't.

"The next newspaper article might have you in it. What about that?"

"Yeah"—he is beginning to chuckle, for he knows he can't straddle this fence easily—"yeah . . . that could happen. It's a chance I'd have to take. I could win, or I could lose."

He tries another ploy. "I would be different. These dudes ain't put nothin' of their lives into dope. They do it for greed. I got greed, too. But I have put a lot of cash in the dope bank; I'm ready for some withdrawals."

He bangs the page again as his mind moves with lightning speed to another facet of the argument. "Somethin' funny is going on—some kind of political thing. These motherfuckers are too big to be fingered. Their cases will be dropped, or they'll get a year or something. Wow! They ought to be axed, but they are just too big!"

"Would it be okay to . . . uh . . . curse your picture?"

Jones lets out a long, sad breath of air. "Yeah . . . I'd be doin' a crime. That's wrong."

End of discussion.

3

More fantasy. Jones periodically cases the Wall Street bank where Jeff works. He will buy a .22 rifle as part of a vague, poorly formed plan. This is a first cousin of the big sting fantasy. After the bank job, he and Jeff will turn the money into cocaine.

"We're gonna start with dimes and quarters [$10 and $25 amounts] until we learn the business. Inside a month, we should be dealing in ounces. Coke moves fast. There aren't that many dudes doin' junk—coke is the thing. If we live the way we should, and stay cool and put money back into the business, we'll get on top of things fast. We'll take forty or fifty dollars a week to live on, and at first we won't touch any of the coke."

He pauses.

"I'm not worried about Jeff, I'm worried about me. I like coke too much. I could fuck things up."

In Jones' neighborhood, dealers make the most money with the least trouble. Nobody gets hurt—nobody they see—and a dealing operation is considered a business. You are an entrepreneur; you are—in some eyes—respectable.

And you make a lot of money.

"I figure I can keep my head. If I had junk around, I'd be in trouble. But I think I can keep coke. We will be building a business. I plan to do a little smoke on the side, too."

"If the business doesn't work out," he adds, "we'll try something else."

Back to the bank.

"You really have to lay on a bank job, check out all the details; you've got to sit down and plan it. Otherwise, you won't walk away."

Jones smiles dreamily.

"If it works, Jeff and me will each get a car . . . because, you know, Jeff likes a Cadillac. So do I."

4

The B bus is crowded. We sit in the back seat as it grinds its bulky way through Lower Manhattan. Jones has the Boone's Farm between his knees, and he steals a swig whenever he thinks the driver isn't looking. Three Chassidic Jews in black hats and long coats climb into the crowded car. Jones watches as they stand in cultural isolation amid the blacks and Puerto Ricans around them.

"I used to make fun of these dudes. We all did. Then I got to thinkin' and I stopped. People laugh at the Jews and the Chinks because they are the way they are. But you got to respect them."

He offers me the bottle.

"They help each other. If you was Jewish and I was Jewish, and I needed some money to start a store, you would lend it to me, dig it? The Chinks are even more that way. I knew this Chink in the Tombs; the people were fucking with him, and I told them to stop. After that I asked him, how come I never see any of you in jail? He said it was because his people stuck together."

He takes the bottle again.

"The Chinks come to the city and get on welfare, you know? But they get *off* welfare. They've even got, like, their own welfare. There ain't no place they can go except up. They are taking over the Lower East Side even now."

More Boone's Farm.

"My father, he gets drunk and he says, 'Them old slanty-eyed motherfuckers!' And I say, Pops, don't you *even* sleep on those people. If black people were like this—if they took care of each other like this—black people would get somewhere. He don't like it when I say this."

We are going to Davy's apartment to do some business among the voodoo dolls.

In the apartment, Jones hands the skinny hustler thirty dollars. Davy counts it, then pulls a gray Valpak out of a closet and opens it. The ancient .22 rifle is broken into two sections. Its wooden stock is gnarled and bruised as if a dog has been chewing on it. The barrel and bolts are spotted with metal corrosion.

"It's stolen," says Davy, "and I think it's hot [used in a crime] too." Davy takes a cigarette out of a crushed pack and sits on the bed.

Jones examines his new toy carefully. He shoves the bolt back and forth and fits the parts together and squints with one eye as he puts his nose against the sighting mechanism. Slowly, he squeezes off rounds, listening carefully to the bolt's heavy click.

They take the sad old rifle apart again, strap it inside, and close up the Valpak. Jones carries the suitcase downstairs as if he is about to catch a plane, waving to people on the park benches as he walks by.

He sees Carol, who has been visiting her mother, and remembers he wants to get some cocaine. He hands Carol the Valpak. She protests.

"Don't you leave *me* with that thing!"

"Be cool . . . I'll be right back. Nobody's gonna stop you."

"I get nervous. Leave it with somebody else."

"Bitch, I done tol' you to be cool. You hear?"

He leaves her scowling and walks toward the basketball courts. He returns with Roland and takes the suitcase back and starts to walk away.

"Where you goin'?"

"Back to the house. I'll see you later."

We walk to the bus . . . the eyes inside my head turn toward the gray case. *How casually he lives with criminality.* Cocaine in his pocket . . . a rifle in the suitcase . . . joints in his coat. I feel as though the walls and windows of the buildings are filled with government agents, their binoculars and guns and walkie-talkies waiting to swoop down on us.

I can't look around . . . that would give us away. Yet my eyes swivel like pinballs. We stand at the bus stop, three men and a hot rifle in a crowd of commuters. Why aren't they curious about the suitcase? Don't they *understand?* I'm a reporter, officer, I'm writing about these people . . . remember the First Amendment for God's sake. I'm the writer—these people, they are . . . well . . . robbers and muggers and dope fiends and gunrunners . . . and I am with them . . . and . . . and . . .

We arrive at Carol's without incident.

While Jones assembles the rifle, Roland tends to the cocaine, mixing the powder and cleaning the equipment. Jones puts down his new toy just long enough to get his works. The next ten minutes is devoted to the usual business of tying belts around biceps, poking around to find the best vein, plunging needles into the flesh, and settling back . . .

Click! Rattle-click! Rattle-rattle! Jones is playing with the gun again, aiming at imaginary targets beyond the billowing curtains. He moves from window to window, chair to chair, sighting targets, working the bolt mechanism and pulling the trigger.

He grabs a box of shells and walks into the bedroom. I'm bent over my notebook, and I don't see him go. Roland is happily collapsed on the couch.

Bam!

He is shooting out the rear window, firing into a construction project next door. I can't believe it!

Bam! Bam!

The Valpak at the bus was nothing . . . this will bring the police for sure.

Bam!

Jones walks into the living room with an alligator smile. "It works good," he announces happily.

I nod dumbly. Roland smiles. We are thinking the same thing.

Jones leans the rifle out the front window, brushing aside a white curtain. "Dig that big ol' cat in that window. Bet I could knock him off with one shot . . ."

Roland and I are suddenly off the couch like puppets on the same string.

"Cool it!" One of us says, I think it was Roland. Jones turns around.

"The cops could hear these shots. Be cool, man. Keep the gun away from the window." That was me in the first part. Roland took it after that . . . I think.

Jones is suddenly embarrassed. He looks at the rifle.

"Oh yeah, wow. I didn't think of that—I'll put it in the closet."

Right. I take a few more notes—it suddenly seems time to wind things up for the night. I get up and put the notebook carefully into my pocket.

"Well, it's late, you know? Gotta make it. Got some places to go. See you all . . ." And I go down five flights of stairs as fast as middle-class legs will carry me.

5

Jones returned from the gymnasium deeply, powerfully, violently . . . angry. In the darkness before midnight he slammed the apartment door closed and reached into the front closet, breathing heavily, eyes red and fiery. One eye was swollen.

He found the rifle and a box of .22 shells.

The apartment was empty except for the lonely dog rattling its chains. Jones dumped the shells on the couch with a clatter and loaded the weapon. He aimed it, squinting fiercely through the sight and swinging the barrel around the room. Then he laid the weapon on the couch and reached for Ritchie's watercolor set.

Next, he carried a kitchen chair into the bedroom, placing it in the room's far corner. He propped two pillows and a board against the chair's back and leaned the lid of his record player's carrying case against them.

The dog whined plaintively while Jones painted a bloody heart in the center of the case with the red coloring.

He picked up the rifle. He positioned himself on a kitchen stool in the far hallway, one knee up to support the gun.

Bam!

The bullet went directly through the bloody heart.

Bam! Bam!

Two more bullets made jagged holes in the red valentine.

"All day," he tells me the next morning, "I knew something would go wrong."

It was an old feud. There are three Johnson brothers in the projects, all street fighters. A year earlier they gave Jones some marijuana and told him to turn it out. He smoked it instead, told them it was poor quality, and refused to pay for it. One Johnson brother pointed a gun at Jones' head.

"I'm gonna kill you, punk," he said, "unless you get the money."

Jones returned with a .22 pistol and caught the brother by surprise. "I fucked up his name. He had to back down. I figured he would be coming back at me sometime, but I didn't know when."

It was a year later.

Jones' eye is dark and swollen as he tells me the story now. His face is puffy with anguish. He talks of the previous night as if it were the most important crisis of his life. He tells the story again and again.

"I was leaning against the wall of the gym, and I was fucked up on smoke and wine. He came over; I saw his hand in his pocket, but I didn't think about it. He hit me fast —I almost went down. It was all I could do to duck and dodge. I tried to move, but I couldn't."

My mind throws out a calculated needle. "You were against the wall like people who get mugged, right?"

He smiles weakly. "Yeah . . ." But he doesn't want to deal with that and goes on.

"I was high, and I couldn't fight. I saw Johnson aiming a punch. It was gonna be a roundhouse, comin' *all* the way around, and I figured, fuck it, I better get one off fast. But I couldn't move because my shoes wouldn't grip the floor. All I could do is duck."

With the dark eye, Jones seems sadly vulnerable. His hands loop and dive telling the story, and he seems afraid that something will crack, his armor will rupture if he doesn't settle this in his head.

"This dude came over to break it up. He was talking to me, and I was taking off my shoes for what I figured was coming. I turned and Johnson was waiting—he caught me with a full punch in the eye. This was it . . . I grabbed ahold of this other dude. It was the only thing that kept me from goin' down. Then some other people came over to break it up."

Jones has worked hard to cultivate his street reputation. Now he fears one fight will cause his fall.

"I decided to shoot him."

He went home to get the rifle. He was inspecting the holes in the painted heart when Jeff knocked on the door.

"He made me see that I would fuck myself up if I went back. It was a pride thing. Besides, the raincoat wouldn't cover the gun."

Still, Jones talks of vengeance.

"I'll let this ride for a month or so. He'll forget about it. This has helped his name, so I'll lay up for a while and chump his hand later . . . he'll be confident . . . I'll get him."

He stops and nods to himself. He paces again—and begins his rationale.

"In a way, I'm glad this happened. I was gettin' too high in my thoughts. These shoes"—the black platform monstrosities with four-inch heels—"make you feel big. I was feeling I couldn't be hurt. I had a reputation in the projects that this couldn't happen. Wow, people are gonna talk!"

"The Johnsons will expect me to hide . . . I won't do it. When I first got down with them, Pops said I would die in the streets. I told him, so what? I don't care how I die, as long as it's quick."

"How about having a *long* life?"

"No way. It will happen sooner. I will die the way I am, or I will die trying to make some money."

He is up and pacing again.

"Now when I go down to the projects, people will want to know what I'm gonna do. I gotta keep my plans secret . . .

Wow, I *hate* to let that motherfucker have one! After that last punch, I had to say, Phillip, fuck it, I'll give it to you. He said, motherfucker, I *got* it. There wasn't nothing I could do . . ."

He lights another cigarette and puffs heatedly on it.

"The thing to do is stay on your feet. I managed it; I stayed cool, and that fucked them up a little. They expected me to leave, but I took a joint out of my pocket and smoked it—that blew their minds!"

Jones pulls back the curtain and looks out at the dark, wet day.

"I *hate* days like this . . . something bad *always* happens. Each time I got busted was on a rainy day; I got my time on a rainy day. It's the dullness of it; I get blue. When it's raining out, all you can do is think. I spent the *night* thinking about this. At times like this I don't go to sleep until five o'clock or so, and I don't sleep sound."

He is straining . . . pushing . . . he has to get the pain and fear up and out.

"I woke up today at seven. I heard this voice, and somebody touched me. A voice said, be cool, better things are coming. I'm serious. The voice could have been in a dream . . . but I don't think so. Maybe it was God; I don't know, it was a voice, that's all. It said things will get brighter. I felt good after I heard it—my turn will come, dig it?"

Jones leans back on the couch and begins nodding solemnly to himself. "I'll probably stay up tonight and think about this some more. It's peaceful in the night. I can get into myself. I look at things I've done, my faults and like that, and I try to get to know myself. I think about the future, too."

4

"You think I should get rid of the rifle?"

"Yes."

"What the fuck . . . I'll take it up to the Bronx and sell it. I'm just gonna hurt myself if I keep it around. It ain't no good for a bank job anyway. I think I can get forty dollars for it."

"What did you pay?"

"Thirty."

Pause.

"You've talked to my family now, right?"

"Yes."

"What do they say?"

"They think you'll change. The new baby might bring you around."

"Wow . . . they *all* think that. The times change . . . so *I'll* have to change. Maybe . . . but I don't see it happening right away. They want me to live through the same things they did, and make the same mistakes. I don't want to do that, not *ever*."

5

Much of Jones' future is today.

"The dude is all right," he is saying. "He sounds like he knows his shit."

We are talking about Carol's legal aid lawyer, whose job requires patience as well as "knowing his shit." This morning's eviction hearing, for example, was postponed. The client missed her court appointment by . . . oh . . . two hours.

"She was supposed to be there at nine. But we didn't get back from the Bronx until four-thirty or so. So we didn't make it until about eleven."

Carol meanwhile has rolled up the rug and packed a number of boxes. She is ready to move in the night, for the landlord has escalated his harassment. An agent came to the door recently; he is said to have shouted at her.

Jones wants to visit Jo-Anne today. He decides to take the dog, and the animal pulls eagerly on its chain as we go out the door.

Below the next landing, a man is climbing. He sees the dog and stops to let it by. He is short and thickly built with fat arms and wrestler's shoulders.

Jones stops, too. Neither man moves. It is an awkward moment.

"Go if you're going," Jones shrugs.

The man wears a gray felt hat with a small brim. A stiff gray beard carpets his face. His sportcoat has patches at the elbows. He edges slowly—somewhat nervously—past the dog and steps onto the landing. Jones starts downstairs.

Suddenly he whirls.

"Hey, I want to talk to you." The bearded man turns around.

"You got up in my wife's face last week. I want . . . I want . . ." Jones chokes back the stuttering and his face becomes savagely angry. "I WANT to talk to you about it."

"What apartment are we speaking of, please?"

"Five–B"

The agent is uncomfortable with so public a confrontation. He speaks in tight bunches of words.

"Oh . . . yes . . . Mrs. Jones. I was up to see her last week, yes."

"Right, and you got into her face, and we gotta talk about it."

"Good, I'm delighted to talk to you—I'm always delighted to talk to a man. Your wife is five months behind on the rent. At first, she said she didn't have the money, she said she would pay as soon as she could. So I said this was all right, I let it go a while longer."

The agent smiles quickly and nervously. His back is against the landing wall—he's cornered—and Jones seems very menacing.

"But then she lied to me. She swore she would put the money in the mail to me. She didn't. I don't own this building—I'm the agent. I have to have something to show for my time. I could understand if she didn't have the money; I can let that go for a while—but she double-crossed me!"

He is tight against the landing wall, talking fast. Jones and the dog are in front of him.

"Man . . . man, with all the people *you've* double-crossed, you . . . you shouldn't feel bad. But wow . . . you got up in my wife's face. I don't *like* it man. That . . has got to stop."

Jones pushes the words out with his usual slowness. He grapples for his sentences with his hands, and the rental agent, faster verbally, uses the same words to keep him at a distance while he eases away from the wall.

He maneuvers toward Jones' far side. He begins wagging his finger at Jones.

"What about the rent, what about it, my friend? I've called the welfare people, they aren't going to pay it. Somebody has to pay."

"If she said she will pay it . . . you . . . you will get it."

"But how, my friend, how?"

The wagging finger reaches out and pokes Jones lightly in the ribs.

"Hey man! We aren't friends . . . don't you put your hands on me!"

The agent pulls his hand back, fast. He begins edging down the stairs; Jones follows him. The dog is jumping about and barking and its chain is rattling and clanking against the stairwell.

"Hey man, you . . . you know the case is in court, don't you? And you know why, don't you?"

"Look, my friend, all your wife has to do is get the apartment fixed the way she wants it and show me the bill. I'll take it out of her rent. I've told her this."

They are halfway downstairs. Jones and the dog tower over the chunky agent, all three are suspended in the darkness above the hallway. The agent is backed now against a cracked, dirty window that peers into a ventilation shaft. He talks fast, cutting in when Jones pauses to stutter, repeating himself again and again, working his way toward the floor.

"I told your wife she could get the apartment fixed. She had only to keep the bill. But she double-crossed me. That's why I . . . went . . . up against her face. She has to pay the rent—it's as simple as that."

Jones becomes increasingly angry as the man dances around him. His case is weak—Carol cannot pay the money either way—and the agent is peevishly persistent. A young black couple walks down the stairs, separating them briefly. The agent eases himself quickly off the landing. Jones hands me the dog's chain. Now they face each other in the tiny vestibule. A small crowd has gathered.

"You know . . . if . . . if . . if I had been there, I woulda *done* something about what you did."

The agent looses an urgent clutch of words: the double-cross, the bill, the back rent, his job, the money, the patience he is showing. His voice is rising.

"Man . . . don't yell at me!"

"I'm not, I'm not yelling, my friend. I'm just talking. What about the rent?"

"Man . . . don't you yell at me ever!"

"Okay, okay, but what about the rent, what about it, who's going to pay?"

"I got one thing to say to you . . . the next time I'm gonna take a swing at you, understand?" Jones is towering over him. The crowd except for me is totally black and Puerto Rican.

"Easy now, easy, I tell you all she must do is have someone fix the plumbing and give me the bill."

Jones spreads his arms and they begin to make motions, and the agent is talking loud and fast.

"MOTHERFUCKER, LET ME TALK! YOU GO UP AGAINST MY WIFE'S FACE AGAIN AND I AM GOING TO PUT A BULLET THROUGH YOUR HEAD!"

"Now . . . wait a minute. Take it easy. Why would you want to do that? It wouldn't do either of us any good, would it? The police would come, and there would be trouble." The agent's eyes move nervously around. "Just calm down now. Let's settle this like gentlemen."

He moves toward the door, and freedom, but Jones moves first, grabbing the dog's chain and pushing the man aside and stomping into the street, throwing a final insult at the money collector.

"YOU GET THE FUCK OUT OF MY FACE AND YOU KEEP AWAY FROM IT, YOU HEAR?"

The words are ended. Jones pushes through the crowd, still raging. We walk to the liquor store and Jones puts a dollar down for a pint of Boone's Farm. Suddenly we see the agent waving at us again.

I can't believe it.

He walks up to us. "A man on the second floor does plumbing and fixing, my friend. Have your wife get him up there. Whatever he does, we'll pay the bill."

Jones looks at him fiercely. "He came up already. He said the sink wasn't worth fixing. She needs a *new* sink."

"Well, I don't know about that . . . but you call him and get the apartment fixed and give me the stub."

The day is bright. In platform shoes, Jones stands about three inches taller than his opponent.

"GET THE FUCK OUT OF MY FACE!"

Jones grabs the dog and stalks away. The agent stands on the corner a moment longer and finally turns and walks in the other direction.

"That motherfucker is stupid," Jones adds in a low voice as we walk. "I talked to that plumber; he said the motherfucker said don't put no new sink in the apartment, no way."

Jones reaches out for a handful of afternoon air to make a last point.

"If he had brains, he wouldn't have tried that shit. I should've took him off . . . that would have fucked him up. But he'll be comin' back; *everything* comes back. The future is a circle. But wow . . . I really wanted to hurt him!"

Fourteen

———————

1

"I'll take care of a man for a while," Carol is saying, "but I can't forever take care of a baby *and* a man."

By mutual agreement, Jones is out this afternoon. Carol and I are talking privately.

"He says his parents spoiled him so he has to live this way. It ain't true. He's healthy. He can work, he can change. He thinks he can live off women . . . but it's got to change."

It is late June; the tension in the apartment remains severe. Ritchie sleeps in the hot bedroom today and one of Carol's younger sisters is next to him watching the ever running television.

"The way he's goin,' nothin' will change. He's got this other girl taking care of him, too."

"How is he treating you?"

She shrugs. "It's all right. He treats me better than her. He takes money from her and gives it to me. But he won't take money from me. He shows me respect . . . he'll ask for money, but if I say no one or two times, he'll forget. But he really collects from her."

Little of this is true. Carol forgets the times I've watched Jones take her grocery money.

"We have our ups and downs. When he goes to see her, he says he's going 'out.' But I know he's been there. I can sense it. He has a big grin; he says hello, sweetie, or hello, baby. It means he's covering somethin'. It used to upset me a whole lot . . . now it don't bother me at all."

Carol sits sullenly in a sweater and Levi cutoffs, watching her hands as she talks. She seems to me almost . . . bent from the weight of her life. In the bedroom, Ritchie begins to cry.

"It's gone too far. I'm ready to give it up . . . I can tell, because it don't bother me so much now. Anytime he wants to leave . . . it's okay."

She glances at the bedroom—"You shut up in there, you hear?"—and leans back on the couch, folding her hands.

"It's all right for him to go see her. But if I go see one of my old flames, there's hollering and shouting. He wants to fight someone and all that. It's not right—if he can go out, I can go out. But he says no. I do it anyway. I haven't found the right guy; but if I do, I'll go see him."

She takes a leather sandal from her foot and walks purposefully into the bedroom—whap! whap!—for a moment the baby cries louder. The sounds quickly subside.

"I can save money. He likes to go out and get high when he gets money. I can take money to my mother's and leave it there for months and months. To him, saving is a dirty word . . . he lives for today and that's all."

She is defiant—and talking more than I expected.

"There's times when he thinks I don't have money; but I do. I always keep a dollar in my pocket. If it was just for me, I wouldn't bother about it."

She sets her mouth tightly.

"But I have a son. He eats first—I get what's left. There's times when him and me and the baby are in the house and we got nothing to eat. I have to go down to my mother's and wait until the next check comes. *He* don't have any money . . . he ain't got a *dime* in his pockets"

In the bedroom, Ritchie suddenly hits his adolescent aunt with the plastic baseball bat. More squawling. Carol goes in to hit him again with the sandal; he cries again.

"I had feelings for him . . . but these are drifting further and further away. I see dudes on the street. They have cars and money . . . something to offer a girl; but he won't work— it drives me up the wall. I thought he would make a good husband. But he's afraid to get married. He spoke about it once; he hasn't spoken about it since."

I am writing as fast as I can in the notebook—I can't believe how much she is talking.

"Once before, I was gonna get married. This dude was the brother of somebody my sister was gonna marry. He was an interior decorator. If I needed money, I'd call him up and say this and that, and he'd give it to me. It got me closer to him. I even had an engagement ring and the wedding band waiting behind it. But I called the whole thing off. I stopped caring for him, I guess."

Ritchie rides his tricycle into the living room and bangs into the coffee table.

"Get outta here before I slap your face!"

Ritchie seems oddly hurt by this rebuff. He begins to whimper.

"I-I-I'm gonna tell dad . . . dy."

"He's talking about Jones," Carol says. "But he knows who his father is, too."

What will happen to this kid, I'm wondering. What is secure in his life? He is beaten every time he moves. Then he is loved—and beaten again. And who, after all, is his father? He doesn't know; and soon he'll have a brother or sister, and who will be *their* father? What can his world possibly be except a confused, constantly changing, frightening place? And how—most of all—can he be expected to be any different from his world?

"What about the new baby?"

"I don't know. The other girl's havin' one, too, you know."

"What do you feel about that?" I hate asking questions like this.

She pulls on the cigarette and stares at the ceiling, and finally stumbles into it. "I don't know . . . I don't know how to deal with . . . that."

"It means he'll have to choose, doesn't it?" I like myself even less as this goes on.

"Yeah."

"What do you think he'll do?"

"I don't know . . . I don't have the slightest idea."

Pause. Silence. I keep writing and hoping she'll go on without my asking.

"I'm gonna have it . . . I don't feel I should have an abortion. I want another baby."

"Won't your life be . . . complicated? Ritchie is a handful already."

She smiles, enjoying this, and I feel enormous relief. "Yeah, he's *bad*. I give him about ten beatings a day . . . it don't do no good." Carol laughs and her face wrinkles happily with maternal pride. She calls to Ritchie, who is standing by the tricycle, sucking his thumb.

"Come here so I can beat you again," she laughs.

"No, mumm . . . my," he protests. He toddles over slowly, She hoists him on one knee and lectures with mock indignation.

"Now what right you got to be hittin' Teresa with your baseball bat?" She wags her finger at him and he grabs it, gurgling happily. She lets him down gently.

"If you want Jones to go," I am asking, "why have the baby? Won't it be a link to him?"

"I don't know . . . why should it? If that was the case, I'd still be with Ritchie's father." Carol suddenly seems very strong.

The door is pushed open, and Jones waves hi-you-all from the kitchen. He stays out of the living room, as agreed; but he rattles pots and pans so loudly that he becomes an obvious presence. Carol ignores him.

The dog begins to whine, smelling food as Jones moves about the kitchen.

"SHUT UP YOU," Carol yells.

"It's always pissing or shitting on the floor and the rug," she adds. "Animal urine is strong. I can't get the smell out, and it's bad for the baby. And the fur shakes off all over the place."

In the kitchen, Jones opens a bottle of soda. Then he starts rummaging through the refrigerator.

"Is this salad good?" he yells.

He opens the freezer and pulls out several ice trays, dumping them noisily in the sink.

"My mother don't like me being with him," Carol observes. "She wants me to find somebody to marry and get a decent place to live. If he got a job and became responsible, it would be okay. But he just stays around, sleeping until twelve or one o'clock, knowin' he doesn't have anything to do. He wakes up, takes a shower, gets dressed, and goes out. It's like that every day."

Jones yells from the kitchen again. "You're gonna make the black-eyed beans, right?"

"There ain't no meat to put in them."

"Hey . . . you can make them without meat." He slams the refrigerator door.

"He's just layin up, free-loading . . . it ain't right. If it was me, I wouldn't be doing that, worrying about where I was gonna eat next. I'd be *doin'* something!"

"What about your life?"

"It's . . . okay. I got the welfare money; my mother is there when I need her. But if I didn't have him around, it would be easier."

Jones waves from the distance and walks out.

"It may end," she continues. "I feel like it will. I'm not doin' that good—so why do I need him to make it worse? I'm not doin' bad, you understand"—she sighs heavily—"but I'm not doin' so good, either."

Ritchie walks into the room holding his hand to his crotch. Carol takes him into the bathroom, pushing the whining dog behind the sink pipes. She stands him in front of the toilet bowl, steadies him, and pulls down his jeans.

"I have to hold him up or he'll pee all over everything. He knows what he's doing, but he likes to see the water go different places—all over the sink and everything."

She returns to the couch.

"Does the baby take a lot of time?"

"Yeah . . . but I don't have much else to do. I stay home a lot. I don't like too much excitement. I stay here . . . listen to the radio, watch TV, read books . . . and I take care of him. Maybe I visit my mother."

Carol leans on one elbow. She is looking at her hands; for

a moment, she says nothing, as if she is straining against some kind of heaviness.

"I'm depressed in some ways," she concludes as I close my notebook. "I guess I'll just live with it until things get better. Maybe he'll go away . . . or maybe he'll get better. It's hard to know. I'll just wait, I guess."

2

"I'm very worried. Where will the money come from?"

Another private talk—Jo-Anne this time. Jones' women are very unhappy. His world is suddenly quite fragile.

"I'm worried about cribs and clothes and doctor bills. And my father says I can't live here after the baby is born. I have to find a place as soon as I can."

She frowns.

"I read somewhere that a baby costs twenty-five thousand dollars to bring up until he's twenty-one. Who's going to pay for this?"

The baby is six weeks away. Jo-Anne is plump and ready, but her life is not conforming to her expectations. Her pregnancy hasn't changed Jones at all.

"Do you still want to marry him?" I ask, hating myself—again—for the question.

Jo-Anne takes this very seriously.

"I was real sure . . . once . . . I wanted to marry him . . . but now I'm not so sure. Everything going on is wrong . . . his other girlfriend and all."

"What do you mean?"

"He lies about it. He said last week he was going to a party alone; he went with her. I've got no chain around his throat —but he can tell me the truth. It hurts worst when I hear these things from people in the streets."

She sits dejectedly on a bench outside the tall buildings. It is a breezy, speckled day. She is tiny and round—and she has a great deal of anger inside her. I feel very divided about Jo-Anne's role in all this for I care about Jones, and I know she would be good for him. But she is crazy to stick around.

"As many times as you sit down and talk to him, it always is his way. He'll listen, but it goes in one ear and out the other. It doesn't penetrate. He wants me to leave my father's apartment and get the welfare. He keeps asking. But I'm putting it off; he would be living off me. The welfare's not enough for three people . . . you've seen how he eats. Sam, it's enough for a horse!"

Everyone in Jones' orbit, I'm thinking, has similar problems. He brings the razor edge of his troubled life tight against the throat of his family and his women. He seems to want to cut everyone, including himself. Those who love him try desperately to find out why his life is so painful—but the cost of this knowledge is high. Jo-Anne and Carol and Stella and Charles pay and pay . . . still trying to find out. And while they try, he takes everything they have as surely as he mugs fifty-year-old men outside of banks. The irony is that the answer eludes him as well.

He, too, is desperately unhappy.

"I still love him," Jo-Anne is saying, "but not like I used to; I won't do crazy things any more, like putting the knife to my father. But I still love him . . . I can't help it."

She smiles at a memory. "When he was on drugs, he was sweet and kind. He was wonderful. I'd hit him sometimes—he wouldn't hit back."

She stops, momentarily triumphant, and turns to me.

"He hits me sometimes now. When he was sick, he'd hit me. But he hasn't laid a hand on me since I've been pregnant."

Jo-Anne's dream of pregnancy remains that much intact.

When she returned from Arizona, he was in jail. She learned of it by calling Stella; after that, she wrote him. His release was a happy time for them. After the month with Jerry in the Bronx, they moved in with Stella and Charles.

Then she found he had other women.

"I felt like a fool. He kept me in the house and went out on the streets to fool around. He'd say 'Stay inside, the streets are dangerous . . . no place for a woman—especially *my* woman.'"

Jones became involved with Carol, a girl named Katie, and

another named Evelyn. Evelyn called the apartment one day; Jo-Anne answered the phone. They met in one of the parks.

"What do you want—something between your legs?" Jo-Anne screamed. "I've been with him for three years; you're trying to get something going *now?*"

But Jo-Anne left. "All this time he had two *other* girls," she remembers. "I didn't even know."

We've left the bench and are walking on First Avenue near Ninth Street. She points toward Avenue A.

"He doesn't like to walk that way. A lot of people from his dope fiend days are still around. He used to run con there, and he's afraid somebody will remember him."

She points west. "He doesn't walk on Second Avenue, either. He got over on people there, too." She grimaces. "I get tired of walking the same streets all the time."

I am searching—again—for reality among the tangled stories of Jones' life. Jo-Anne says she left him after discovering his girlfriends. Jones says he sent her away; she'd become too entangled in family fights. The ideas are only vaguely related.

Another question. What of Jones' love for "deep" conversations? What about his praise for her warmth and understanding?

Jo-Anne explodes.

"Sam, do you think we *talk?* We talk for an hour on the phone and say *nothing.* We have nothing in common! We don't get along when we're together. We always fight! What kind of life is that? He says he loves me—that's *words.* Words are something you write down; you buy a card in the store, it says I love you. *He hasn't done anything to prove it.* A man is someone who gives you money . . . if you give him money, are you putting on the pants . . . and that is what I've been doing for *four years!*"

"It's a rare day when he's nice. He comes around when he feels like it, three, four times a week, maybe less, and he's got to be *on* something to act nice, wine or smoke or something else . . . because when he's sober, he thinks of all his problems. He gets evil. He comes here and they'll all flow out on me. He'll start his roaring—not yelling, but a different thing, words with an attitude behind them, something you can sense."

Jo-Anne watches an ice cream wagon pass the corner, then sets her jaw firmly.

"He hasn't mentioned marriage in a long time. He don't want to be tied down again. He lost ten years of his life to heroin; he wants to go around and meet people and be a teen-ager again." She pauses. "But he can't do that. He's too *old* to be in the streets, hustling and all that. He's a man, now."

"What do you think will happen to him?" She is caught between anger and sadness now, and I feel a thickness gathering in my throat as I listen.

"If he has *deep* problems, he'll go back to heroin. I fear this a lot. I see him going further and further into doing wrong. Hustling and mugging means risking your life every day. Suppose somebody knifes him in the back. God forbid." Jo-Anne tosses her head nervously. "There's *got* to be easier ways to live."

We've walked back to the bench. Children are playing in a park behind us.

"I used to make him fight for money he got. I couldn't *give* it to him. He had to show some manhood, and he did. He would force me to give it up; and then *he* would make the rules. I would be doing something wrong and he would tell me to stop . . . and I would stop."

She wrings her hands and looks painfully at me as she talks. I dive hurriedly into my notebook. It is as though she is bleeding.

"I do care for him. I don't pity him . . . I used to when he was on dope, but I know he can do for himself. Some people would say you don't get to see your baby if you don't support him—I can't be that cruel. My girlfriend says she would raise the baby alone and say his father died in Vietnam. I can't do that . . . it's his flesh and blood, too. I want my child to see his father."

She is deeply saddened, but then I ask another question—

and she squares her shoulders, sits upright, and smiles bravely. She is a strong, brave woman of twenty—a woman in love.

"What about *your* life?"

"I suppose . . . I'll . . . keep sitting around and hope—pray, I guess—that he changes. I sat around four years; five or six weeks more ain't gonna hurt. By the end of the summer, I'll know how everything is working. He won't let his kid go out in the street with nothing; he's not . . . that cold-hearted."

She smiles half-bravely again.

"If I saw he was straightening out, I guess . . . I'd take that one chance . . . of marrying him and moving out. I still love him. I can't change that."

Dusk is moving down on the city, the young woman shifts nervously on the bench to keep warm. Time for her to leave, time for me to go and see Jones. I ask how the pregnancy has been.

"Terrible—the worst thing that could happen to anyone. I get back pains and stomach pains; I get sick all the time. I'm not scared because I have a good doctor and I'm going to a good hospital. If I had to go to a welfare hospital, I'd be scared. I wouldn't know anyone; I wouldn't know what to do."

She waves goodbye as the evening begins to settle. The baby is expected in August—but it will enter her life sooner.

Fifteen

———◆———

1

Midnight. In the small bedroom, the window overlooked a long line of tenement rooftops. On the edge of a narrow bed in the corner, Jones sat and smoked a cigarette, watching the smoke drift in half-circles toward the ceiling. It was wet-hot; the lights of buildings to the north poked through the fog in clusters of yellow and orange. Jo-Anne lay in the bed full of child and warm and wet in the early-summer stillness. Then she shifted her Madonna bulk under the sheet—and suddenly felt something. She said nothing.

In the heavy darkness, Jones got into his gray slacks, hoisted the brown suede and wool shirt over his shoulders, and pulled on his high-heeled platform loafers. He killed the cigarette in an ashtray next to an empty Boone's Farm bottle on the dresser. Jo-Anne wrapped herself in a cream-colored bathrobe, torn slightly at one pocket, and followed him to the door.

The baby was not due for another month.

A quick goodbye; he loped through the doorway, heels clicking. Morris would be home within the hour and he did not wish to be there. Jo-Anne turned the bolt and again felt the rush, the draining. It was not right; it was too soon. But there was pain. She wrapped the robe around her and walked to the bathroom.

There was blood in her urine; she felt pain and water draining. She knew that her water had broken, that the baby, early or not, was coming. Leaving the bathroom, she moved fast toward the telephone. Dr. Katz was on vacation, summering in Long Island, but his service reached him and he called back. The pains were beginning—sharp, piercing jabs. Wait an hour, Katz advised, then call his associate. If the baby came quickly, there would not be time for Katz to reach Manhattan.

The hour passed. The pains were now twenty minutes apart, sharp, jabbing contractions. Jo-Anne began to give way to panic. She called the associate; he said wait another hour—don't go to the hospital until they are four minutes apart. But she was upset. She had heard the stories of babies born in stairwells and back seats of taxicabs. There was no way to reach Jones. Carol's apartment—if Jo-Anne would call him there—has no telephone.

Morris, quiet and gray-haired, finally came home.

He moved quickly. The pains were less than fifteen minutes apart as Jo-Anne dressed in blue maternity slacks and a puffy beige blouse. It was nearly two in the morning; father and daughter left the apartment house and took the slow elevator to the street. They walked to First Avenue and joined a foggy population of shuttered liquor stores and late night clusters of street people. Morris saw a cab.

The ride to Mount Sinai was long and bouncing and painful, cars careening in and out of the fog in front of them. By the time the taxi pulled into the maternity wing's canopied entrance, Jo-Anne's contractions were six minutes apart. She was registered at the front desk, half in a fog now, then taken to a room with four empty beds.

2

Jones lifted another bottle of Boone's Farm to his mouth. In the warm night, the coarse sweater rubbed against his skin. Time for another shower. Carol's apartment was ten minutes away. He brought the bottle to his mouth again and threw back his head for a long pull.

The climb to Carol's door, up the five flights, seemed long

on this steambath night; he was breathing heavily as he reached the top. Carol and the baby were asleep; he settled into the small bed in the far corner of the room. An hour passed. He heard firecrackers, dogs barking, Spanish door-stoop chatter, the engines of cars and trucks. He peeled off his clothes and crawled into the other bed with Carol, who stirred and turned over to accommodate his presence.

Dawn. Then day brightened slowly and the street began to take on life, trucks, vendors, children. Carol nudged against him; they made love. He was sluggish from the short hours of sleep, rank from the wine on his breath. He turned over again and slept blissfully through the morning's gathering heat.

3

Hot lights, people with costumes and hidden faces . . . Jo-Anne was awake. A dark face mask was descending, a black cloud coming down. She flailed at her tormentors, slapping the man with the mask. Arms reached out and pulled her down, belts and buckles slid into place, and she was pinned to the operating table. The gas mask fell . . . one . . . two . . . three . . . four . . . and she was gone. Time passed and she rose out of the darkness briefly. "Push! Push!" someone was saying, and she knew her child was coming down.

Miles away, Jones slept on, turning fitfully now as the morning heat increased.

4

"It's a girl," the nurse smiled.

It was a six-pound, six-ounce baby, twenty inches long, the first child of a mugger, confidence man, and former heroin addict, and of a woman who once robbed her father to bring him money. The child was healthy, despite its premature ap-pearance. It rested in a cardboard cradle behind thick viewing

213

glass: it was wrapped in a pink blanket and displayed with half a dozen other human beings who did not ask to be born. Its existence thus far had been financed by the quiet man in baggy pants who stayed with his daughter until 5 A.M. In two days he would pay the hospital more than six hundred dollars. His granddaughter, he would be told, could not come home otherwise. And he knew the doctor bills would equal the hospital charges.

The baby, soon to be named Barbara, had puckered lips, red, wrinkled feet, and eyes clamped tightly shut as if she'd been drinking Boone's Farm for three days. She had dimples; occasionally she yawned toothlessly.

5

"It's Sam." The police lock turns and I walk into Carol's apartment. Her fourteen-year-old twin sisters, wearing owlish glasses and school dresses, are watching television; Jones is half out of the bedroom, showered and dressed, working the last of his tight curls into place.

It is a routine day; no one at this address—including me—knows the baby is born, no one expects it for another month —no one here will talk of it when it is. Jones is wearing his virmilion tank top plus the gray slacks of the previous night. He is not fully awake; he mumbles hello and walks past me to the bathroom. The dog, chained as always to the sink, raises its ears and moves carefully toward the back of the tiny toilet area. Jones unhooks it and motions toward the door. I follow him out and we climb the stairs to the roof.

"I'm training it," he says, choking the dog tightly as she tries to leap ahead of us. "Stay!"

The black tar is sticky in the afternoon sun. We sit on a low concrete wall between this building and another roof, passing Boone's Farm back and forth.

"All I want to do is buy time," Jones begins. "I want about five years on top, then I'll go to jail with a smile on my face."

He laughs in a low, dreamy way, taking a long pull on the wine. "Yeah, I could do that time with a *smile* on my face. I would have money, I would have made it."

He turns and looks at me.

"If Jo-Anne and the baby couldn't live on what I sent them, then wow, I don't know *what* they could live on!"

He is talking, again, about dealing cocaine. A stake of several hundred dollars to begin, then the money would turn . . . and turn . . . and turn. He hands me the bottle, shifting now to another part of the dream.

"Does that sound dumb—being willing to go to jail?"

I say it sounds . . . destructive . . . as though he is . . . almost happy to give up his freedom. I never know precisely what to say in these moments. I can't change him; it isn't my role. But I keep hoping—however naïve it seems—that something I say will make sense to him, that something will make him change his life.

He pulls out a crumpled joint and smooths it with his fingers.

"Yeah . . . maybe. But the streets do weird things to you. You live for the time you've got—and you gotta live right—a Cadillac, man, clothes to change into five or six times a day."

He lights the joint. "Jeff's old man is doin' one-to-five on a federal bust now. But he had the money to make it right. He got busted with three pounds of cocaine. But he was making a lot of money, and he kept makin' it while he paid lawyers to delay things."

"But he's in jail."

"Yeah, but you know, one night Jeff and I went over to his house and he was doin' some business. This dude brought him money, and he had this roll in his pocket. He took part of it, oh, say, twenty-three hundred, and he gave it to his wife. He said, here, you keep this for me. Then he asked us if we wanted to go out and shoot craps with him."

Jones hands me the joint.

"That seemed cool. I had a hundred and fifty on me and Jeff had gotten paid, and he had his leg money and his school money, so we was feelin' flush, you know?"

The dog, which had been nosing around the wall at the other end of the building, suddenly bounds across the Tarvia. Jones shifts his weight off the wall, bracing himself. The dog will jump.

"We went to this house in Brooklyn. It was full of people and they said, good, come on in, we've got new blood. They invited me to roll the dice. That was cool; I stepped up and I put a hundred on the table, and wow, everybody got quiet. I thought they were impressed, you know? I rolled on fifty of it, and I blew it, and Jeff came up and he put down fifty and it got quiet again. He fell through his money fast."

Jones grabs the dog and pushes it away. He looks at me with a pie-eating grin.

"Then . . . then . . . then Jeff's dad came up to the table, and I looked to see what he was gonna throw—and he starts with *fifteen hundred dollars*! I couldn't believe it! Everybody got noisy again, and I realized what was happening. I had really chumped my smitty, chumped it good! The place was full of dealers and people who really had theirs—we had nothin'!"

Jones has his hands in the air, fingers spread wide, combing the hot afternoon air.

"I couldn't believe the things Jeff's old man did. He kept throwing that bread down, and he was smilin' and drinking and it meant *nothin'* to him. He lost fifty-five hundred. Can you dig that? *Fifty-five hundred dollars.* He didn't even blink. He went out to the car afterward, and he was feelin' just fine. He went to this bar, and you know he bought everybody in the house a drink!"

In his enthusiasm, Jones bangs his heels with a thud into the hot Tarvia.

"I heard later he got the twenty-three hundred he left with his wife and lost that, too. Wow, that is showing something—a dude who has really got *his*. I've been in his house in Brooklyn, you know? There is a stereo set in every room! Big, deep carpets and fine furniture and all the best booze—and his clothes, wow, I mean he is *fly!*"

The bottle is drained, and the joint is gone, and the dog

has returned to nuzzle Jones' legs. He slips the chain over her neck and we go down the stairs. A quick handshake and I leave.

6

All through the housing projects, narrow, crowded elevators rose and fell like pistons while people talked. In the park, the benches were filled with gossip. Word of Jones' new baby was passing. Charles Jones stopped his son's friends. Jo-Anne's girlfriend Sally made the rounds; both were searching anxiously for the missing father. Sally walked into one elevator, saw Carol's mother, and breathlessly blurted out the news. Inadvertently, the connection was made.

All day, Jones had an odd premonition that he should call home. He dismissed it. That afternoon, he decided to visit Jo-Anne. He stopped to telephone her—no answer, and he wondered about it; he'd said he might come by.

He called again an hour later . . . still nothing. He let the phone ring for several minutes. Again he had the odd feeling he should call home—he didn't.

At the hospital, a smiling nurse brought the baby, all wrinkles and pouty facial expressions, for the six o'clock feeding. Jo-Anne had watched the telephone nearly all day. She remembered that she once asked Jones to be with her in the delivery room; he said no, he wanted nothing to do with that. She grew angry at his absence.

Jones returned to Carol's apartment, which was empty. He sank onto the couch, threw his feet onto the coffee table, and turned on the television. But something bothered him. He should call his mother. Carol's apartment has no telephone— so he pushed the thought from his mind.

In the middle of "Kung Fu," Carol returned with a girl-friend. She looked at him strangely.

"I want to talk to you."

He nodded and kept his eyes on the set. Carol said she'd talk when the girlfriend left.

"Kung Fu" ended and Carol agreed to walk the girl to the bus; she asked Jones to wait. He nodded; but then, because the night was hot, he decided to take the dog up on the roof.

Carol returned and waited nearly an hour without knowing where he had gone. She finally climbed the stairs. He was sitting on a wall smoking a joint. She said nothing; Jones ignored her. He could see she was angry, but he preferred to wait for the complaint, the fight, or whatever was coming. Carol stood silently beside him for several minutes.

He walked to the other end of the roof. She followed him.

"You know what, motherfucker?"

"What?" He turned toward her.

"Your friend had a baby."

"What friend you talkin' about?"

"You know I hate to say her name. Jo-Anne had the baby."

Jones looked at her with surprise and disdain. "No, Carol, no . . . no, that's a lie. The baby isn't due for a month."

Carol thrust her chin at him. "It's no lie. Your father says it happened. Call him, *see* if I'm lying."

It was too early, it was impossible . . . it was beginning to sink in. The unanswered telephone in Jo-Anne's apartment, the premonition he should call home—Jones reached for the dog and slapped the chain on it hurriedly. He moved fast. The dog was quickly chained in the bathroom, the police lock put in place . . . he and Carol walked to the street to find a bar with a pay telephone.

7

Midnight. I am reading and halfway to bed when the telephone rings.

"Sam!" A jukebox booms in the background, mixed with a low roar of nighttime voices. "Sam, Jo-Anne had the baby!"

I'd asked him to call me when it happened. "Tonight?" I begin, pulling my sleepy self together. "It's too early."

"Yeah, dig it, but she had it. I called my parents. It's a girl."

"Is it okay?" I am thinking that premature babies die, or at least spend time in incubators, and if they spend time in incubators, it costs money that nobody in the fractured Jones family really has.

"Yeah, as far as I know."

"Are you going to visit it tonight?" I had wanted to be with him the night it happened.

"I can't. The hospital doesn't open until the morning."

"Which hospital?"

"I don't remember. I forgot to ask my dad."

We agree to meet in an hour. I want to be with him, hospital or not. I feel moved by this event as if something has happened that everyone should know about. The fog is up again as I walk outside. A man and a woman talk in front of my door, and their dogs, a Husky and a Great Dane, nuzzle. I want to tell them. I detour past an outdoor restaurant and watch couples lingering briefly before closing time. Past the all-night restaurant on the corner, past cleaners and drugstores and florist windows, past another man and a woman talking in front of another apartment building.

Something monumental has happened. Don't these people realize?

In my crazy idealism, I am thinking this one child will make a difference, a change in a violent man's life, even a *metaphysical* change in the city's life—then I stop myself. I don't believe that. I don't believe that Jones' first child will change him. A new child brings only hope . . . and hope, like everything else, must confront life.

"What can I teach my child except mugging?" Jones asks, and on a foggy Manhattan night I am offering up the middle-class religion of rebirth, the new child as the hope of the world. Wow!

But as the subway rumbles into the tunnel, and I am telling myself, no, I do not believe one more child will make a difference, another part of me insists that it will. Jones' humanity is the key. Even with all that has happened, we must *still* reach out to it.

I'm surprised to see Carol. She plans to spend the night at her mother's—at least that is the rationale—and she'll walk with us to the projects. Jones plans to walk and talk all night; she is not anxious to let him alone with his thoughts. We begin walking vaguely toward the projects.

Carol's presence is an immediate problem. It is difficult to talk about your newborn child by one woman when another, who carries your three-month-old fetus, is walking beside you. So we are silent. The streets are dark lines of grim buildings, garbage cans out front, cats among them. The city lamps stick yellow tongues through the mist.

We pass several tall, empty buildings. They surround a long courtyard. Jones breaks the silence to offer some social criticism.

"This here's the project that was closed down because they would only let Jews in." He laughs loudly. "It cost a lot of bread—so I guess they'll have to let everybody in to start gettin' their money back."

Still no mention of the baby. The development's dark windows are sleeping eyes.

Jones laughs again. "They built this project because Jewish people was complaining they couldn't go to synagogue down here without getting mugged. Wow, that would be a drag—going to church and thinking of God and being mugged."

"Orthodox Jews don't take much money to temple, do they?" I'm playing the game, too.

"No . . . but muggers ain't heard that." Jones laughs loudly at this. "Wow, you are going to the house of God, but you got curses on your mind now. That old motherfucker—he mugged me! You got these bad thoughts and you can't pray, wow!"

It is after 2 A.M. We pass a flophouse called the Atlantic Hotel.

Carol screams and jumps behind me, grabbing my jacket. A large furry rat sits boldly in Atlantic's hallway.

At the East River, Carol leaves us . . . protesting, sullen. We sit on a wooden abutment overlooking the water, and I watch the river's waves wash against the muddy bank.

"I like water," Jones begins. "I got to liking it in the Navy. It calms you down."

Below us a cement seawall drops six feet to a shoreline of black sand. We sit at the cross hairs between the Brooklyn and Manhattan bridges; each is a string of lights rushing across the river like tracer bullets. A skyscraper's neon time-and-temperature sign says 2:45 A.M., 73 degrees. Behind us the abutment touches a parking area for garbage trucks; now and then one lumbers in and works its machinery with loud clanking and spitting sounds. The dark water is animated by lights from the shore.

"I'm lost, man, I'm really lost. I wasn't ready. My head isn't where it should be."

He hands me the Boone's Farm. His face is dark with blood and emotion.

"Before there was only me. I only had to please *me*—but I've got a child now. This is one hell of a change!" He throws his head back as if to howl. "Wow, I don't know what to do!"

Jones lights a joint and exhales with a whooshing sound.

"I have to go one of two ways . . . it's hard to know what to do. I want to see my child, you know? If I go one way, I see my child a lot. That means a job—and fuck that! But if I live the way I want to, I won't see my child but once in a while, you know?"

He is resting on his elbows, shoulders collapsed under the weight of his thoughts. Suddenly he laughs again and gestures toward the water.

"And so-o-o-o, king of the sea," he intones loudly, "t-a-l-k to me."

Silence. I am drinking Boone's Farm and watching him out of the corner of my eye.

"And wow! I can't even talk to Carol about this. I can see the look on her face."

Wine and smoke begin to compete with the conversation. The water—and the light bouncing off it—seems very close, almost washing over us. It is 3 A.M. Suddenly Jones throws up his hands.

"How the fuck do you react to something like that—being the last one to know? My life is nothing but trouble. All this time I kept thinking, 'Call your mother.' I can't do *anything* right. I mean how do I even go *up* there?"

"Take some . . . flowers, maybe?"

"Ain't that a kick in the ass—I'm broke!"

"If you need it, I've got money."

"Yeah, but what do I *say*? Everybody else heard about it. When I go up there, and her father is there, he'll look at me with a mean face. Man, I feel dumb! I can't stay away from the hospital—Jo-Anne would feel I had a cold heart—but if I go up there, he will be there. He will hate me."

Jones takes a long pull on the Boone's Farm and slumps forward again, dropping his hands to let the bottle sink into the sand.

"Wow, I am the father . . . and I haven't seen the baby yet. The people at the hospital will look at me funny. They will talk about me. I've worked in hospitals, and I know how they talk."

He drops his head into his hands.

"Sometimes I think my life is timed wrong, you know?"

More silence. The river is blinking at me.

"Check this out. I'll get her candy and flowers to fix things. No, wait, can she eat candy? Maybe she can't—what the fuck, I'll get it anyway."

He takes a long drag on the joint. The river keeps moving, and I say something about how it'll be all right once he gets there, how the gifts will help, but if he was listening, it passes by.

"Water keeps moving, you know? It keeps moving, like life; it just keeps going around and around."

I know he is saying something, but it is bouncing off the outside of my head. A boat goes past, and its waves lap loudly against the shore.

"It goes around, you know? The water you see here, it washes against the shore and some of it stays behind and is picked up by the sun. The sun makes it into air and this goes up and into the clouds, where it turns around and comes back down as rain."

He turns to me.

"It's a circle, man . . . it's like life, going around and around and you can dig that there is no way to stop it. Nobody can change what is happening—nobody."

He suddenly thrashes the air with his open hand, fingers spread wide.

"Wow, it sounds so stupid. You're the father, the nurse will say, how come you didn't know? If I was a businessman I'd say I was gone on a business trip—but I haven't got a suit. I'm serious . . . they will *know* I'm not from some office. All I've got is two-piece suits. Nobody wears them to offices. They will look and they will know I've been to jail, and they will talk and say, wow, that's one strike against the baby."

Jones wags his forefinger in the air, imitating an angry nurse. Then he begins to chuckle—it is absurdly, darkly humorous.

"Excuse me, nurse," he begins, moving his shoulders and hands in a mimic stance, "can I talk to you? The mother of my child is Jo-Anne, and my child was just born. Could you tell me where she is? I was indisp-o-s-e-d, and I couldn't make it to the birth. Uh, you see, I work in the space program, and I'm not supposed to tell you"—Jones makes a conspiratorial face—"but we are working on a nuclear aircraft for the Nam and we had to work late."

He stops. "No, wait, how about this? I work in this observatory, and you know, we were checking out this star shining in the daytime, and it's a top-secret project, and I couldn't be reached." He stops again. "No, man, my clothes will give me away! I could wear pressed slacks and a good knit, but my shoes will tell them what is happening.

"Fuck it, I'll tell her I work for the FBI and we are working on drug arrests and dig it, I have to look like one of the people."

The river keeps rolling and Jones and I are really . . . drifting.

"Now . . . maybe I could still tell them I am a businessman. I do have this gray suit, the one at Carol's. I could wear it with a light-colored mock turtleneck and . . . fuck it, Jack, I still don't have the right shoes!"

"What about the brown loafers?" I'm getting into this, too.

"Yeah . . . but then I'd have to wear a brown knit to match it. That would look too flash."

"Right . . .yeah," I'm thinking. "That makes sense."

"Hey, wow . . . dig this. I walk into the hospital looking right with the slacks and a nice knit, and I have got my father's briefcase. I go up to the nurse and say, uh, excuse me, miss, but my child was born and I would like to see it. You see, I am a hit man for the Mafia and I was out of town on a job. I couldn't be reached. And she will go, 'Oh! oh!' and step back and that will take care of things."

The wine is nearly drained, and the joint is down to a tiny roach.

"Hey, check this out . . ." He begins to laugh that peculiar half-embarrassed laugh that emerges when he is deeply into himself. "Excuse me, nurse, but I am a mugger and I was out on a caper and I didn't hear the news. No, I'll do this . . . I'll say I'm a mugger and I was waiting for you, nurse. I was waiting outside your home; I thought you were on the day shift—but you didn't come out, so I came up here to get the money."

We are both nearly falling over with laughter.

"That will put her off guard. *Nobody* will talk."

He finally winds down. A garbage truck turns its lights on us for a moment, clanking noisily; we both turn to look.

"Uh, you see, nurse, I was taking a shower in Brooklyn, and I couldn't be reached. No . . . I had to take my dog home, nurse, and he lives in Philadelphia. Uh, you see, nurse, I work for an elevator company and we were out on a job and I got stuck between floors . . ."

It is past 4 A.M. according to the skyscraper clock in Brooklyn. The wine and the smoke are gone; it is time to move. Jones will walk to his parents' apartment and wait for his mother to get up. I need sleep. He walks me to the D train in the darkness. I am still wondering if this is really happening. Tomorrow, we'll visit the baby.

Sixteen

————◆————

1

The hospital complex occupies half a dozen blocks of high-priced land between upper Fifth and Madison Avenues, sprawled about like an elegant housing project. To the south, down Fifth Avenue, its neighbors are millionaires who have doormen, drivers to bring around limousines, and private schools for their children. Harlem lies in the opposite direction. The buildings begin to deteriorate several blocks north, showing greater numbers of garbage cans, more broken windows, and considerably fewer doormen. Further uptown, they become tenements. Whole families spill out of single rooms, junkies nod on the doorsteps, dealers and prostitutes work the corners.

The clinic entrance has a canopy and a uniformed doorman to call taxis. Barbara's father uses neither; he frequents a wine shop on Madison Avenue, slightly south, which makes it more efficient to lope down a side walkway meant for wheelchairs.

Jo-Anne and Sally are chattering excitedly while the new father sits silently nearby as I arrive. Jones and Sally do not get along; they talk to each other only in high school-style putdowns—"so's your sister," or "don't talk to me anymore."

Jo-Anne, meanwhile, holds court from her bed, blonde hair pulled tightly back. A bottle of hard candy sour balls, a box of butter cookies, and Erle Stanley Gardner's *The Sun Bather's Diary* sit at the foot of her throne. Directly outside the room, eight babies lie in cardboard cradles. It is a pet shop window; visitors gathered outside make faces at the puppies inside.

The baby, though premature, is healthy. So—for the moment—is the parents' relationship. Jones arrived a day late, but he arrived; Jo-Anne soon forgot her anger as they gazed through the thick glass at their daughter. ((All Jones' fears of the previous night were nothing. No one at the hospital said anything.) Jo-Anne pads happily behind us at the window now, all smiles; it soon becomes feeding time. Hospital regulations require me to leave, and Jones suggests a trip to the wine shop to kill time. As we turn to leave, Barbara soundlessly turns on her stomach behind the window, hands failing, head down in her blankets as though she might drown in an inch of bathtub water.

Jones presses his hands urgently against the glass.

A tall black woman pulling the blinds notices Barbara's curious predicament. She takes the baby's tiny head in one hand, spreading her fingers as one might grip a melon, and twists. Barbara's body follows easily, without discomfort.

Jones is horrified.

"Hey, wow, whatta you doin' to my child, *my child*, you ole bitch . . . don't move my child that way!" If the woman hears his voice or the tapping of his hardened fingernails on the glass, she doesn't look up.

In the liquor store a clerk wraps the Boone's Farm in a small bag. We drink it on the corner near the luncheonette.

A Puerto Rican girl wearing fiery lipstick, tight Levis, and platform shoes walks by. "Hey, baby," he grins drunkenly, "I would like . . . I would like . . . to be the father of *your* child." He leers serpent-like as she walks away. He has been drinking and smoking joints without sleep for more than thirty-six hours.

He drifts a moment. "I guess I'll have to get a job." Pause. "Wow, fuck *that!*"

Back inside the hospital, a nurse pulls the curtain around the young family. Jones throws a cloth on his shoulder—the Official Burper. He also provides the guiding hand for a bottle-and-nipple insertion of an ounce of glucose water after Jo-Anne and the baby finish the main event. "I feel strange," he says afterward. "I'm not used to holding babies, you know?"

2

Visiting hours again. Jerry arrives, and we go to the window again to watch the baby. Jo-Anne clucks at her child through the window. Jones and Jerry stand on opposite sides of her.

"The baby don't look nothin' like him," Jerry says. Everyone laughs. There follows some jocular discussion of the origins of Barbara's ears, nose, cheekbones, hands, eyes, and other anatomical parts.

"Oh, wow!" Jones cuts in, high from drinking and drugs and no sleep. "You trying to tell me I don't know my own child. Man . . . man . . . man, she's got *my* features, my nose, my ears. I'm serious, man, She's got Jo-Anne's nose, that's all, and she's got Jo-Anne's thumb. But check this out. She's got *my* brain. She *thinks* like me."

"Yeah, she sleeps all the time," says Jerry.

"No . . . no, I'm serious. When I sleep and I hear a noise, I jump. She hears a noise, and she jumps, too."

"She's like you, all right," Jo-Anne smiles oddly. "She has that evil look in her sleep, she grins up at you with it."

"Yeah, she's fly, she's really together."

Behind the glass, a white-clad East Indian woman lifts Barbara and rocks her gently. Jones questions whether she is holding his baby correctly.

"Hey, man . . ." But visiting time has ended again. The woman returns the baby to its box, then closes the window. The timing is bad. Jones isn't ready to stop basking in the limelight provided by his firstborn.

"Wow," he blurts out drunkenly, "this funky broad is gonna pull my child away. Hey, don't *do* that!"

But the woman, hearing nothing, moves the boxes into a

row against the far wall. Jones' baby, having first come to her attention, is positioned farthest away.

"Wow, you are a foul broad!" Jones yells, evoking a wave of tittering from others around the window. "Wow, you old broad, I'm gonna take you off. I meeaan . . . don't *move* my child like that!"

It is for naught. The orange-striped shades crash down. The maternity wing is closed. Jo-Anne must return to the hospital's womb.

3

Jo-Anne will be home tomorrow.

"Wow," Jones is saying. "I gotta get Pampers . . . I gotta get a *lot* of stuff " He is bleary-eyed and swinging free and easy between the effects of little or no sleep, gallons of wine, smoke, pills, and fatherhood. He spent the night at Jerry's, falling asleep about sunrise.

Today, the ward is crowded. Sally is sitting by the bed. Jerry has brought Ruth and their baby. Jones, red-eyed and unshaven, has gone through yet another pint of Boone's Farm this morning.

I complete the list. I've arrived in a car, so my importance is considerably exaggerated. I agree, in fact, to drive everyone to the Lower East Side. A confrontation with Charles Jones is promised.

"My old man wants to talk," Jones says. "I think he wants to give me money, and that can't *even* happen. This is my child, not his."

As we arrive, the brothers suggest a refueling stop—a six-pack of beer and more Boone's Farm; Ruth also wants milk and groceries.

"All I need now," Jones announces as he passes the bottle, "is to see Carol. Fuck it, man, that would be *too much*."

Times passes. Then the inevitable. Carol walks by the car in pink hair curlers—and sees us.

Jerry and Ruth say hello in husky voices; I nod. Jones

gets out, and they walk to the next parked car and lean against it. Carol's face is wooden.

A pudgy housing cop, pockets bulging with notebooks, handcuffs, and flashlight, walks by.

Then a middle-aged black woman waves. "Hey, how come you ain't boastin' about your daughter? You had a daughter, right?"

"Right," Jones smiles. Carol smiles, too, acknowledging the woman's greeting. They sit on the hood of the car drinking beer. Jones puts his arm around her waist and pulls her in. She resists. He wraps the arm around her shoulders . . . kissing her cheek . . . gathering her in for a full embrace.

They talk for a moment longer. Then, arms around each other, they walk to the doorway of a nearby drugstore.

For a moment, Carol stands beside him, head down. They disappear inside, where Jones tells her not to worry; he is coming back.

Then he returns to the car alone.

4

Music from the stereo set floods the empty living room, its crest pushing into the hot, busy kitchen where the family is gathered. Charles Jones stands over the table slicing ham on a grinder with a circular blade. The pink meat falls into ragged rows like torn playing cards. Hands all around the table reach for it. Biscuits bake in a small electric roaster.

As we enter, there is silence. Charles continues to work the grinder, neither looking up nor saying hello. Stella sits at the table, smoking a cigarette and surveying the commotion. Bruce is wolfing down ham and biscuits.

"Hey, Pops," Jerry says, "that record is bad. You gotta get rid of it."

"You know the way out," Charles Jones answers in crisp words, cranking out pink, ragged slices like an organ grinder. "The door is open." He does not look up.

Charles Jones turns to his oldest son.

"You've got a child now—when are you going to settle down?"

Jones turns heatedly. "Father, when you . . . you had your first child, did *you* settle down?"

Charles Jones continues to slice ham. His face, a fragile assembly of lines and large eyes, reads suffering, martyrdom, and the patience of Job. He is nervous about my presence—but a genial host. I am offered biscuits, ham, and beer; when I take them, he seems to relax.

Jones retreats to the bedroom to change clothes.

"How do you think all this will turn out?" I begin.

Pops pours beer into my glass and says nothing for a moment.

"I don't know." Pause. "I *do* know he's got to do something about Carol. She's not for him; what he's doing is wrong. He's got to get out of that nigger's house. Carol's got to take a long walk."

He opens another can of biscuits.

"I can't manage him. He's got too hard a head—I don't want to break his spirit, but how would *you* like to see your son in jail?"

"You think all this talk about a job means anything?"

"I'm wondering. He has been a *bit* excited." The delicate lines on Charles' face become darker. "But with him, this can last twelve or twenty-four hours—that's all. I've seen it before. The other night he asked me how to raise a daughter. I said, you start *now*."

He glances over his shoulder nervously to check on the biscuits.

"*I* can't raise the baby. It's time for me and Stella to take trips and *enjoy* the money we've saved."

He leans forward angrily. "I'll tell you this: I am going to be the blackest member of *my* family. *He* is going to get rid of that nigger—and I mean lowlife, I don't just mean black—and do the right thing by his child. He's *got* to!"

"What about Carol's child?"

"He's got to make a choice, doesn't he?"

A large shopping bag filled with Pampers, pink blankets,

and baby clothes leans against a nearby wall. Charles watches his son moving about the bedrooms.

"Look at that," he announces to the room. "He's found my cologne!"

Jones walks out holding a shimmering blue sweater against his gray pants. "How about this?"

"It's too warm tonight," asserts Pops, assuming the role of fashion coordinator. "Are you going to Jerry's tonight?"

"Yeah."

"Then wear a tank top. I've got one in the bedroom."

Charles turns to me, smiling and shaking his head theatrically. "He's *so* vain." But Jones is right behind him. He slaps his father playfully on the shoulder. "This is my teacher," he grins.

"You know," Charles continues after Jones returns to the bedroom, "he had the nicest singing voice. He was on 'Star Time.' But every time he went to an audition, he messed it up."

Charles sighs deeply, shifting to his martyred look.

"*That* is his problem. It's been the same all his life. If he has a job, he'll get up at seven like he's supposed to, but then—no matter what—he'll send two hours in the bathroom. Then he'll get to the job and say, "I'm here, let's get started.' "

Charles Jones spreads his hands as if to say something profound.

"Life isn't like that," he concludes.

Seventeen

1

The highway is a blur of red and orange metal-light motion. I am driving Jones to the hospital and it is past visiting hours. He is slumped in the front seat, saying little. He returns to a familiar theme.

"I love my daughter, you can dig it, right?"

I'm harassed by erratic traffic moving around me in jerky patterns. Jones is a silhouette in the corner of my eye.

"Right."

"I loved her the first time I saw her. I would fight the world for her."

I'm preoccupied with traffic. I make a minimal response.

"I have talked to the Families," he continues, still slumped oddly forward. "I want them to set me up in drugs—but they won't do it because I was *on* them. So maybe I will do it with Jeff's uncle, who has got some of his old man's action now. I have got to have five good years. I've got to do it right so my girl can live her life with the things she needs."

He sits up.

"What do you think?"

I am stopped stone still by the question.

Wildly different parts of me start to talk. One voice is yelling: *"Why don't you get a job you son of a bitch and live like the rest of us? Stop making our lives miserable, stop frightening us. Give us our cities back!"*

But the law-and-order man in me has nothing constructive to say. We all know Jones is selfish, neurotic, destructive,

232

ruthless . . . the problem is what to do about it. In wealthy communities like Shaker Heights, Beverly Hills, or Riverdale, he and fellow neurotics might joyride, take pills, and impregnate shop girls. In the Lower East Side, they become heroin addicts and muggers.

As long as our society, led by it's law-and-order advocates, tolerates ghettos, we will have muggers. It's as simple as that.

The question, then, is what to say tonight. He has so much strength—he quit heroin, for example—so much potential that I am searching desperately this moment for an answer that will serve him. We are friends, this mugger and I, *this human being and I,* and somehow I must say something to help both of us.

"Look," I begin, "I can only be straight with you."

We are so different. Who in God's name am I to tell him how to live?

"I have to turn you on to one thing which is missing," I go on. "The missing part is that money won't matter to the little girl. Love is what matters, and if you have to do time, love won't be there. She won't have love because she won't have you."

He lights a cigarette and drags deeply on it.

"I can dig that, yeah. But there's another thing." He stops to let his thoughts fall into a comfortable cadence.

"When I was small, you know, Pops was out of work and I had to go to school without the right clothes. I didn't have enough lunch money either. I felt bad about this. I don't want my daughter to feel this way. She's my *own.*"

The argument is joined. Son of the Middle Class Craftily Convinces Evil Mugger to Go Straight.

"Yeah, but if you go to jail, she'll feel worse. She won't have you and the love and teaching you can give her. You won't be there—and if you stay in crime you will go to jail, it's inevitable. You can dig *that.*"

"Fathers are a dime a dozen, you dig it? There is always somebody around to do that thing."

He has begun to hiccup from the wine and drugs. It is even harder than normal to talk.

"It's the (hic) mother that counts, and she will be there to give (hic) love. If I do things right, she will have what she needs to raise my (hic) daughter right."

"Little girls need their fathers . . . they want to be around them; they need to have a man around, a father, you know, so they can know one man well enough to make comparisons with others . . ."

I am talking off the top of my head—I have no children.

"It's important to have a father around the house to play with, you know, someone who will really get down with you when there are things to learn the mother can't teach."

"Yeah . . . yeah . . . yeah, I dig."

But he puts his head in his hands as if to wipe away the information. Prison and martyrdom seem more romantic.

"Yeah . . . what the fuck."

The debate falls away from us. I pull up to the clinic. Jones disappears inside for about fifteen minutes. It is late, but the nurse lets him upstairs long enough to give Jo-Anne the gifts that Charles bought. He gets into the car again, and we drive to a liquor store for another bottle of Boone's Farm.

2

Nearly midnight now, a hot summer night filled with poor people. We sit in the parked car near the projects, finishing the bottle. All around us, kids are learning to fight, fists up, feet raised for karate thrusts at each other, shadowboxing. It is all the business of growing up: identity, manhood, ego—and survival.

"There's one thing I haven't told you," Jones says, cupping his hands around a cigarette. "I don't know if it should be in the book."

I hold the bottle in my lap and wait.

"I've done some hits—you know, a contract. It was right after I got out of prison, and I needed some bread."

"Oh . . . wow!"

That's me, not Jones.

In an instant, a fog of shock covers me. I thought I had everything. But I hadn't expected . . . the cold, calculated robbing of life. For I believed all along—and I still want to believe—that Jones hurts his victims only as a last resort. Murder! This time *I* need the bottle; and in the hot night I lift it high to drain a generous slug of cheap apple-flavored forgetfulness.

Silence; a stillness in the air smothering sound. The walls of my mind are soundproofed by shock. The law-and-order man suddenly has nothing to say. The liberal college student is mute. So the reporter, the fellow with the job to do, takes over—and hopes this is a joke, or a neurotic bit of braggadocio.

"Tell me about it."

Jones shifts in the seat. He takes the bottle back. He starts slowly. "It was . . . up in the Bronx. I was known to some people up there . . . I had the rep that I could come down heavy if there was a fight. So one night I'm high on smoke, and I walk into this bar. I see a dude named Cuba. He is from the island, you dig it, and he is into numbers and he does some things in drugs."

Pause.

"I had sold him a TV set when I was doing the burglary thing, and so he knew me."

Jones pulls on the bottle, a full quart, and across the street two kids in their early teens are slap-boxing.

"We started rapping, and after a while, he was telling me he had some business to do. I asked how much it paid. He said four thousand, and I said, wow, I'll do that thing! He said okay. He would give me half before I did it and the other half afterward, he said. I was high, you know? I didn't really know whether I would do it, but the money looked good. I figured maybe I would beat him for it."

He lights a joint and the glowing end of it burns bright orange in the dark car.

"Anyway, I was high on smoke and I said I'd do this thing. But I really figured I would beat him for the two thousand. He gives me the money and takes me down to this place to get a weapon. They had everything there except tanks! He gave me a .38 and told me to throw it away if I used it, or bring it back if I didn't."

A police car pulls into the block. The cop at the wheel barks something at the two teen-agers in the middle of the slap-fight. They become robots, shoulders drooping, arms dangling uselessly, heads down. The patrol car pushes on into the steamy night—one of the kids yells something at its receding red tail and the fight continues. Jones is loosening up now.

"I had this gun and I was still gonna beat him, but then I remembered something my uncle, my mother's brother, said. Moms don't like to admit it, but he's with the Families. He said you don't take money from the Family unless you do the job. Or you don't get to spend it."

I nod.

"So I went to this street where these two dudes lived. They were black dudes and they had done wrong, I guess. I laid for them one at a time. I caught the first one in a hallway, and I cut his throat. It was very fast."

He stops. He doesn't like talking about this, and I am not taking notes. I'm thinking suddenly of Danny who talked of the alternatives of Jones' life. A portfolio of stocks would influence him one way, the violence of his environment make him behave another, right?

But a contract? Jones would end a life simply to enhance his own? It reaches to such primitive levels that after months and months of questions and talk and shared experiences and . . . and . . . I am speechless. Here is the man Hobbes talked about; he can remove all civilized restraints when he wishes, all the carefully worked-out spiritual and legal codes thought to keep people from tearing each other to pieces . . . they mean nothing to him.

And yet I still find Jones disturbingly human.

"What about the other dude?"

He is finishing the Boone's Farm and offers me a last chance at it before he takes the final swill.

"I laid for him the same way. I caught him from behind in

another hallway and did the job with a hammer. I left fast. I don't even remember seeing him hit the ground."

"What did you do with the gun?" I ask numbly, at bottom with my emotions about this writing project.

"I took it back. I didn't use it because I figured I could do the jobs better with my hands. It's safer to do things quietly."

Jones throws his head back, finishing the bottle with a long pull.

"The man was impressed, real impressed that I didn't use it. He asked if I wanted to do other jobs. I said no. I didn't want to be a hit man. I didn't feel there was any future in it."

He throws the bottle out of the window.

"Besides, I had enough money to keep me going for a while."

Silence. I can't think of a thing to say. All I can do is hope he's lying.

Jerry and Ruth lean in the window of the car. Carol and little Ritchie are trailing behind. Ritchie has ice cream on his face, and Carol has combed out her curlers. I look over my shoulder and see other groups of kids slap-fighting. Jerry proposes loudly that we all go to the Bronx. It is agreed.

I beg off, tired of all this, anxious to extinguish it with sleep. Jerry and Ruth and their baby and Carol and Ritchie and Jones crowd into the car and I agree to drop them at an uptown subway stop. Jones is due at the hospital at 11 A.M. to help Jo-Anne and her father take the baby home.

3

It is three days after I've left Jones and his entourage at the uptown subway stop. He has money today—a lot of it—and he wants to go shopping. Father and daughter, all of five days old, are "steppin' out" . . . gonna show the neighborhood what style really is.

So he needs clothes, new ones, fly ones, and the baby needs

a carriage. He's checked out a stroller modeled after a Cadillac (with a fringed top), but the price is too high, so we are going to try S. Klein's.

We walk down Houston Street, past the delicatessens and open shops; the sunny day is stirred by a light breeze.

"How was it bringing the baby home?"

"I didn't wake up in time." His eyes are aimed at the sidewalk.

"I went to my parents' house, and we all went to Jo-Anne's Monday. It was a big family thing. Morris talked to my father and mother—the usual stuff. Jo-Anne shouldn't of had the baby and I was a dope fiend, and who was gonna pay for everything and all that."

He jams his hands in his pockets.

"I didn't even want to hear it. Man . . . man, they know I can take care Jo-Anne. I did it when I was on drugs, that ain't no small thing. I am tired of all this bullshit!"

Right. Now, let's move on to another totally unresolved subject.

"What about Carol?"

"She knows it's over. All night in the Bronx, she wanted to fuck, and I kept telling her I wasn't interested."

"Are you still at her place?"

"I got some clothes there. And I have to figure out what to do with the dog. She can't go to my parents'—Moms is afraid of dogs."

He points toward a men's store around a corner and down a block.

"You gotta see this suit I'm buying, man. It is fine!"

"How'll you support the baby?"

"I guess I'll have to try something else—you know, work."

"You believe that?"

He is silent.

The men's store is filled with cheap, flashy clothing. "Now dig this," Jones says, pointing to a two-piece suit with suede shoulders. Its front pockets are secured by outsized buckles. The suede trim is brown; the suit itself is butter-colored cotton. "I seen this in the window, and I got to have it!"

We walk inside. A wall rack holds fifty of these suits. The store is filled with assembly-line outfits of similar color and flash.

Behind the counter, where cash is taken, two white men lean sleepily against the wall, arms folded. A black security guard in a dark blue uniform watches the door. Though the store is empty, the white men do not move at Jones' appearance. Their indifference is palpable. A young, Afro-coiffed black salesman in blue polka-dot pants, stack heels, and an off-white body shirt, stomach bulging at his stylish belt buckle, appears.

Jones describes the suit. The salesman guesses he is about size 40 and pulls a visibly crumpled outfit from the crowded rack. Jones tries on the coat—the salesman immediately tells him how good it looks. Jones walks to the mirror and turns around several times. He asks the salesman how it looks in back.

"Fine," the man says authoritatively. "It's a nice fit. It looks good on you, man."

"It's too big in the shoulders," I cut in. "Try a smaller size."

"There's nothing wrong with that fit," the salesman barks. "What you talkin' about?"

The shoulder seam hangs over the fall of Jones' arms. The coat is baggy. The salesman is afraid of losing Jones' momentum. He scowls at me and tells Jones to feel under his arms. If the armpits are "tight," he says, the suit fits right.

Jones looks at me. I shrug. I am a journalist, not a tailor, and I do not belong in this neighborhood, and the salesman knows this.

"It won't hurt to try another one," I venture.

The salesman scowls again, and pulls a size 38 out of the rack. This suit is not so crumpled, and the shoulders are right.

Now the question of pants. Jones wants his alterations today.

The salesman, seeing that momentum is with him again, nods gravely. Yes, he can do that; he'll talk to the tailor.

No one else is in the store.

We take a slow elevator to the second floor. A fat man in horn-rimmed glasses appears. He wears a tape measure where Jones might wear a string of African beads.

Jones stands on a wooden box in front of a three-way mirror while the man makes chalk marks and inserts pins in the cuff area.

Downstairs Jones asks what the cash discount is. It is twenty percent. Now the price falls to sixty-four dollars plus tax. Jones pulls a thick roll out of his pocket and gives four twenties to one of the white men behind the counter.

We walk next to the London Character Boutique, a shoe store.

The store is a fast-moving mix of noise and people—rock sounds cascading out of speakers near the front windows. A black man with short curly hair jumps up when we enter.

"Number 2-40-42-42," Jones says.

The man smiles. Not many customers walk into the store so decisively.

"That's green on beige, right?"

Jones nods. The salesman disappears into the storeroom.

He returns with a pair of high-heeled green and tan platform loafers. Jones has asked for size eight; when the salesman shoehorns his foot into one of them, he wiggles his toe and asks what size it is.

"Try it and see if it fits," the salesman urges.

Carole King croons "It's Too Late, Baby," and Jones rises and stands on the shoe pushing it down and testing the fit. It feels all right. He goes to the counter and pulls out the roll of green again.

The cash register rings up $52.43. I'm thinking that little Barbara is going to have quite a walk. Three Dog Night sings "The Road to Shambala."

Next we come to Don Julio Joyeria—Jeweler, a dusty little watch and ring shop. Don Julio is a sour little man who ignores us while he talks in rapid Spanish to an older man leaning over the counter.

Jones decides to buy a small square watch with mock-gold trim worth about eleven dollars. But he doesn't want its Twist-O-Flex band.

Don Julio watches him with an expression that indicates he expects little or nothing out of this deal.

"Uh . . . can you change the band?"

"Not for that price."

"No . . . no, I'll pay for the new band."

Don Julio throws up his hands. "You want to spend more money, hokay with me." He replaces the metal band with a thin leather one.

"How much?" Jones asks.

Don Julio looks at us with mild distain. "Fourteen dollars."

Jones pulls out his big head of lettuce again. Now we go to 14th Street to retrieve the famous ring. It costs forty-seven dollars today; Jones rubs it with Kleenex as he walks out of the shop.

Now we are in a shoe store shopping for green socks to match the shoes. The clerk, a Puerto Rican kid, suggests an alligator-green shade, translucent, calf-length. Jones shakes his head.

"That's an *off* green. I need a darker color."

Then a stop for similarly shaded underwear. A green sleeveless undershirt must show slightly through the zippered front of the suit, adding color-coordinated input to patterns of yellow cloth, beige suede, and green and beige shoes.

One last stop at a shoe repair for metal taps.

The shop is filled with men in green smocks; they have bent shoulders, foreign accents, and their hands are permanently stained by shoe blacking. The back of the shop has dark, whirring machinery, and the air is choked with malodorous fumes of leather, rubber, and glue. All around us, broken shoes lie like battlefield casualties.

Out of this comes a little man with kind eyes. Can he help? It is a simple enough matter—taps on the heels and toes—so the man takes the first shoe and turns it upside down on a metal platform. He pounds the tap into the heel with two small nails. He does the same with the sole, but his face has an odd expression. He bangs the sale again tentatively, cautiously, then finishes with a flourish.

He tries the second sole. The tap bounces off and falls on

the floor. He squeezes the base of the shoe, and shakes his head.

"Cork," he says almost inaudibly.

"What?" Jones asks, leaning forward.

"Cork," he repeats, reaching under the counter to pull out a sole-shaped piece of it which he crushes easily in his hand.

"Cork," he says again, and hands Jones his shoes.

"Ain't that a kick in the ass," Jones says in loud disgust. "Fifty-two dollars for cork!"

The little man's eyes are bulging. "Fifty-two dollars!" he exclaims in disbelief. He goes back to the whirring machinery.

S. Klein's, we are told, doesn't carry cribs and strollers. But a security guard—surprisingly, the person Jones immediately gravitates to—directs us across the street to Mays Department Store.

The cribs and strollers at Mays are in a basement alcove. A young man of Caribbean origin, clearly unimpressed by our arrival, manages this concession; he stands at least twenty feet away as we look at beds, and when Jones asks the price of a stained walnut model with white decorative sides he shouts across a sea of cribs that it costs $49.99. The mattress is $18.99 and the crib liner $3.99 Jones says he'll take it. We walk to the stroller section and select a vehicle with a visor and front tray. The salesman has disappeared into the stockroom; Jones becomes angry.

"I got this money and I want to buy something and nobody will even *talk* to me," he whines. We wait a few minutes and then he shouts: "*Hey, where's the man in charge of this here department? I want to see the boss. I want to buy something and nobody will wait on me.*"

The young salesman springs out of the stockroom as if shot by a cannot. "Hey, man, take it *easy*. I had things to do. What do you need?"

Jones points to the stroller and the bed, complete with mattress and liner. The salesman rips the tags off each one and tells Jones to find a cash register on the adjacent basement floor. He has to pay there and return with the recipts.

I'm wondering how it would work if Jones were white, educated, and equipped with credit cards. Would he have to find a cash register by himself?

We struggle up the escalator and across the floor with three huge cardboard crates. Outside, a taxi driver ignores us when he sees our packages. A larger Checker cab has the room, and we head triumphantly back to Jo-Anne's. Today's bills are $116.58 for little Barbara and over a hundred and eighty for Papa Jones.

4

Jo-Anne's bedroom is crowded with trash, cardboard crates, and odd-lot pieces of wood. The television set on the dresser rocks with "I Love Lucy" reruns. David Cassidy covers the hole in the door. And the object of all this confusion, less wrinkled now, lies in her temporary cardboard home, shaking her fists, jerking, and sniffling. If Barbara cries, Jo-Anne, who is playing a minimal role in crib construction, goes to her. The rest of us circle around the main business at hand— the baby bed.

The sides go up. Then we take them down. There are springs, metal supports, and far too many wiggle-shaped bolts. I can't believe this is the baby bed we saw assembled in the store a few hours earlier! Jones sits cross-legged on the floor fastening and unscrewing bolts as Jerry and I read and reread the directions, give advice, change it, then vow vengeance on the manufacturer.

Jo-Anne's father, Morris, who has been sitting quietly in the kitchen, pokes his egg-shaped face in the door . . . quiet, expressionless, watching.

"You try," I say, handing him the instructions. But his advice is no better than ours, and it is burdened by the obvious tension between him and Jones.

The manufacturer hasn't included enough screws; or they have been lost in the confusion. Or something.

After an hour's struggle, we've reached the point of collective despair. Someone suggests returning to the store the following day and looking at the floor model. Everyone slumps onto the bedroom floor in defeat.

Jones is deeply, petulantly angry.

"You know what I feel like doing?" he whines menacingly. "I feel like kicking this thing apart!"

He sits in the middle of the half-formed baby bed, screwdrivers and bolts around him.

"We ought to go back tomorrow and kick that guy's ass!"

He is close to exploding, almost in tears. "Wow . . . wow, I bought all this stuff for my baby, *and I can't even use it! I can't even put my baby in her bed!*"

But the issue is dropped. Our inept construction gang breaks into smaller parts; someone produces a bottle of wine from the kitchen. Jones walks over to his sleeping child and leans over the cardboard crib, regaining a macho pose.

"I tried, girl," he sighs, exhaling heavily as if he holds up half the world. "I tried."

Jo-Anne brings him a glass of wine.

5

The kitchen seems miles from the bedroom, and Morris sits at the table reading the afternoon paper, turning his back to the hallway. Our eyes met briefly during the attempt to assemble the crib.

I sit down facing him. He stares hard at the paper. I light my pipe . . . lean back in the chair . . . sip a glass of wine. He seems to be receding further into himself, a rabbit looking anxiously at his watch.

I am partly wrong. He is willing to be drawn out. A few opening lines are necessary.

"How do you think this will turn out?" I motion toward the bedroom.

He says nothing for half a minute.

"Hard to say." The sound is almost inaudible. He is still looking at the newspaper. "Depends on what *he* does."

Pause. I pull on my pipe. He turns a page of the paper . . . slowly . . . and folds it back.

"Will you let Jo-Anne stay?"

"Guess I'll have to."

He is beginning to put the paper aside. In the bedroom, Jones and Jo-Anne have started to fight. I wait a moment longer.

"How do you feel about all this." Come on, Morris, say something.

He smiles almost defiantly. "You're a writer, am I right?" We are getting somewhere at last. His voice is muffled with shyness; but for a moment he is in charge, and he is enjoying it.

"You want to ask me some questions, right?"

"Yes. Will it bother you if I take notes?"

"No . . . no, don't do that. We'll just talk."

I repeat the question about his feelings.

"It isn't right," he begins. "There's no privacy here now. They can't live here. This isn't what you do when you get married—move in with your in-laws. I can't keep them here; anyway, my wife may come back from Arizona. And the financial burden, it's just *not right*. I can't be supporting three people."

He pours more wine for both of us.

"I just got out of a hole. I had to send a lot of money to Arizona." He spreads his hands, turning the palms up in exasperation. "Now, this . . . I might have to go back to the book-of-the-month club again."

"What?"

"You know, the First National City Bank. I'll have to borrow money again, and I don't like it. I can't be going to the book-of-the-month club all the time."

"How do you feel about *him?*"

He veers away from the question, smiling shyly again, embarrassed . . . looking down at the table.

"Kids today live . . . looser . . . than I did. It used to be that I had a pair of sneakers to last the summer. Mom would mix hamburger with dough to make dinner. We didn't have butter, so we put garlic on the bread—it was good. Now you look in the refrigerator and you see steaks and chops, you know? The kids think everything comes easy; they don't get ready for their responsibilities."

The anger is obvious—yet he remains low-key, a radiator barely hissing in the middle of a cold winter. Does he ever shout?

"You've got to plan for things; these kids just live for to-day and assume tomorrow will take care of itself. You've got to *plan*."

Enough steam. He slows up.

"I don't exactly blame them for what happened, I mean, I'm glad to help as much as I can. But who's gonna pay for this? The baby's got to have clothes. The baby's got to eat. This isn't something I should have to worry about."

I rise to get ice cubes from the refrigerator. Morris is beginning to enjoy the conversation thoroughly. I understand his predicament. I'm not one of "those kids." I talk his language. He thinks I share his values.

"I haven't got that much money, you know. I haven't been to a movie or a play in a dog's age. I go out to the Holy Name Society, get dinner, go to a dance and see people. And that's nice. But I can't do it every week. I spend most of my nights at the tavern across the street or sitting on the benches talking to my friends. I should be able to take it easy now; I'm almost fifty-seven."

The anger remains at war with the shyness. Morris feels strongly about this, but his face, even at the most difficult moments, is gentle and soft, almost pink-cheeked with embarrassment at being so open.

"I can't take it easy—I'm in the hole because of this thing. I had to pay the hospital to get the baby released. I got an anesthesia bill for eighty-five dollars and other things, too. I figure I can hold the doctor off for a couple of months—but who's gonna keep paying for things. His parents? Me? *He's* not working."

6

Jerry is standing at the kitchen door.

"We're ready to go when you are, man. I've gotta get up to the Bronx tonight."

I get up from the table and shake hands with Morris, who follows me to the hallway as if he owns more of his house than he did an hour ago.

"Be careful what you write," he says, "Don't make me look bad, okay?"

In the bedroom, Jo-Anne is pacing in angry circles, and crying. Jones smokes a cigarette and stands silently before her in his glittering new suit.

"I'm home all the time," she is saying, red-faced and sniffling. "*You* go out. Now the baby is here, and it will be worse! You spend all that money on clothes and shoes, then you visit *her!*" Jo-Anne bursts into tears again.

Jones starts to say something. He gestures with the hand holding the cigarette—then turns and walks out of the room in anger and shame, eyes aimed at the floor.

"Let's go," he says in a low voice.

It is raining lightly as we reach the street, scattered drops bouncing against the sidewalks and park benches, a watery film on the street reflecting the colors of First Avenue's neon lights.

Jones looks up and curses at the sky.

"You would know it," he growls. "I got my new clothes on, and the motherfucking rain starts. Maybe I should go back and change."

"It ain't so bad," Jerry says. "Let's go across the street, man, and get some wine." Nobody wants to go upstairs again.

A few minutes later, we are leaning against the outer wall of the liquor store, half-shielded from the rain and mist. Jones is working hard on the bottle.

"You know what they are gonna do, don't you?" he announces bitterly. "They are gonna try to keep me out of raising my baby. They paid for it, they are going to say, so I don't have anything to say about what happens."

His voice is scratchy and deep from an anger that is close to tears.

"You know what? Jo-Anne says I can't take the baby out tomorrow. Her father says it's too young. *Bullshit* . . . it's my child . . . now they won't let me raise it. My father will be trying to raise it, too. *And it's my child!*

"What the fuck," he says, cooling off . . . but still bilious with pain and frustration. "I'm goin' out tonight and do it right, get it *on*."

He turns to Jerry. "You comin' with me?"

"I gotta get to the Bronx," Jerry says hesitantly, caught between conflicting loyalties. "But if you're goin', I'm goin', too."

A girl in a green dress walks by, moving fast, looking straight ahead.

"Hey, baby," Jones yells drunkenly at her. "How'd you like to go steppin' out with *me*? I got lots of money in my pocket and we'll have a good time!"

He pulls on the bottle, leaning back against the wall. Two girls in Levis pass us on the corner.

"Babeeeee!" Jones leers. "I got a whole lotta money, and we'll do the town. Whatta you saaay?"

But Jones walks into the rain alone. Jerry goes to the Bronx after all, and I am ready for some sleep. He walks me to the subway. The rain is falling lightly on our heads, and we shake hands, each of us bracing the grip with his other hand.

"Take care of yourself," I say haltingly.

He nods, avoiding my eyes, and he smiles to himself and walks away into the darkness.

Afterword

I've seen Jones several times since that night outside the liquor store. Almost a year has passed, and his life has changed in some important ways.

Jo-Anne has left him. She took the baby to Arizona for a while to live with her mother and sister. It caught him completely by surprise. They'd fought and made up several times during the summer—sometimes over the hospital bill, most often over the future. For a while, she wouldn't let him see the baby. Then he took a job as a hospital orderly, insisting this meant steady money and a good future. And he asked her to marry him.

"I finally said yes when he promised he'd leave Carol alone," Jo-Anne told me afterward. "Then I found out he was still living with her. I bought the plane ticket that night. It didn't make sense to be with him anymore."

Jones still lives with Carol. They left the Clinton Street apartment one night without paying the back rent. Carol eventually had a healthy baby girl. And again, Jones managed to be somewhere else when his child was born.

I visited him at his parents' place that Christmas Eve. A tinfoil Christmas tree laden with blinking blue lights and candy canes stood in one corner of the living room. Dozens of Christmas cards were pinned to the hallway wall, and the stereo was stacked with Mahalia Jackson albums. Moms served pot roast, and we all crowded around the tiny kitchen table to get at the rolls Pops was pulling out of a small toaster-oven.

As far as I could tell, Jones was getting his money from the hospital, his parents, and from Carol. He'd dealt smoke for a while, but it didn't work out. He hadn't mugged anyone for a long time, he said—and probably wouldn't as long as he was working. The dinner table conversations rose and fell like an angry north wind. Pops and Jones and Jerry argued and threatened each other and then laughed and talked after each angry confrontation. Stella sat quietly through the evening, smoking cigarettes and reminding everyone it was nearly time for Midnight Mass. Pops made eggnog and poured brandy into it.

Jones had little to say. His life seemed to have stabilized somewhat, though Pops kept saying he wanted him out of "that nigger's house." Jerry and his family had moved from the South Bronx to upper Harlem. Everyone wanted to know about the book. I said I was still working on it; and I warned them that it would not hide anything. They nodded and accepted this.

I felt that I was seeing Jones' family—in some ways—for the first time. I hadn't realized how much they loved each other, despite all that had happened between them. Pops said that he and Jones had fought the previous night, and both men had cried afterward. They insisted again and again that they loved each other. And Jones nodded as his father talked, and Stella smoked. And Jerry stood behind the table and agreed with all that was said. And everyone wished Jo-Anne would come back from Arizona.

Shortly after that, she did. But she doesn't see Jones any more.

Moms and Pops had given Jones a blue winter overcoat with a white fur collar. He'd had his hospital whites tailored with white high-heeled shoes to match. The hospital was hassling him, he said. He looked too fly.

For several days after that I carried a picture in my head of this besieged family sitting around the hot, crowded kitchen table. And I remember Jones standing on the street corner in his new coat and hospital whites as I left. I will see him again and again until I know where his life is going. If he goes to jail, I will visit him. And if he is ever married, I'll want to be at the wedding.

As for me, I've stopped looking for simple answers. I know that Jones is shaped by his environment; everyone is. And I know that good and evil can live together in the same person. And lastly I know that each of us must continue to look at each other without ever turning away.